GROWING PLANTS INDOORS

the text of this book is printed
on 100% recycled paper

FIG. 1. THE NICEST PLACE IN OUR HOUSE.

GROWING PLANTS INDOORS
A Garden in Your House

Ernesta Drinker Ballard

PHOTOGRAPHS BY

EDMUND B. GILCHRIST, JR. & OTHERS

BARNES & NOBLE BOOKS
A DIVISION OF HARPER & ROW, PUBLISHERS
New York, Evanston, San Francisco, London

CONTENTS

FOREWORD

by John M. Fogg, Jr.

The practice of growing plants in the home is not a new one. At a very early date man learned from experience that it was possible to keep plants growing indoors throughout the long, bleak season when the world of plants about him was dormant. Doubtless these early plants were valued for their culinary or medicinal properties: potherbs to relieve the tedium of a diet of dried meat, cereals, and roots, or standard home remedies for bruises or indigestion.

Down through the ages man learned how to prolong his enjoyment of the growing season by bringing into his dwelling plants which would provide not only the lustrous green of their foliage, but with proper care, the cheerful and infinitely varied colors of their flowers and fruits. Thus centuries ago human habitations in the colder portions of the world were adorned with pots, tubs, and baskets containing living bits of field and woodland. This gradual transition from the utilitarian to the aesthetic is closely paralleled by the development of horticulture which, starting with the kitchen and physic garden, became primarily concerned with the growing of ornamentals.

Until about the middle of the eighteenth century the devotee of house plants had only a limited variety from which to choose. At about this time, however, world exploration was in full swing and rare and exotic species began to flow into Western Europe from the Orient, from Africa and from the Americas. Soon there was an embarrassment of riches and breeders were able to select those best suited for use in the home. Today many hundreds of species are available to those who desire to bring nature indoors; they include plants from as widely differing habitats as the tropical rain forest and the desert. No house is too small, no apartment too confined, to offer a window sill or two suitable for the successful culture of a few carefully selected subjects.

The present volume brings to its reader all of the knowledge needed to grow and care for plants in the home. Problems of soil, watering, fertilizing, and control of pests and diseases are all dealt with by a writer who has "learned by doing," one who has long been recognized as an expert in her field. Over 500 different species and varieties of plants are described; the largest number, we believe, ever to have been included in such a work. That which began as a useful hobby has become an art and Ernesta Ballard is one of its foremost practitioners.

ACKNOWLEDGMENTS

First, I owe an acknowledgment to the men and women who operate the greenhouses and nurseries listed in the Appendices. Their willingness to propagate and make available literally hundreds of different species of plants makes indoor gardening possible. The fascinating plant lists and descriptions and the excellent cultural suggestions in many of their catalogs not only have whetted my collector's appetite, but have provided information not obtainable through the formal literature. Those I have visited have been unfailingly generous in sharing the teachings of their long experience.

In connection with the preparation of this book, thanks are due to many individuals, particularly to Ann Newlin Thompson for her careful reading of the manuscript as well as for her able assistance in the greenhouse; to Margarete Segebarth for the insect illustrations; to Edmund B. Gilchrist, Jr. for his skillful photography—except for the pictures with a credit line indicating another source, all of the photographs for the book were taken by him; to Dr. George H. M. Lawrence and the Staff of the Bailey Hortorium for information about plant names; to Dr. John M. Fogg, Jr., who read the manuscript and made many helpful suggestions and corrections; and, most of all, to Frederic L. Ballard, without whose interest, encouragement, and editorial assistance this book would not have been written.

E.D.B.

INTRODUCTION

Happiness depends, as Nature shows,
Less on exterior things than most suppose.

WM. COWPER

The nicest place in our house is the sunporch where I keep most of my house plants. Built into a corner facing east and south, it is an almost perfect location for an indoor garden. Here, the warm winter sunshine coaxes blooms from flowering plants and timid growth from tender tropicals, a delightful contrast to my other garden that lies outside the glass, bare and dormant. This is the place I visit two, three, or even four times each day, to water the plants that look to me for their very life, to care for them, and to enjoy them.

A combination of circumstances led to my first attempt at growing plants indoors. Two small children kept me at home; weeds discouraged my efforts outside; and a pair of south-facing window sills in the old Pennsylvania farmhouse where we lived cried for decorative contents, if only to hide the weather-beaten paint. The catalyst was a Christmas present, a book on house plants given me by a friend. Starting with six wax begonias and three ivy plants that first winter, I have since acquired about five hundred different species and a bigger house and two greenhouses to keep them in. Each acquisition brings with it not only the reward of growing a plant through the winter, but the interest of something new, the pleasure of adding to my collection, and sometimes the satisfaction of understanding better the nature of the plant world.

Two comfortable chairs and a little table are squeezed between the plants on our sunporch, and often during a winter weekend we sit there for a few delicious moments enjoying the warmth of the sun and the growing things. Each plant is a treasured possession, an intimate friend, a special child whose progress we mark from week to week. Each new leaf is a gift, and eagerly we watch each bud from its embryonic beginnings to the ultimate perfection of a freshly opened flower.

My plants have taught me many things. I have learned to value every ray of winter sun. I have learned to enjoy the various shapes and textures of the leaves as I wash the dust from the foliage and leave it clean and shining. And above all, I have learned that indoor gardening brings the same peace of mind that I get from the feel of earth on my hands outside in spring and summer.

One of the pleasantest discoveries is that while December 22 marks the start of winter outdoors, it brings spring indoors. Almost immediately the lengthening days put new life into dormant plants. Each year, the first to respond in my indoor garden are the geraniums. One day in early January new shoots pop out, and flower buds soon appear. By February my crown of thorn is naked no longer; the sun has coaxed its leaves back and makes it respectable once more. Then flowering maples, African violets, and begonias, which have languished during the short days, come to life again. Buds whose predecessors have withered prematurely now stay on the plants and begin to swell. To see them bloom is the culmination of my efforts, the reward of waiting through the winter days.

Make no mistake about it, effort is required to produce these little miracles, and in effort lies an important ingredient of success. Green thumbs are not a matter of luck; they belong to those whose plants and gardens are part of their lives; to those who are not too busy to care for their plants endlessly; to those who will take time to know and enjoy them.

This porch of ours is but one of many indoor gardens that I know. Just as there are all kinds of gardeners, so are there all kinds of gardens—from a custom-built greenhouse, complete with automatic controls and thermostats, to a tiny window sill in a city apartment. The dedicated grower will have plants in every situation.

For some, a greenhouse or sunny window is a place for exploration into the tropics. Theirs are often miscellaneous collections of everything under the sun.

Others find satisfaction in becoming expert in a particular group of plants— the gesneriads, the begonias, the succulents from Africa, or the American cacti. Any of these families presents an almost infinite diversity of form and color.

Again there are those who really want a garden in the house. With them design and color take precedence over the collector's enthusiasm for a hetero- geneous gathering of plants or the specialist's concentration on his specialty.

Finally, there are those who decorate with plants in pots. A large philo- dendron in a handsome container adds life to an otherwise drab expanse of wall or dreary corner. In contemporary houses, masses of plants are a vital step in the process of "bringing the outdoors in." Indeed, many of these houses need plants quite as much as did the conservatories of the Victorian era.

The ultimate in indoor gardening is a greenhouse; and the nicest ones are those which are part of the house, easily accessible to work in and enjoy for an hour here and there, or, on occasion, for a whole wonderful day.

When I began this book, I planned to write on house plants and not to discuss the aristocrats of the greenhouse. But the more I worked with plants and visited greenhouses, window gardens, and modern houses with wide planting beds, the more I became convinced that no line can be drawn between house and greenhouse plants. What one person can grow to perfection in his house, another may have trouble with under glass; what I can grow under fluorescent lights in my warm kitchen will die if I move it to my chilly sunporch; and what many grow with ease in a greenhouse may often, with a little extra care, do well indoors. It depends on the ingenuity of the gardener in reckoning with problems of light, temperature, and humidity. And above all it depends on his determination to succeed.

And so this book became more than just a description of the plants I have grown, though it is true that I have grown every plant described or pictured in these pages. In Part I, I have begun with a review of some horticultural principles which are basic to successful indoor gardening but which are often not explained to the indoor gardener in concise and simple form; and because principle and practice go hand in hand, Part I includes cultural practices as well.

Part II describes indoor gardens—not for the traditional Victorian conservatory or humid, stove-heated farmhouse, but for the kinds of houses and offices we live and work in today, with a picture of each and a practical discussion of how the effects can be duplicated under similar conditions in an average house. If your eye is caught by a detail in the picture, you will probably find it explained in the text.

Part III includes pictures and descriptions of indoor plants (including those in the gardens described in Part II) with suggestions for use and culture based on my own experience. I believe you will find there most of the plants discussed in gardening magazines or offered by growers today. Because a knowledge of plant geography is essential to successful growing, I have included in most of the descriptions a reference to the plants' native habitats.

Finally, the Appendices are indoor gardening in a nutshell—formulas for potting soils, lists of plants for various exposures and temperatures, sources of supply, and helpful books. Here, as well as in Part I, I have emphasized such modern developments as packaged soils, inert growing mediums, water-soluble fertilizers, plastic film, and insecticide bombs, which have rendered obsolete much of the traditional lore of indoor gardening and have made it a great deal easier for beginner and expert alike.

PART ❦ ONE

The Culture of Indoor Plants

Horticulture is applied botany. Almost everything there is to say about indoor gardening refers back to the principles of botany. Advice about such different problems as watering, fertilizing, propagating, the choice of plants, and summer care—often bewildering when considered alone—makes sense in its relation to botanical laws. Part I of this book is an attempt to set out familiar rules in the light of botanical principles and thus to make them easier to understand. I don't expect that experienced gardeners will find anything revolutionary in my discussion of the location of indoor gardens and the importance of light, humidity, and temperature; nor in my descriptions of cultural practices. I hope they may find my explanations helpful.

Plants are the result of their environment. The characteristics of different species have been developed in response to the conditions in which the plant grows naturally, and each plant is adapted to withstand the unfavorable factors in its environment and to exploit those that are favorable. While most of the varieties grown indoors are surprisingly amenable to unnatural surroundings, the more nearly your indoor garden resembles the natural habitat in ways important to the plant, the better the plant will do.

The characteristics of an indoor garden begin with its location, and this in turn begins with the place where you live. The latitude and climate of your city determine the length of the days, the intensity of the light at different seasons, and—excepting air-conditioned houses—the summer temperature and humidity. My house is in Philadelphia, where days tend to be dark in winter and hot and moist in summer, fine for tropical plants but not so well suited for those from cooler places. Residents of the northern part of the country will find that their longer summer days and cooler summer nights produce some different results from those that I describe.

Wherever you live, the best place in the house for plants is one that gets several hours of sun each day, where the humidity can be kept fairly high, and where the temperature does not fluctuate too much. All too often the spot chosen for plants by the modern architect or interior decorator is deficient

3

in some or all of these respects. There are a few plants that will survive in even the most unsuitable places, and you will find them described in Part III; but if you want a variety of plants and satisfactory growth and bloom, you must put botany ahead of esthetics and choose the place where the plants will grow best rather than where they might look best.

LIGHT

Light is the source of energy for plant growth, and the horticulturist must concern himself both with how much light is available (the light intensity) and with how long it lasts (the day length).

Day length

The most specific effect of day length is on flowering. Plants that bloom in a particular season know when the season arrives by the lengthening or shortening of the days. Christmas cactus and poinsettia, for example, flower only when the days are short. Plumbago and fuchsia, on the other hand, will not bloom until the longer days of spring and summer.

A more general effect of day length is on metabolism—the rate of plant growth. During fall and winter, when the days are short, growth virtually ceases. I well remember the first winter I had my greenhouse and my mounting despair as November passed into December and December into January with no visible change in many of my plants. Fortunately spring comes early under glass, and by February new shoots appeared to restore my faith.

Light intensity

In addition to the shortness of the days, another factor which contributes to the dormancy of so many plants in fall and early winter is the diminished intensity of the light at that time of year. In summer the sun is high and shines through the atmosphere almost at right angles, taking the shortest course through the enveloping layer of air and reaching the earth with a minimum of diffusion. In contrast, the winter sun is low in the sky, even at noon. It slants obliquely through the atmosphere, taking a longer path in the course of which particles of dust and moisture absorb and deflect the light and lessen its intensity. The magnitude of the effect is striking. At noon on a clear day in midsummer, the level of illumination may be as high as 10,000 foot-candles. In December the corresponding figure is rarely above 5,000 and will fall as low as 500 on a rainy day.

When you consider that the scanty winter light is reduced still more as it passes through the window glass and sometimes through curtains as well, it is easy to understand why only plants like African violets and philodendrons —accustomed to the dim light of the jungle—show signs of life at this time of year. And even they need all the light they can get. I know of no plant, not even the tenderest African violet or begonia, which if grown in the house in the northern half of this country, will not welcome full winter sun.

In spring and summer, of course, the case is different, and many jungle plants need protection from the noonday sun. Indoors this can be achieved by placing the plant where the foliage of a tougher species will filter the glare, or by the use of very thin curtains. Even a screen noticeably reduces the illumination.

The intensity of the light also has an effect on flowering. As a general rule plants will not bloom unless the level of illumination approximates that in their native habitat, although they may survive, and even grow, with considerably less light. This explains why geraniums, which grow naturally on the sunny plains of South Africa, are reluctant to bloom indoors in winter. It also explains why the greenhouseman, with glass on four sides and a roof of glass set at the optimum angle, can produce winter blooms no one can duplicate in the house. The great popularity of African violets is due to their unrivaled ability to flower in subdued light.

Proper exposure for plants

The controlling effect of light makes it the prime consideration in choosing a site for an indoor garden. A southern exposure gets the most light and makes the best location. As between east and west, the former is to be preferred because it gets the morning sun. For reasons that are not wholly understood by science, plants, like people, seem to find the sun's rays more life-giving in the morning. Northern exposures, which get no direct sun, considerably restrict the choice of plant material, but even in a window facing due north varied and pleasing effects can be obtained.

Artificial light

Recently it has been found that artificial illumination, especially from fluorescent bulbs, can supplement or even replace natural light. However, the intensities that can be obtained in this way rarely exceed 500 to 1,000 foot-candles; and while these levels are ideal for African violets and other natives of the deep jungle, they are of much less benefit to plants from the mountains, deserts, or plains. A spotlight carrying a 150-watt incandescent bulb will also keep foliage plants alive for many months, even in a corner with no natural illumination. However, because of the heat given off by a large light of this type, it should be placed three or four feet away from the plants.

Virtually all plants grown under artificial light need twelve to sixteen hours of illumination per day. Traditionally, it was thought that they also needed a few hours of darkness in order to grow properly. However, scientists have recently shown that plants do not actually need a nightly "rest," and nurserymen have found that they can speed the vegetative development of many newly rooted woody plants by subjecting them to continuous illumination around the clock. Nevertheless, since constant illumination interferes with the flowering of many species, I suggest, for general purposes, a fourteen-hour day. If the plants being grown are known to be sensitive to day-length, there should be sixteen hours of light for long-day plants and no more than thirteen hours for short-day plants.

No matter how long you leave your lights on when you are at home to care for your plants, it is wise to turn the lights off if you have to leave them unattended for two or three days. This precaution greatly reduces the risk of drying out, since plants transpire much less in the dark than under illumination.

The making of a garden under artificial light is described on pages 46 through 48.

HUMIDITY

The second respect in which it is important for the plant's environment to approximate its natural home is humidity, the dampness of the air. The place in which a particular species developed may have been characterized by air which was extremely moist or extremely dry or something in between, and the plant has adjusted its life processes accordingly. The desert air may contain as little as 5 per cent of the water vapor it is capable of absorbing; a jungle may have a relative humidity as high as 90 per cent; and the sunny subtropics have average humidities in the high fifties and low sixties.

Effects of low and high humidity

Humidity affects the rate of transpiration—the process by which water from the interior of the leaves and stems escapes through the plant's pores and evaporates into the surrounding air. If the air is dry, evaporation takes place speedily, drying the leaf surface and stimulating more rapid transpiration. If the air is already saturated with water, both evaporation and transpiration slow down. The structure and functions of the plant have been developed to maintain a balance between the intake of water through the roots and the output through the leaves. If the air is very dry, output becomes too rapid and the leaves and stems become dehydrated, lose their turgidity, and wilt. This cannot be prevented simply by supplying more water to the roots. Increasing the humidity of the surrounding air is also a vital necessity. The only plants that can live for any length of time without moisture both at their roots and in the air are the succulent plants of the desert, which carry a supply of water in their swollen leaves and stems and have structures on the leaf surfaces to reduce transpiration.

Inadequate moisture in the air has other deleterious effects, less serious but still important. For example, the roots of jungle climbers, which in moist air are pliable and able to grip rocks or bark, become hard and lose their tenacity in a dry atmosphere. The leaves of plants grown in dryer than normal conditions are neither as large nor as crisp or colorful as those produced where there is more humidity.

The opposite condition—too much moisture—is not nearly as frequent, nor as harmful to the plant when it does occur. Succulent plants, adapted to desert conditions, will become leggy and flabby if grown in a humid greenhouse, and flowering plants from the temperate plains will develop thicker and spongier foliage than usual. So long as they remain in the moist air they grow satisfactorily, but upon being moved to the dryer atmosphere of the house, which they would normally tolerate easily, they lose most of their leaves or even wilt and die. They are, indeed, the traditional "hot house plants."

What does this mean to the indoor gardener? Just this: the air in most houses in wintertime is too dry for most plants, and the grower's constant concern must be to alleviate this hardship. Remember that the humidity in question is relative humidity—the amount of water in the air compared to the maximum the air could absorb. Remember also that the capacity of air to absorb moisture increases rapidly with temperature. Thus, if on a winter day the temperature is 30° and the relative humidity outside is 50 per cent—a rather good figure for most plants—it means that the amount of water in the air is just half what the air could absorb at that temperature. But if the same air is brought into your house and heated to 70°, its absorptive capacity increases so that the same water represents only about one-tenth of what the air could absorb at the higher temperature. A relative humidity of 10 per cent is a poor figure for any but desert plants. Finally, remember that the characteristics of the particular location in the room may have considerable effect on humidity. Cool spots are more humid than warm spots. The worst place of all is a spot directly in the path of hot air pouring out of an outlet in a hot-air heating system.

Pebble trays to increase humidity

One of the simplest and most effective methods of increasing the humidity around plants is to provide a layer of damp pebbles in waterproof trays under the pots. The moisture evaporating from the surface of the stones will add water vapor to the surrounding air. For best results, the pebbles should be relatively small and porous. I use the kind sold for forcing bulbs. Crushed granite, sold in feed stores as turkey grits, is also satisfactory, and coarse sand or gravel will serve in a pinch.

As for the trays, they should be at least an inch and a quarter deep and, of course, watertight. Copper is the best material. Its color makes an attractive

contrast to the foliage of the plants, and it lasts indefinitely without mainte-
nance. It is also the most expensive. Galvanized iron is an acceptable substitute, less expensive but requiring paint on the outside to hide the zinc
galvanizing and on the inside to prevent rust, which will otherwise appear
sooner or later.

Unless you are a metal worker, you will have to have copper or galvanized
trays made by your plumber or roofer, but a third available metal—aluminum
—can easily be fabricated at home. The basic material is the aluminum sheets
sold at almost any hardware store. They can be cut with tin shears and bent
with a pair of pliers or, preferably, two strips of wood clamped along the line
of the bend as illustrated. The result is a cheap tray which will last for several
years and can either be used unfinished or painted to suit the owner's fancy.

Before the advent of plastics, it was essential that the trays themselves be
watertight. Now, I find that the life of a rusted or pitted tray can be pro-
longed indefinitely by lining it with polyethylene. You can also achieve
perfectly satisfactory results by constructing a simple wooden frame in the
shape of a tray and putting a plastic film inside it to hold the water.

Once the trays are in place beneath the plants, your task is to keep the

FIG. 2.   MAKING ALUMINUM PLANT TRAYS.   The right-hand end of the tray on
the left has been folded over so that the fold will form the edge of the tray, stiffening
it and making it smooth to the touch. The left-hand end of the same tray shows how
the corners are cut to permit this fold. Bending along straight lines is facilitated by
clamping the aluminum between two laths as pictured. The tray in the center shows
the "breadpan" fold used to keep the corners watertight. The tray in the foreground
contains the pebbles I use under my pots, the kind sold for forcing bulbs. The tools
shown are all that are needed for making a tray, although a mallet and square ended
board to hammer against are helpful in obtaining neat corners.

pebbles moist. Fill the trays until the water level reaches the bottom of the top layer of pebbles, and refill them whenever the pebbles look dry. On damp cloudy days one watering may be enough; on sunny days when the humidity is low you may have to add water several times between breakfast and supper; but no matter how great the temptation, don't fill the trays to the point where the bottoms of the pots are immersed. Pebble trays are not for bottom watering; if they were, neither copper nor aluminum could be used in their construction, as both these metals can become toxic to plants.

Spraying to increase humidity

The second easy way to raise the humidity is to spray the plants with water from a hand sprayer—one of the kind supplied with insecticides or one of the "fog-type" sold for the purpose or an electric paint sprayer. In theory your sprayer should produce a fine mist which will fill the air around the plants with water vapor without excessive condensation on the leaves. In practice, even with a very fine nozzle, drops of water will collect on the foliage. When this happens, don't be alarmed. Under greenhouse conditions, wetting the foliage on a cloudy day encourages fungus disease, but in the house such diseases are comparatively rare and the wet foliage discourages insects and spiders, much more serious menaces to the indoor garden.

Incidentally, if any of your plants are climbing on totem poles, don't forget to spray the roots and the surface around them. It helps them to get and hold a firm grip.

Spraying should be part of the daily routine. I try to spray at least as often

FIG. 3.   INCREASING THE HUMIDITY AROUND SOME AFRICAN VIOLETS WITH A FOG-TYPE SPRAYER.   Those shown are (left to right) 'Wild Girl,' 'Geneva Beauty,' 'Sailor Girl,' and (in back) *Episcia cupreata* 'Variegata' and *Saintpaulia* 'Snow Prince.'

as I add water to the pebble trays, more frequently if possible. It gives me two or three occasions each day to visit and enjoy my indoor garden. I use an attractive copper sprayer which can be kept close at hand and in plain view as a reminder of my plants' needs.

Are pebble trays and spraying effective? The best answer will be the improved appearance of your plants, but you can satisfy your curiosity more quickly and directly by buying a humidity indicator. The inexpensive models sold for house use or the somewhat better ones sold for tobacco warehouses are accurate enough to register the difference, although they cannot be relied upon to show the actual humidity. For that you need a wet and dry bulb hygrometer. Whatever instrument you use, you will find the readings consistently 3 per cent to 5 per cent higher over your pebble trays than in the middle of the room. After spraying, the reading will be raised another 10 per cent, and an hour or more will pass before it returns to normal.

Humidifiers

To some, this watering and spraying may seem more trouble than the plants are worth. There is another way—a humidifier. You can use the reservoir type or a small commercial unit permanently connected to your water line and controlled by a humidistat. These humidifiers operate by electricity, are relatively noiseless and trouble free, and reduce the water to a vapor which will not form drops under normal circumstances. The capacity of the humidifier is the important thing. Last winter I kept account of the water I used in my sunporch each day for watering and humidification, and it was often as much as nine gallons. A humidifier of less than five gallons output would make only an insignificant impact on the humidity in a normal-sized room.

Grouping plants to increase humidity

Finally, the more plants you have together, the more their combined transpiration will raise the humidity around them. It is possible to grow many jungle plants successfully in a group, while the same species will dry out and die in isolation. Indeed, only the hardiest plants can be relied on for the dramatic locations of which interior decorators are so fond—the center of the picture window, the focal piece in the entrance hall, or the top of the grand piano. Most will do better in a group with their fellows, where each can contribute toward making the environment healthier for all.

TEMPERATURE

The third environmental factor to be taken into account in locating and managing an indoor garden is temperature. It is only natural that plants adapted to the tropics will require more heat than those that have developed in temperate climates. However, in practically every case, the crucial temperature is the low, not the high. We have all experienced summer days in the temperate zone when the thermometer reached 100°—a point almost as high as the hottest day on the equator. On the other hand, many tropical countries never know temperatures below 60°, whereas most of the temperate zones have considerable spells below freezing. So when the greenhouseman speaks, let us say, of a 50° house, he refers to the minimum temperature, the point at which his thermostat calls for heat. And because greenhouses receive heat by radiation through the glass during the day and lose it by a reversal of the process at night, the minimum temperature is synonymous with the night temperature.

In this respect a greenhouse is really no different from the plant's natural habitat. Out-of-doors, too, nights are cooler than days, and the plants have woven this daily change in light and temperature into the pattern of their functions. During the day the plant builds carbohydrates out of water from the soil and carbon dioxide from the air, using light as its source of energy to accomplish the chemical change. At night, when the absence of light makes photosynthesis impossible, the plant digests the basic starch into sugar and uses it just as we use our digested food to build the more complicated compounds of cells and tissues.

Having developed this cycle of activities in an environment where nights are cooler, plants do not perform satisfactorily without the stimulus of a drop in temperature at the end of the day. Since most house plants are grown near windows, this is usually no problem indoors, the heat loss through the glass producing the desired temperature drop. Indeed, the problem is more apt to be keeping the night temperature high enough. In any case, plants, like people, will be healthier if the night temperature is several degrees below the daytime reading.

Different temperatures for different plants

As for specific thermometer readings, it can be said generally that tropical plants need a minimum of 65° and temperate and desert plants need a minimum of 50°. Of course, the various species differ widely in their adaptability to temperatures below or above those recommended. For example, the florist's cineraria will scarcely endure temperatures as high as those normally maintained in the house; fuschias will not set buds if the thermometer is above 65° at night; and camellia buds are apt to dry out and drop off if the night temperature gets this high. At the other end of the scale, episcias will not survive many nights below 65° and are said to "freeze" at 55°. By contrast, cacti and a number of other plants such as Hoya and Aspidistra seem almost oblivious to the temperature as long as it is above freezing.

All this does not mean that a person who keeps his house at 65° during the winter nights is forever deprived of camellias. The fact is that in almost every house there are wide differences in temperature between rooms, and even between different parts of the same room. Window sills, for instance, are almost always cooler at night than the center of the room; so cool-growing plants should be put nearer to the panes than those from the tropics. Or, if you particularly want a tropical plant near a window pane, as is frequently the case in north windows where the light is too poor for anything else, you can reduce the heat loss by installing a second pane between the window and the plants, or by lowering the shade behind the plants or putting a sheet of cardboard or several thicknesses of newspaper behind them whenever the night is clear and cold.

With a little experimentation you will become familiar with the climate of the various plant locations in your house and with the needs and tolerances of your plants. In this process a thermometer is a great and often overlooked aid. You will be surprised how frequently a corner you have classified in your mind as warm because it is warm on a sunny day will prove to be cold at night. Even the sunniest window will not develop day temperatures above 90° during the indoor season, and almost any plant you can think of has become inured to more heat than this in its native land on summer days.

SOILS AND POTTING

For many people soils and potting are either shrouded in mystery or hedged round with a disheartening array of "do's" and "don'ts." Actually, the key to potting—just like the key to selecting the proper plant in the first place—is an understanding of the plant and its habitat. If you know something of the conditions in which the species grows naturally and also something of its growing habits—how fast it develops, what size it attains, and whether its rate of growth is relatively constant or varies with the seasons— then the correct culture is almost self-evident.

Plant geography—a fascinating study—tells us that the many different places in which plants grow present almost every imaginable variation and combination of light, temperature, humidity, and soil characteristics. However, I have found that as a practical matter the indoor gardener need only keep in mind the general characteristics of three environments: the tropical jungle, the warm temperate zone, and the desert. A great majority of the plants grown in the house can be assigned to one of these and treated accordingly.

Jungle soil

Let's consider first the jungle—and a rather generalized and stylized jungle at that. Temperature and humidity are uniformly high; plant growth is lush and constant. The plants range themselves in layers: tall trees and a few high-climbing vines forming the roof; terrestrial plants that have learned to survive with a minimum of illumination carpeting the floor; and, in between, vines and epiphytes, that great group of plants which have learned to live in the crevices of trees and cliffs, deriving nourishment from the particles of decaying matter carried by the jungle rains.

Under such conditions, decay—the breakdown of dead vegetation into humus needed for new growth—is very rapid. Rapid, too, is the use of the decaying matter by the fast-growing, overpopulated plants struggling for survival. As a result, a tropical jungle does not develop the thick layer of fully decayed humus we associate with forests in the temperate zones. Its floor is covered by a relatively thin layer of porous, spongy vegetable matter in active decay, and similar material is lodged in the crevices of trees and rocks where many of the plants live. The surrounding air is damp and the water washing over the layers of vegetation above carries with it more decaying matter. An exposed root may absorb nearly as much nutrient and water as one thrust into the soil in the traditional manner; the roots of plants accustomed to these conditions tend to be fleshy and the root system sparse.

Warm temperate zone soils

The soils of the warm temperate zones resemble more or less the soils we meet in our gardens—a mixture of clay, sand, and silt with varying proportions of well rotted organic matter or humus. There are, of course, wide variations in soil structure, the friability of the soil and its capacity to retain moisture, and also in its acid-alkaline balance, measured by the pH factor. But in general all these soils have smaller particles, are less spongy, and retain less water than the half-decayed humus on the jungle floor. The plant species that grow naturally in such soils develop much more complex and extensive root systems.

Desert soil

Finally, there is the desert, where the great bulk of the soil is sand, often marked by particularly sharp particles. The proportion of humus is small, and the soil structure allows water to percolate rapidly to a considerable depth.

These different kinds of natural soil are the models for the basic soil mixtures described in Part IV of this book. What I call my jungle mixture is an attempt to duplicate the forest floor; epiphyte mixture simulates the conditions found in the nooks and crannies of trees; desert soil is self-descriptive; and my all-purpose mixture is patterned after soils of the temperate plains, but with a bigger proportion of humus to counteract the packing effect of daily watering.

There are many other types of growing mediums and soil mixtures. Jungle plants grow well in completely soilless mediums such as sphagnum moss or decayed leafmold. The standard substance for orchids—one of the largest groups of epiphytes—is osmunda fiber, with shredded bark as a recently developed alternate. Indeed, epiphytes will thrive in almost any medium that will retain a film of moisture and at the same time allow excess water to drain away rapidly, exposing the roots to the air without which they cannot function.

As for the all-purpose mixture, it cannot be expected to encompass every kind of soil from the rich muck of river bottoms to the impoverished sand or rocks of semi-arid regions. You can profitably alter the formula for plants from one of these extremes. Thus, geraniums may do better in a heavier mixture—some commercial growers use a soil almost as heavy as clay—while many Australian plants prefer a blend of all-purpose mixture and desert soil, doubtless because it resembles conditions in the inhospitable interior of their native country.

Pots and containers

Having chosen the proper soil, your next problem is to select the container in which to plant it. The most important characteristic of any container is the drainage it permits, because drainage is vital to the plant. All species except those specially adapted to swamps or bogs grow above the water table in the soil, which means that the surface water drains downward from around their roots, permitting air to penetrate the interstices between the soil particles. The oxygen in this air is used by the plant roots in much the same way as the oxygen obtained by breathing is used by animals. If drainage is impeded so that the soil spaces are filled with water rather than air, the plant fails to obtain the necessary oxygen and drowns. Drowning as a result of overwatering and poor drainage is one of the commonest fates of house plants.

How then do philodendrons, Chinese evergreens, ivy, and the like grow in water? By developing specialized roots that can breathe the air dissolved in the water—as a fish does. Incidentally, these specialized roots are not well adapted to growth in soil, which partly explains the difficulty many house plant fanciers experience when they root cuttings in water and then attempt to pot them.

Containers with holes in the bottom provide better drainage than those without. Unglazed pottery—which allows evaporation through the walls—disposes of excess water faster than glazed pots or other containers that are impervious to vapor. Thus, the risk of drowning is least in the traditional unglazed pot with a drainage hole and greatest in a metal planter with no drainage. Conversely, plants need watering much more often in conventional pots than in planters.

Plastic pots with drainage holes are popular with many growers. They are light and easy to handle, and do not develop either the fungus growth or the salt accumulation which appear on unglazed clay. On the other hand,

I do not find either the color or the texture as attractive as those of clay, and the risk of overwatering because of reduced evaporation is serious. I still get the best results with old-fashioned pots.

A word on planters without drains, of which dish gardens are an example. Plants in such receptacles cannot be expected to look well for any great length of time, and it is virtually impossible for them to grow in any receptacle without a drainage hole.

Pot size, too, affects the danger of drowning; a large ball of earth holds in the water and prevents aeration. I make it a rule never to give my plants more than a half inch of soil outside the root ball, with the result that they are in smaller pots than most persons would expect. A glance at the pictures in Part III of this book will show you better than any words the sizes of pot I have found suitable for various kinds and sizes of plant.

Repotting

As the plant grows, the root system extends into the surrounding layer of soil and gradually fills the spaces between the particles, producing a tight-packed mass which interferes with plant functions much as a too heavy soil would. When this happens, the plant's development slows down, and it is time to repot. Turn the plant upside down and let the rim fall gently on the edge of a table, holding your fingers across the top of the pot to catch the ball of earth as it comes loose.

If your diagnosis was correct, and repotting really is in order, you will find a mass of roots pressing closely against the wall of the pot, with no loose soil. If this is not the case, your diagnosis was wrong. Perhaps the slowing in plant growth was due to the onset of dormancy—which might have been predicted by a check on its growing habits—or perhaps it is due to too little light, a food deficiency, or an insect pest. Whatever the cause, you can put the plant back in its old pot. There is nothing to be gained by giving more space to a plant that hasn't used up the space already provided.

If the plant needs repotting and you want to encourage its growth, make the new pot half an inch or an inch larger than the old. If the plant (or the pot it is in) is already as big as you want, prune the roots to make space for some new soil and put the plant back in the pot it came from—but remember whenever you do this to prune the top of the plant as well. Otherwise it will lose more water through its leaves than the reduced root system can replace, and the result will be severe wilting, loss of foliage, possibly loss of the plant. I make it a fixed routine with almost all types of plants to prune whenever I repot, not only to prevent a setback from the repotting, but also to encourage bushy growth and a compact shape.

In the actual technique of potting (or repotting), drainage is again the keynote. In order to keep an unobstructed path for excess water to escape through, put a piece of broken pot across the drainage hole, concave side down. In larger pots a layer or two of these potsherds is a good device, with possibly a layer of sphagnum moss above them to keep the soil from clogging the drainage channels. Next should come a layer of fresh soil thick enough to raise the plant to the desired level—about one half inch below the top of the pot. Finally comes the plant itself, surrounded by more fresh soil.

At this point a warning is in order: do not tamp the soil around the plants; to do so compacts and destroys the spongy soil structure, prevents aeration and impedes growth. Instead, set the full pot down with a slight jar several times to settle the soil particles into place and then water thoroughly, or better yet, immerse the pot in water to a point just below the rim and leave it for several minutes. When you pick it up, the water draining out through the bottom will compact the soil more gently and evenly than your fingers ever could.

Sterilized soil

No discussion of soils and potting would be complete without mention of the value of sterilized soil. The traditional ingredients of potting soil—manure, leaf mold, compost, and the like—contain weed seeds, insect grubs, and numerous bacteria, some of which can cause disease. All these can be eliminated by sterilization, either by heat or by chemicals such as chlorpicrin, methyl bromide, or formaldehyde.

For heat sterilization of small quantities of soil, your kitchen stove is all the equipment you will need. A good-sized roasting pan of soil can be cooked free of pathogens, nematodes, insect grubs, and weed seeds in two hours at 200°. Be sure to moisten the soil first, or it will come out a powdery mess, and be prepared for the fact that the house will be pervaded with an unpleasant odor. The results are worth it.

The chemical procedures, while very effective, are too exacting to recommend themselves to the average house plant fancier. Growers with large indoor gardens or home greenhouses would be well advised to investigate them.

In considering soil sterilization, you may wonder about the beneficial bacteria, the ones that break down organic matter into compounds suitable for plant nutrition. Are they destroyed along with the pathogenic organisms? In the case of heat sterilization, the answer is yes. In the case of chemical sterilization, the manufacturers claim that the answer is no. In any event, as explained under *Fertilizing*, the organic processes are much less important indoors than out. The benefit from eliminating pathogens and weeds far outweighs any harm from the incidental destruction of desirable organisms.

Packaged soils

All the advantages of carefully mixed and sterilized soils are available today in the packaged potting mixtures sold by house plant supply stores and growers. While these differ somewhat in ingredients and analysis, most of them, whether advertised for African violets or for house plants generally, are based on peat moss or some similar spongy substance with a small proportion of leafmold or other source of humus. I always keep a bag on hand and use it without hesitation for any jungle plant for which I would normally recommend African violet or begonia mixture, and for many flowering plants as well. I have grown succulents in these mixtures too, with great success, though plants of this kind do better in a sandier soil.

WATERING

Of all the factors in the natural environment of a plant, the most difficult to reproduce under artificial conditions is the moisture content of the soil. The top layer of the earth's surface—the topsoil in which most plants grow—is kept constantly moist by capillary action, which draws the water up from the water table below. During a rain the spaces in the topsoil are temporarily filled with water, but soon the rain water drains away and the upward passage of moisture through the soil begins again. Thus, plants are accustomed to live in soil which is damp but not flooded—with a layer of moisture around each particle and air in the spaces between. The root hairs are adapted to absorbing the moisture from the surface of the soil particles, and the roots themselves use the air in between for the respiration process.

How thoroughly to water

Watering is not only the most important operation in plant culture, it is also the most difficult to master. The first commandment is: when you water, be sure to soak the soil thoroughly so that every particle is wet. Thus, when the excess water drains away, the soil will be uniformly damp and the roots will be encouraged to use all the space available to them. Spotty or inadequate watering will tend to concentrate root development in the damper part of the pot. Also, any soil left dry will absorb water from the damp soil in competition with the roots, reducing the effectiveness of the watering almost to nothing.

How often to water

How often do plants need water? There is a story about a lady who bought a selection of cacti and then subscribed to the Tucson newspaper so she could water them whenever it reported rain. She was on the right track in trying to reproduce the natural growing conditions of her plants, but she forgot that soil in pots indoors loses moisture much faster than it would in the earth outdoors—and cannot draw on a subterranean reservoir to replace its losses. Water is lost by evaporation from the surface and if you are using unglazed pots, from the sides of the pots as well. Because the air indoors is dry, evaporation is much more rapid indoors than out. And, as we have seen, this same dry air causes the plant to put out more water in transpiration. The cumulative effect of all these factors explains why plants indoors must usually be watered at least once a day, whereas those outside may be rained on no more than once or twice a month.

Factors affecting the need for water

The object, then, is to water the soil thoroughly just as it is beginning to get so dry that the plant can no longer obtain the moisture it needs. We have already discussed most of the factors which affect the rapidity of the drying out process. They include pot size—evaporation is faster from small pots than from large ones—drainage, soil composition, and the relative humidity of the atmosphere.

Two other important factors are temperature and light. Plant activities, both photosynthesis and transpiration, speed up as temperature rises and light increases. Also, evaporation is faster at higher temperatures. Taking all these into consideration, you can see that, generally speaking, plants in smaller pots will need water more often than those in larger containers; plants in a fast draining soil or pot will need it more often than those having slower drainage; and all plants will need it more often on hot, dry, sunny days than on cold, damp, cloudy ones. Finally, remember that resting and dormant plants do not need water as frequently as those that are growing vigorously.

Observation is the key

Beyond these generalities, you must rely on close observation and experience. Be alert for signs of wilting, and when you see them, water immediately. A plant which really wilts may take months to recover and may lose irreplaceable foliage, generally the lower leaves, in the process.

The things to watch are the rigidity of the stalks and the crispness of the leaves, and always the appearance of the soil, so you will know how it looked just before the first indication of trouble. Plants with thin, light green leaves—such as Lantana, flowering maple, and Browallia—are prone to wilt on sunny days, and show their distress by drooping stems and limp foliage. Philodendrons and similar jungle plants with thick, dark green leaves rarely wilt in the generally understood meaning of the word, but their foliage becomes a little less full and crisp looking, a little wrinkled where it used to be smooth. The same is true of cacti and succulents, although both of these groups can survive for astonishing periods without water.

Harmful effects of cold water

Another cause of wilting in many species is the use of cold water. At lower temperatures the tempo of plant activities decreases. If the entire plant is subjected to a drop in temperature, all its functions slow down more or less uniformly, and the effect is merely to retard growth.

If, however, on a sunny day with air temperatures in the seventies or eighties, a plant's roots are suddenly bathed in cold water, their ability to absorb and use moisture will be slowed for several hours, during which time the moisture loss through transpiration may be enough to cause serious dehydration. This effect is more noticeable in some plants than in others. If you can't supply tempered water for all your plants, keep a container at room temperature for use with those that seem to need it most—generally African violets, episcias, anthuriums, and other natives of the tropics.

There is a second reason for using warm water on African violets and other gesneriads: the fact that water 10° or more below room temperature harms the cells in the leaves of these plants, causing yellow spots and lines. Many African violet experts avoid this risk entirely by watering from the bottom, putting water in the dish under the pot and letting it work up to the surface by capillary action. If you adopt this practice, remember two things. First, you must not let the pot stand in water indefinitely, or the moisture will fill the soil spaces and produce the same effect as lack of drainage. Second, the flow of water upward through the soil causes an accumulation of fertilizer salts near the surface, which is harmful to the plant's crown. An occasional watering from the top will flush these salts out through the drainage hole.

FERTILIZING

It is common knowledge that certain elements found in the soil, particularly nitrogen, phosphorus, potassium, and calcium, are essential to plant growth; and traditional potting composts, based on loam, manure, and bone meal, are designed to be rich in these elements. However, modern inorganic and water soluble fertilizers have, to a large extent, eliminated the necessity of having your potting soil "complete" in these necessities of life. Physical structure of the potting soil is now more important than nutrient content.

In this, indoor practice differs from outdoor. Rich soil in your outside garden will remain satisfactory for several seasons; but in the house, no matter how rich the soil is to start with, it rapidly loses many of its nutrients as a result of the frequent watering, which literally washes away the food elements, particularly the nitrogen. This is why frequent fertilizing is necessary for plants growing indoors. If plants are growing in soil, fertilizing is the difference between mere survival and vigorous growth. For plants growing in sphagnum moss, osmunda fibre, and other soilless mediums, it is an indispensable necessity.

Different amounts of fertilizer at different seasons

In fertilizing, as in other aspects of plant culture, close daily observation, together with a knowledge of the growth habits of your plants, is essential. Most plants have a dormant or semi-dormant period, usually during the short days of fall and winter. At such times continued fertilizing not only is a waste of time but may be harmful, because the nutrient salts, which the resting plant is unable to use, may accumulate to a point where they become toxic. With the lengthening days of late winter and early spring, growth resumes; from then until autumn, plants should be fertilized every two weeks or so.

Within this broad pattern there are many variations which only a study of individual species and specimens will reveal. Geraniums, for example, are among the first to notice the coming of fall. Philodendron, on the other hand, continues to grow well into December and resumes growth again in January. Individual plants that are pot-bound have little soil in relation to the mass of their roots and may need periodic applications of very weak fertilizer solutions to keep alive, even in the dormant season.

There are also some plants whose need for periodic rest is not entirely dependent on the time of year. Gloxinias are a good example. Their growing season is always six to eight months, but the length of their dormant season can be controlled within limits by the length of time they are kept dry and out of the light. If you start gloxinias at intervals, it is possible to have one growing during all months of the year. With species like this, only the appearance of the individual plant will tell you when to stop fertilizing. Gloxinias signal their dormancy by stopping the production of new leaves and eventually losing the leaves and stems they have, but Hoya, for instance, simply stops growing without any marked change in appearance.

Selection of fertilizers

When it comes to choosing fertilizing materials, there are a great many balanced mixtures for house plants on the market, and I have found most of them satisfactory. Gardeners accustomed to mixtures used outdoors will notice that the proportions of nitrogen, phosphorus, and potassium are somewhat different in the formulations for indoor use, the purpose being to compensate for the rapid leaching of nitrogen indoors. Also, most mixtures designed for house plants are water soluble and contain the nutrient elements in inorganic form, the form in which they are immediately available for plant use.

Organic fertilizers—so popular with many outdoor gardeners—are of doubtful value indoors. They require bacterial action to convert them into usable form, and the necessary bacteria may be lacking in the potting medium (especially if it has been sterilized); or the plants may be kept at temperatures well below 70°, which is generally considered the lowest temperature at which the bacteria can operate effectively. Even if conditions are right for the breakdown of the organic compounds, the process is so slow that the nutrients may well be washed out through the drainage hole, or the plant may reach the dormant stage, before real benefit is obtained.

For these reasons it is wise to buy a fertilizer specially recommended for indoor use, and not try on your house plants the same mixture that works well on your lawn or garden. Remember, though, that overdoses of these fast-acting inorganics can cause weak stems, lanky growth, susceptibility to certain diseases, and in extreme cases, the death of the plant. Read the label and follow directions. To be on the safe side I usually use a weaker solution than is recommended and make up for it by more frequent applications. The only supplement I use at all regularly is bonemeal (to supply phosphorus and calcium) in my all-purpose potting mixture.

Application

The most practical way to fertilize indoors is to apply the fertilizer to the soil in a water solution. There are a few products designed to be put in the soil in tablet form, but I have found them unsatisfactory because of the difficulty of knowing when the tablet is used up.

Another fertilizing method is foliar feeding, in which the fertilizer is applied to the leaves in water solution. Foliar feeding is a comparatively recent development. Formerly it was thought that only the roots could absorb water or nutrients. Now we know that the leaves of many plants are also capable of absorption, and that this capacity is more marked in jungle plants and especially epiphytes.

Under natural conditions, plants of this kind derive a large part of their food from the jungle rain and condensation, which carries decaying vegetation and dissolved bird droppings to the foliage below. Even in the temperate plains the rain carries far more organic and mineral matter to the plant leaves than does the tap water with which house plants are sprayed. All plants have learned to use this organic and mineral material; all benefit from occasional foliar feeding, although few can depend on this method exclusively. In my experience, the benefit is most noticeable in the case of bromeliads, ferns (especially the epiphytic varieties), and jungle plants like anthuriums and philodendrons.

Proper fertilization produces vigorous growth, even in small pots, and large, healthy-looking leaves with strong, vivid colors. While it has some beneficial effect on flowering, it is by no means as important as light. Sunlight, not fertilizer, produces flowers.

PESTS AND TROUBLES

No less important than light, temperature, watering, and fertilizing is plant hygiene. The comfortable 70° temperatures and dry atmosphere in our houses are ideal for insects, and if they are permitted to multiply, they will soon make the most vigorous plant look stunted, messy, or neglected. As much as any other factor, control of pests and diseases makes the difference between vitality and drabness in house plants.

I use the word "control" advisedly. The pests are always with us; and even if it were possible to eradicate them from your plants, the next new purchase, perhaps even the next touch from an admiring visitor, might reinfect them. Some growers have become so conscious of the danger of infection, especially by cyclamen mite, that they ask visitors to refrain from handling plants and will not permit new plants to be brought into their greenhouses until they have been sprayed. Fortunately, however, it is not necessary for indoor gardeners to exercise such care. Pests and diseases can be kept within bounds by simple hygienic procedures—plus unremitting vigilance.

Buy healthy plants

The first rule is to buy healthy plants and to dispose ruthlessly of those that develop an infestation you cannot bring promptly under control. The apparent saving in picking up a plant as a gift from a poorly kept collection is almost always outweighed by the effort involved in curbing the pests it brings with it. By the same token, misplaced sentimentality over a sick plant can doom a dozen more. Only where you cannot replace the particular species are you justified in keeping a diseased specimen, and in such cases the strictest isolation is in order.

Washing

The second rule in house plant hygiene is to wash your plants routinely, regardless of whether they show signs of trouble. If each plant is taken to a sink at least every two weeks and washed thoroughly with a forceful spray of lukewarm water—insects, insect eggs, mites, and dust will be swept away. The plant will look better, its clean leaves will function better, and any infestation will be halted early.

Don't worry about warnings that wetting the foliage may harm the plant. The winter sun, even in a south-facing bay window, is too weak to burn the wet leaves, and fungus diseases are not much threat in the dry atmosphere where you and I and our house plants live. If I had to choose just one piece of advice to give a beginner with house plants, it would be to follow the practice of regular plant washing.

Of course, washing is not the complete answer. Some plants are too big to wash, some collections are so large that individual washing is impracticable, and some infestations resist washing. To cope with such circumstances, indoor gardeners should be able to recognize at least the kind of insect or organism that is causing the trouble, and should be generally familiar with the type of pesticide that is effective against insects or organisms of this kind.

Sucking insects

Perhaps the most common and easily identifiable pests are the sucking insects—aphids, mealy bugs, white flies, and scale—below and on pp. 24-26. Not only are they themselves visible to the naked eye, they also leave a sticky excrement—euphemistically called "honey dew" by entomologists—which, if not attended to, collects on the leaves and stems of the affected plant, where it becomes host to a black fungus which is even more repulsive.

In most cases, these sucking insects will be seen and disposed of before they do real harm to the plant; but if they are not checked, the plant will suffer severely from the punctures of its leaf and stem by their needle-like proboscises and the loss of the plant juices on which they feed.

The regular biweekly washing, by removing eggs and mobile young, will

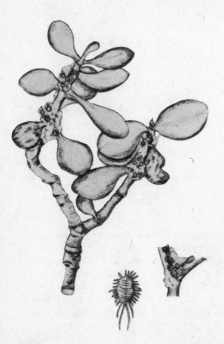

FIG. 4.   MEALYBUGS CLUSTERED IN THE STEM CROTCHES OF A CRASSULA BRANCH.   They are white, cottony insects, which, once they reach the adult stage, seldom move.

ultimately bring sucking insects under control. If more drastic measures are indicated, the standard prescription is nicotine sulphate (applied as a spray), malathion, or the pressurized house plant "bombs" containing rotenone or pyrethrin, both of which are lethal to insects of this type and nontoxic to people or pets. A toothbrush or cotton-tipped toothbrush dipped in alcohol

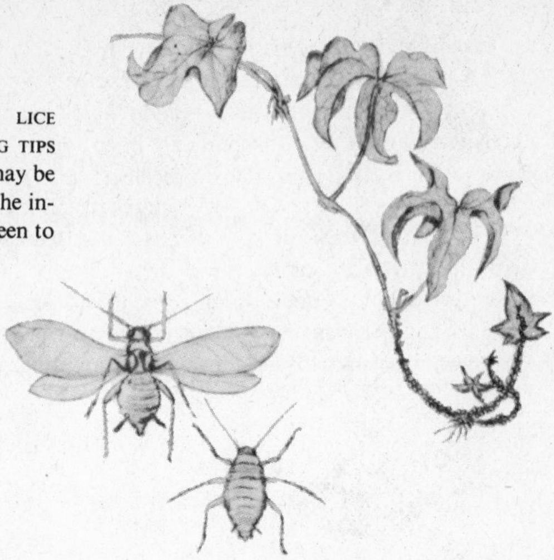

FIG. 5. APHIDS OR PLANT LICE
CLUSTERED ON THE GROWING TIPS
OF AN IVY PLANT.   They may be
green, brown, gray or red. The individual insects are seldom seen to
move.

or nail polish remover is also sure death for a mealybug, scale, or aphid,
but a little tedious to use on an army. Finally, a badly infested plant can
often be saved by dipping its foliage into a warm, soapy solution containing
a teaspoonful of nicotine sulphate to each gallon of water.

FIG. 6.   SCALE ON THE UNDERSIDE OF A FERN FROND.
The scale is actually the thickened and hardened
skeleton. It protects the insect in its adult stage and
also its eggs, which the female lays inside the scale
before she dies, a single scale often housing as many
as thirty eggs or newly hatched young. After a short
period of development, the young insects move to
new locations a short distance from the original scale
and there develop scales of their own, completing
the cycle. Scale is found almost exclusively on
smooth and strap leaved plants.

FIG. 7. WHITE FLIES CLUSTERED ON THE UNDERSIDE OF A GERANIUM LEAF. The adults are tiny and white and will fly off a little distance when disturbed, returning when the disturbance has subsided. The young are wingless and appear as motionless green dots. They can be easily washed off.

In passing, I should warn you to heed the manufacturer's directions for the use of "bombs." The reason he says to keep them at least eighteen inches from the foliage is that if they are held closer, the rapidly expanding gas literally freezes the leaves, causing them to turn brown and drop off.

Red spider mites

The other common enemies of house plants are the tiny creatures known as red spiders, red spider mites, or on occasion, simply as mites. The telltale indication of their presence is the appearance of yellow flecks on the leaves, caused by the mites' sucking juices from the cells in the under surface. You can confirm the diagnosis by finding the tiny webs on the underside of the leaf or by shaking the leaf gently over a piece of white paper, on which the dislodged mites will appear like reddish-yellow dust. Unlike the sucking insects, mites often do serious damage to the plant before you notice the infestation. Leaves that have been subjected to their activities frequently dry up and drop off, spoiling the shape of the plant and if defoliation is severe, retarding its growth. Red spider mite is pictured on page 26.

Because mites are so easily dislodged, biweekly washing is the best cure. There are also a number of miticide sprays on the market, and the multi-purpose sprays containing malathion are lethal to these creatures. Unfortunately, what is toxic to mites is also toxic to humans and animals, so if you use any of these sprays keep them away from people, pets, and food.

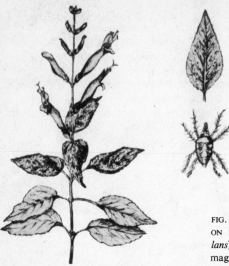

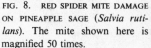

FIG. 8.   RED SPIDER MITE DAMAGE
ON PINEAPPLE SAGE (*Salvia rutilans*). The mite shown here is
magnified 50 times.

Cyclamen mite

A less common house plant pest—but by far the most difficult to control—
is cyclamen mite. This microscopic creature lives and feeds on the growing
tips of the leaves, causing the deformed and stunted foliage which is the usual
indication of its presence. If the new growth on your African violets appears
too furry and too tightly curled, or if the new growth and flower buds on other
species are wrinkled and turn grey or black, cyclamen mite is a likely suspect.

The control of cyclamen mites is extremely difficult. Washing will not dis-
lodge them from the crevices and folds in which they live. Sometimes the
infestation can be checked by cutting away the infected parts with a sharp
knife and dipping the remainder in a solution of miticide. Even then the plant
should be isolated for three weeks and dipped in miticide again at the end of
this period.

Sodium selenate, a systemic poison, which the plant takes up from the
soil and incorporates in its tissues, is effective against cyclamen mites and
some other pests. However, the only sure cure, and the one I would recommend in all cases except where the plant is irreplaceable, is to throw the
victim away. And remember that cyclamen mite is easily transferred from
one plant to another. Wash your hands carefully after touching a plant
suspected of harboring this pest.

Nematodes

Another group of organisms beyond the average indoor gardener's ability to control are the microscopic worms called nematodes, which attack the roots of certain species, causing dwarfed or stunted growth. If you suspect their presence, knock the soil from the roots and examine them for the small round galls on the root branches which are caused by the nematodes' activities.

Sterile soil is the best preventive for nematodes. If they do appear, I generally burn both the plant and the soil that was around its roots, for though there are at least two chemicals on the market which are effective against them, the plant is usually so badly stunted by the time they are discovered that curative efforts would be a waste of time.

Slugs and earthworms

By comparison with such microscopic pests as we have been discussing, slugs and earthworms are readily apparent and easily curbed. Slugs are shell-less snails that eat seedlings and chew holes in leaves. Since they need a very humid atmosphere and a damp, dark place to hide during the day, they do not thrive indoors; you are most apt to encounter them while your plants are outside during the summer. However, if you are not careful, you may bring several inside on the pots when you return your plants to winter quarters, and occasionally a colony may get started in a large planter or ground bed. Wherever they appear, they can be controlled by spraying the lower leaves of the plant, the pot, and the surface on which it rests with one of the liquid solutions sold for the purpose or by putting snail bait (available under a number of brand names) around the affected plants at night when the slugs are most active. Be sure to remove the bait next morning, since it soon loses its effectiveness against slugs but may still remain harmful to pets.

As for earthworms, these beneficial inhabitants of your outdoor garden soil can do a surprising amount of harm if allowed to share a pot with a plant indoors. While they do not actually feed on plant tissues, their motions disturb the contact between the root hairs and the soil particles and may even break off the root hairs entirely. Worms signal their presence by leaving droppings on the surface of the soil. When these appear you can find and remove the offender by knocking the plant out of the pot and probing with a finger in the soil, or by watering with a solution of a teaspoon of dry mustard to a gallon of water or a solution of permanganate of potash strong enough to have a deep pink color. Either of these should bring your unwelcome visitor to the surface.

Diseases

Plants are also prey to many bacterial and fungus diseases causing wilting, galls, blights, tumors, and other symptoms. Exact diagnosis is sometimes difficult even for the trained scientist, and a cure is frequently impossible. Fortunately, such diseases are not common indoors, and when they do occur, they are unlikely to spread from the species afflicted to the other different species in your collection. Intensive study of diseases is a waste of time for the average house plant fancier.

There are, however, at least two common and curable diseases you should watch for. Occasionally the leaves of seemingly healthy plants are marred by brown spots or curled brown edges. This may mean that they are playing host to a fungus which can be controlled by a spray containing the ingredient "captan." Great care should be taken to follow the manufacturer's directions, as too strong a solution does more harm than good. Mildew, another controllable fungus disease, occurs on the leaves of various plants under warm, humid conditions. Your garden supplier will have a fungicide especially formulated for this.

A great many of the plant diseases are carried by the insects discussed earlier in this section, so control of these pests will keep the diseases at a minimum. Conscientious plant hygiene is the best preventive medicine for your indoor garden.

Fresh air, ventilation and heating

House plants benefit from a gentle circulation of clean air. They are harmed by drafts, particularly when accompanied by abrupt changes of temperature, and by many of the toxic substances that pollute the air in our cities. The atmosphere of warm, stagnant air, saturated with moisture, is also undesirable, because it encourages mildew, mold and disease.

This means that you must pay attention to the quality and circulation of the air around your plants. In my experience it is much easier to grow plants in a house heated by hot water than by hot air. Hot-air systems, at least the old-fashioned kind, tend to produce hot dry blasts, interspersed with periods of cold—a poor environment for tender plants. Such a system can also pick up combustion gases from a leaky furnace, which are quite harmful to growing things. I have also found that the circulation of air near a cool window keeps most plants healthy, but, of course, if the window is very leaky, the resultant cold drafts can make trouble.

One caveat found in older texts is now out of date. That is the warning that plants cannot be grown successfully in houses heated with gas. This warning dates from the days of manufactured gas, which was, indeed, poisonous to plants and people as well. Today, the gas in general use is natural gas, which has a different chemical makeup and does not seem particularly toxic. The garden under artificial lights described in Part II is in the kitchen of my house where natural gas is used for heating and cooking.

I have had little experience with air conditioning. The rather tough plants in my air-conditioned office seem to thrive, and I would expect the same to be true of plants in an air-conditioned house, subject always to the caution that tender tropicals should not be placed in the direct path of cold air.

SUMMER CARE

Summer is the season when tropical plants are at their best, for only then is there enough light, heat, and humidity for them to grow the way they do in their native homes. Wise gardeners make the most of this by putting their larger plants outside at this time of year, but this does not mean that the plants can be scattered around the garden indiscriminately and abandoned to the summer's drying winds and drenching rains.

A knowledge of the natural habitat of your plant will help in determining the best location for its summer vacation. The jungle plants, which have evolved wide, heavy leaves to expose the broadest possible surface to the filtered jungle light, will need a protected and partially shaded place, perhaps along the northern side of the house or under high bushes or trees. Plants of the semi-tropics and the warm temperate zones should be put in a spot that receives full sun for several hours every day, but the transition from their winter quarters must be made gradually, or many will develop scorched leaves. Desert plants will grow and flower profusely if given every available hour of sunlight. Their thick leaves and stems will protect them from drying or burning, and the intense light is just what they were born to enjoy.

Leave the plant in the pot

Regardless of what location is chosen, plants that are to be taken back into the house (with the exception of cacti and succulents, which do not wilt) should be left in the pot. If allowed to grow without this confinement, the plant develops a sprawling root system, most of which is lost when it is dug up and repotted in the fall. This unintentional root pruning causes severe wilting, which will undo all the summer's benefit.

Plants in pots dry out fast during hot summer days. This danger will be considerably lessened if you sink the pots in the earth up to their rims. And this practice has the added advantage of keeping the root ball cooler than it would be if the pot were exposed to the summer sun. When you dig the hole to sink the pot, put an inch or two of pebbles, broken crock, or cinders in the bottom to discourage the roots from growing through the drainage hole and down into the earth below. But don't rely solely on this discouragement. Regardless of obstacles, the roots will grow down and seek the earth, and you should lift the pot and break them off every two or three weeks.

July and early August will be a busy time for the gardener with a large collection. By then the plants will have put on prodigious growth and most will need repotting to a larger pot and pruning to induce compactness. August is also the latest good month for making cuttings of plants that have become too big for the window sill. Cuttings taken after midsummer are apt to be finicky and difficult to root.

People with large collections will find that a lath house offers the best conditions for summering their tropical house plants. Some of these shelters, particularly on the west coast, are a great addition to the garden, affording a shady place to sit and enjoy summer weather and winter plants at the same time. Old-fashioned porches used to answer the need for many, but they are too often surrounded by large shade trees so that the plants do not get enough sun to put on the desired growth. Also, deep cold frames have served me well. Lath sash replaces glass, and the plants thrive in half sun and half shade. Unfortunately, so do armies of slugs.

If you are tempted to dispense with all this summer care, remember that much as you might wish it otherwise, summer is the season when most tropicals bloom, grow, and prosper. The only way you can have beautiful plants in winter is to give them care, feeding, and above all, extra light in the summer.

PROPAGATION

For me, propagating my own plants is half the fun of indoor gardening. No matter how often the process is repeated, it seems a miracle when full-fledged plants develop from seeds I have sown or cuttings I have taken. So my advice is to try. You will find propagating easier than you expect, and success will add immensely to the satisfaction you get from your plants.

There are, of course, two methods of reproducing plants—seminal propagation (growing from seed) and vegetative propagation (rooting cuttings, dividing clumps, air layering, and similar processes).

Seminal propagation is the sexual method of reproduction. The seed results from the fertilization of the egg cell in the female part of the flower (the pistil) by the pollen from the male part (the stamen), the pistil and stamens being sometimes in the same and sometimes in different flowers. As a consequence, each seedling has its own unique hereditary traits, and seedlings vary just as people do. In many well established species, the variations are so minute as to be insignificant; such species are said to breed true. In others, such as coleus and some begonias, there are marked variations among seedlings. Hybrids, being crosses between species or varieties, generally will not breed true.

Vegetative propagation, on the other hand, does not involve any new combination of hereditary factors. The new plant has the same heredity as the one from which it was taken. In effect, they are as like one another as identical twins.

With most house plants either method will work. There are, however, quite a few plants that must be reproduced vegetatively—species that do not flower readily and hybrids that bear sterile flowers or do not breed true from seed. There are also a very few species that can be grown only from seed, either because they are so formed as to make vegetative propagation impossible, or because none of the vegetative methods meet with success in their case. Finally, there are genera, like coleus, which are highly variable and should be reproduced seminally if new varieties are wanted and vegetatively if the existing variety is to be carried forward. The descriptions in Part III tell my methods of propagating most species.

Propagation from seed

While vegetative propagation is generally considered easier (think of the number of African violets produced from leaf cuttings), it has been my experience that in many cases plants from seed grow faster and are stronger and more compact than those from cuttings. Also, seeds are the cheapest way to acquire a new item for your collection. A packet costs about twenty-five cents, whereas a small established plant is seldom less than one dollar, and often much more. Don't be discouraged by the fact that the seeds are sometimes tiny and the techniques delicate. Growing plants from seeds requires more patience than skill.

The first thing to remember is that fresh seed is the only kind worth using. If you fail with anything but fresh seed, you will never know whether to blame the seed or your own efforts. Fresh seed may be bought from reliable dealers or collected from your own or your neighbor's plants. You will be surprised at how many species set seed naturally even in the house or greenhouse, and there are a few more, notably oranges and lemons, which you can hand pollinate in the winter when bees and other insects are hibernating outside.

Generally speaking, in the case of the tropical and subtropical plants grown indoors, the seed is ripe and ready to plant when the pods have turned brown and appear dry. No long maturing period, such as is needed with many plants from colder climates, is necessary.

Seed sowing and germination

There are a hundred and one methods of germinating seed, all intended to accomplish the same ends: to keep the developing seeds moist but not wet, and to provide ventilation and light for the seedlings when germination has taken place. You will find differences of opinion as to the growing medium, the kind of container, methods of watering and conserving moisture, and even the amount of light and ventilation needed by the tiny plants. This variety of views shows that there is no definite right way to proceed, no magic formula for success. Any of the alternative methods will give good results if faithfully and understandingly followed.

For a sowing medium I prefer milled sphagnum moss. It holds a large proportion of water and gives unmistakable indications of dryness when it needs more. The roots of the seedlings grow vigorously in it, and it is virtually free of microscopic organisms, which means that it entails little danger of "damping-off," the insidious fungus disease that causes tiny seedlings to disintegrate where the stem emerges from the soil. Of course, there are a number of other sterile substances—notably vermiculite, perlite, sand, and sterile soil—which share this advantage; but all of them present more problems in the control of moisture.

The question of what kind of container to use is much discussed, but the one point frequently overlooked is that the indoor gardener generally wants only one or two plants of a variety, so there is no need to use the large containers or flats recommended for outdoor gardens. A 2¼-inch or stubby three-inch clay pot is large enough for the tiny seeds of the gesneriads, begonias, and many other tropical plants and does not take up too much space in a crowded indoor garden.

Fill the bottom half of the pot with broken crock or stones and the top half with whatever growing medium you decide to use. If it is milled sphagnum, be sure to wet it thoroughly in a bowl, squeezing the excess water out, as it is practically impossible to wet in any other way. Sowing is easy. Scatter the seeds on top of the damp moss and then immerse the pot in a bowl of water until moisture is visible on the top. When the pot is removed from the bowl, the receding water will settle the seeds. Small seeds will need no covering, but larger ones should be covered to a depth of about their own thickness.

Keeping the growing medium moist during germination is absolutely essential; one thorough drying out may be fatal. On the other hand, too frequent or too abundant watering can rot the seed or encourage "damping-off." Bottom watering lessens the danger of flooding and also the danger of washing the seeds all to one corner of the pot. In order to conserve moisture, reduce the frequency of watering, and minimize the risk of drying out, cover the pot with a moisture-proof seal. But in so doing, remember that the seal must not be airtight, because stagnant air encourages mold and rot. Also, seedlings need light as soon as they emerge. Transparent polyethylene plastic makes a good seal because it retains moisture and still permits the passage of light and air. The plastic film sold under the name *Saran wrap*, which also adheres to the rim of the pot, is especially convenient. If you use another kind of seal, glass for instance, it must be opened periodically to allow a flow of air.

The seeds of tropical plants need heat to germinate, and this is best supplied from underneath. Radiators are generally unsatisfactory because they go on and off too frequently and do not afford the constant heat that is needed. The low voltage 2½-watt electric cables sold for heating seed flats and cold frames are ideal. They present no fire hazard and can be left on all the time, supplying a mild, steady heat ranging between 70° and 80°, such as would be found in tropical soil. I have also known some determined gardeners to use an electric bed heating pad to good effect, but I suspect the cost is high.

There are wide differences between species in the length of time required for germination. Browallia seed, for example, often germinates in ten days; Ardisia seed takes eight or nine months. The average germination time for a particular species can generally be found in the catalogs or on the seed packet. If such information is not available, my rule of thumb would be not to throw anything away in less than six months.

Thinning and transplanting

Once the seedlings are up and have developed a second pair of leaves, they can be thinned and transplanted. If you need only a few plants, thinning is all that is necessary. Leave the seedlings in the seed pot until they are big

FIG. 9.   SEEDS AND SEEDLINGS.   The seeds are planted in milled sphagnum and are watered from the bottom. During the germination period the pots are covered with *Saran wrap* to retain moisture. When the seedlings begin to emerge, the covering is removed. Bottom heat is supplied by low-voltage 2½ watt cable, which keeps the temperature at the level of the plant tray about 70°. On the left are recently potted seedlings which have been put in the moist atmosphere under the cake cover until they recover from the shock of being transplanted.

enough to handle easily, thinning them from time to time with tweezers and throwing the extra ones away. If you want more than a few plants, you will have to transplant some out of the original pot; this is best done before the seedling has put on too much root growth. I often use tiny 1¼-inch clay thumb pots, giving each seedling one of its own.

After the seedling has been transplanted, some sort of terrarium or moisture proof covering is essential. It will take the transplants several days to get over the shock of being moved; and if they dry out and wilt during this period, they will probably die.

Beginning with the appearance of the second leaves, the plants will benefit from weekly watering with a weak fertilizer solution. However, a word of caution is in order. Fertilizer, water, and too little light will produce weak, spindly growth. Fertilizer, water and good light, preferably sunlight, will produce strong bushy growth.

Vegetative propagation

Vegetative propagation is the basic method of maintaining a collection of house plants, and every indoor gardener should have at least the elementary equipment and a working knowledge of the different techniques—rooting cuttings, making divisions, air layering, and planting runners and offsets. Quite a few plants can be propagated by one or more of these methods, so if you find, for instance, that the cuttings of a particular species are hard to root, try air layering.

Rooting cuttings

The first thing to keep in mind in regard to cuttings from the tropical plants grown indoors is that nine times out of ten these are softwood cuttings —quite different from the hardwood cuttings generally taken from hardy woody plants grown in the temperate zones. Rooting hardwood cuttings can be tricky and time-consuming; rooting softwood cuttings, at least those from tropical plants, is usually fairly easy. So don't be confused by the extensive literature on vegetative propagation, most of which is written for the nurseryman rather than the indoor gardener.

The first step in rooting cuttings is to choose a rooting medium. Sand, perlite, and milled sphagnum moss are all widely used for the purpose because they are virtually free of harmful bacteria and their structure retains moisture and at the same time permits the aeration which is essential for root formation. Of the three, perlite is the easiest for the indoor gardener. It is light and clean and holds more than ten times its weight in water without becoming water logged; plants seem to root in it at least as readily as in any other substance. Slips rooted in water never seem to adjust as well or make as vigorous growth as those rooted in sand, perlite, or moss, probably because the roots they develop in the water are not adapted to soil.

Cuttings from tropical plants, like tropical seeds, develop faster if the rooting medium is supplied with bottom heat, the optimum soil temperature for cuttings being about 70°. Cuttings, however, need more humidity than seedlings because they have been deprived of their roots and cannot replace water lost through transpiration. Fully equipped greenhouses use mist propagation systems which maintain the relative humidity at 90 per cent or more. The indoor gardener can achieve somewhat the same effect by enclosing the cuttings in a vapor-proof canopy. Small plastic "greenhouses" and boxes serve this purpose well; or the cuttings can be covered with an inverted glass jar, bowl, or a plastic cake cover. Whatever is chosen must admit a reasonable amount of light and the cover should be raised periodically to permit circulation of air. Excessive bottom heat and stagnant air both contribute to rot.

The time of year also has an effect on the successful rooting of slips or cuttings. Those taken in early spring are by far the surest to root, for at this time practically all plants are awakening from their winter dormancy and are actively growing and developing. Cuttings taken in late summer and early fall usually root less quickly, and those taken in late fall and winter are apt to rot before roots form. If off-season propagation is necessary, it is much facilitated by the application of bottom heat.

Cuttings can be taken from any plant that has a stem or branches. They should be three to five inches long and should be green growth, not brown or hardened woody growth. Use a clean, sharp knife, and for best results take the cutting from the end of a branch or shoot. Shoots thrusting up from the base of the plant are generally considered the best, though any tip growth may be used.

After making the cuttings, trim the leaves and bracts from the lower two inches and wrap all but the newly cut end in a wet paper towel for an hour or so to let the cut end dry. With some plants, like geraniums for instance, the drying period should be extended to several hours, and with cacti and succulents to several days. Then make a hole in the rooting medium at least one inch deep with a pencil or your finger and insert the cutting in the hole. Firm the medium around the cutting and water it. Be sure to label it too, or you may find yourself with that most pathetic of horticultural specimens, a plant without a name.

Don't pull your cuttings out to examine them in less than two weeks. Except for a few very fast rooters like coleus, all plants require at least this long to root or to develop the clearly visible enlargement of the cut end of the stem which is called a callus, and which is a sure sign that roots will eventually form. Some take an astonishingly long time, as much as six or eight months. As long as the cutting hasn't rotted, there is a good chance it will root.

When the roots are one-fourth to one-half inch long, dig the new plant out carefully, pot it in your smallest pot in soil appropriate to the species, water it, and return it to the place it was rooted for at least four days. This will reduce the inevitable shock that this first crucial operation brings. After about a week, knock the plants (root, soil, and all) out of the pot. If you can see new white roots, you have a new plant to be added to your collection and treated like the others there. If you don't see new white roots, continue to baby the cutting until you do.

Leaf cuttings

Rex begonias, and many of the large leaved rhizomatous group as well, can be propagated from a single leaf. Under favorable conditions, as in your cutting box, new plants will develop where the main veins of the leaf are cut. You can lay the leaf on the rooting medium (holding it in place with toothpicks), or you can cut wedge-shaped pieces of leaf with a main vein in each of them and insert these in the medium like cuttings. These cuttings should be given the same treatment as stem cuttings. With adequate bottom heat the new plants should develop in two to four weeks.

Crassulas and many succulents are also propagated from leaves. As an extreme example, plantlets will sprout in the marginal notches of kalanchoe leaves that are severed from the plant, without any further action by the gardener. Indeed, in a few species the plantlets will appear even while the leaf remains on the plant. Sedums also are virtually self-propagating. A sedum leaf needs only to fall on damp sand or pebbles to develop into a new plant.

Peperomias, African violets, gloxinias, and most other gesneriads are readily propagated by leaf-petiole cuttings. Cut the leaf and its petiole (stem) from the main stem of the plant and insert the petiole in your rooting medium with your other cuttings. The new plants (in the case of violets, several from

FIG. 10. CUTTINGS AND TRANSPLANTS. These cuttings are rooting in perlite in a plastic box which retains moisture and prevents drying out. The lid is opened a little for about an hour a day to permit circulation. When the perlite gets too dry, I sprinkle it with water at room temperature, using the syringe sprinkler shown at the right. Low voltage 2½-watt cables running under the box keep the perlite at about 70°. Also in the box you will see newly potted cuttings put there to get over the shock of being potted.

each cutting) appear at the cut end of the petiole. They are ready for potting as soon as new growth is visible above the surface of the rooting medium. I pot the whole mass of growth and divide it later when it is sturdier and easier to handle. Tuber-forming gesneriads like gloxinias will form a new tuber on the end of the petiole. It will be several months before new growth appears.

Divisions

Plants with a multiple crown—that is, more than one stem emerging from the ground—can often be divided into several parts, an operation which at the same time yields one or more new plants and reduces the size of the original plant so as to prevent it from outgrowing its pot. Take a sharp knife, muster your courage (you will not hurt the plant), and slice cleanly through the crown, root and all. Then cut the foliage back quite severely to encourage new growth, and pot the divisions in the appropriate potting soil—not in the cutting box. The result will be two or more smaller, more compact plants to replace an overgrown and possibly leggy one. Cane-stemmed or "angel-wing" begonias, African violets, succulents, ivies, and many others lend themselves to this procedure. Just be sure that each division has a growing point (a place where growth is emerging), or "eye" (a bud-like protuberance).

Air layering

Occasionally you will have a plant which you want to propagate, but which is too large for your cutting box—a large-leaved philodendron, a rubber

FIG. 11. PROPAGATING REX BEGONIAS FROM LEAF CUTTINGS.   Cuts are made across the main veins as shown. The cut leaves are then placed on damp perlite in a cutting box in such fashion as to bring the cut portions in contact with the perlite. If necessary they can be held in place with toothpicks or hairpins. If you look closely, you will see a number of plantlets growing from the cuts in the leaves in the box.

plant, or a dracena. These are natural candidates for air layering, as are the few species that are hard to reproduce from cuttings and unsuited for division. Air layering takes time, sometimes as much as six or eight months, but it is worth trying, particularly if you want a good sized plant to replace your overgrown one.

The first step is to girdle the stem where you would like to have the roots appear; I usually remove a strip of the outer layer of bark about one half inch wide at, or just below, a node (a place where branches or leaves emerged). An alternative procedure, which sometimes seems easier than girdling, is to cut a notch or wedge in the stem. If you do this, pack the opening with damp sphagnum moss to keep the wound from healing.

When the bark has been removed or the notch cut, wrap that portion of the stem with a good handful of damp sphagnum to keep the wounded area moist. Then wrap the moss in polyethylene film and seal it at the top and bottom with electrician's tape. If you achieve a moisture-proof seal, you will have nothing more to do until the roots develop. If not, the moss will dry out in a short time and you will have to remoisten it and try again.

When the newly formed roots are visible through the film, cut the new plant off just below the roots, remove the film but not the moss, and pot the root ball. Do not automatically discard the parent plant. It will often sprout new leaves where the new plant was cut off, and in some cases will have a more branched and bushy growth than before.

Runners

Some plants do all the work for you by producing small plantlets on runners like strawberries. These root if they touch damp soil or pebbles, and can be detached from the parent plant and potted. They do not need the special nursing and care that cuttings or seedlings require. Episcias, Boston ferns, saxifrages, and spider plants are all in this group.

Offsets

Bromeliads, agaves, aloes, haworthias, and various other plants produce offsets—small stemless replicas of the parent plant (often called suckers), which grow out from its base or stem, sometimes in great profusion, and sometimes only once a year. These can be cut off with a sharp knife and rooted like cuttings. They seldom rot and are generally a very reliable way of getting a new plant.

PRUNING AND SHAPING

Most house plants, if allowed to develop without restraint under natural conditions would become full-sized trees, shrubs or vines or rangy herbaceous plants. Only a very few are naturally small or compact. The challenge of pot gardening is to keep the naturally large ones at manageable size and in pleasing proportions. The basic technique for accomplishing this is pruning.

Horticultural basis of pruning

A young tree must elevate its foliage above the surrounding underbrush and into the light in order to survive. Accordingly, for the first year or so it is apt to consist of a single, leafy stem growing straight up. Many single-stemmed woody house plants are really tropical trees in this juvenile stage.

As the growing tip of the young tree extends upwards, additional leaves and ultimately branches appear at intervals along the new growth, and the older leaves lower down on the stem die and fall off. This is inevitable. Proper culture may prolong the life of a leaf, but sooner or later every fiddle-leaved fig and every rubber tree will lose its lower foliage and look leggy. At this point, pruning will induce the plant to branch earlier and oftener than it would in its natural development, thus restoring its attractiveness.

The explanation for this is the presence of lateral buds along the stem—so-called axillary buds in the niches (known as axils) where the leaf stalks join the stem, and adventitious buds scattered in between. Each of these lateral buds is capable of developing into a branch, but its development is inhibited by a hormone-like substance produced by the terminal bud at the end of the growing shoot. When the terminal bud is removed by pruning, the lateral buds, both axial and, to a lesser extent, adventitious, begin to grow, and new leaves develop along their growing shoots.

Techniques of pruning woody plants

When the terminal bud is pruned, a new growth will usually begin in one or two axillary buds immediately below the cut. This means that the cut should be made just above the height where you want the branch to appear and at a place where there is a bud to develop into a new leader—*i.e.,* at the base of a leaf if the leaf is still attached, otherwise at a node, the swelling that marks the place where a leaf previously grew. Cuts made at axils or nodes will heal readily without dying back. An internodal cut dies back to the next node, forming an unsightly stub.

Once the branches have begun to grow, they, in turn, can be induced to develop lateral branches by pruning. Removal of the end bud of a branch has the same effect on it that removal of the terminal bud has on the stem. And the same is true of the multiple shoots of woody shrubs. Repeated pruning will produce numerous branches and twigs from which the gardener can retain those that are pleasing to the eye, cutting away and discarding the others.

Pinching

The foregoing explanation shows that the horticultural effect of pruning comes from the removal of the terminal buds. The same result can be obtained simply by pinching off the terminal buds from time to time. Pinching is particularly effective on fast-growing plants during the spring and summer, when the pinched bud is rapidly replaced.

Shaping herbaceous plants

Begonias, philodendron, geraniums, African violets and other herbaceous plants are just as amenable to shaping by pruning and pinching as trees and shrubs. Frequent pinching during the growing season keeps them compact and encourages the multiplication of side branches. Occasional severe pruning, usually in late winter or early spring, will result in a renewal of the entire plant. When a tropical perennial is grown in the house, protected from the vicissitudes of the weather and devouring animals, there is nothing but the gardener's clippers to remove the old growth and make way for the new.

PART ❧✦❧ TWO

Some Indoor Gardens

Indoor gardens are as varied as those outdoors, and like their outdoor counterparts, they reflect the personalities of their owners. Some are neat, restrained, and orderly. Others grow in happy confusion. Some are planned so that foliage and flowers compliment each other. Others serve as a home for every plant the owner can lay his or her hands on.

In the following pages are pictures and descriptions of gardens of different kinds and in different locations. Except for the greenhouse garden, which was set up as an educational exhibit in a flower show, and the desert garden, which was put together for the picture, I followed the principle of showing actual gardens with the plants that actually grow in them rather than a collection of greenhouse specimens arranged for the occasion. However, photographic demands required a few changes and substitutions among the plants, and in two cases I compromised with principle to the extent of reconstructing the garden in a more attractive location. The descriptions of growing conditions are based on first-hand observation, and the discussions of ways and means reflect the gardener's actual experience. In short, these are real gardens and can be duplicated under similar circumstances.

The plants shown are described in Part III, and the cultural practices mentioned here are explained in Part I. Particular items in a garden—plant benches, hanging baskets, and the like—are described in the text accompanying the pictures.

A SOUTH WINDOW
(*Fig. 12*)

This charming indoor garden grows in a dining room window facing almost due south and gets five or six hours of sun each day. The nearest radiator is six feet away, so the temperature in the window often drops as low as 55° at night. The sill itself is sixteen inches wide, which means that there is a considerable difference in light and temperature between the interior and the exterior edges.

FIG. 12.   A SOUTH WINDOW.

KEY TO FIG. 12:

1. *Manettia bicolor*
2. *Begonia* 'Orange rubra'
3. *Heliotropium arborescens*
4. *Davallia fejeensis plumosa*
5. *Pittosporum Tobira variegata*
6. *Citrus ponderosa*
7. *Beloperone guttata*
8. *Pelargonium* 'Happy Thought'
9. *Cissus striata*
10. *Davallia Griffithiana*
11. *Malpighia coccigera*
12. *Pellionia Daveauana*
13. *Polystichum adiantiforme*

Such a cool, sunny spot is well suited for flowering plants. Heliotrope, shrimp plant, Mexican firecracker, and the orange-flowered begonia were chosen because of their everblooming habit and because their flowers and bracts, together with the fruit of the lemon, make a pleasing combination of orange, blue, and yellow. But even these reliables falter in November and December. To tide the garden over this bleak period and provide an interesting background for the flowers as they appear, I chose variegated Pittosporum with its shining crisp leaves, and balanced it with a fancy-leaved geranium, 'Happy Thought.' There is further variety and contrast in the feathery plumes of the ferns which frame the two lower corners.

The interior edge presents conditions different from those near the glass. It is warmer, and the plants there are partially shaded by those nearer the light. Also, they must be low, even trailing, to hide the pots but not the plants behind and to break the straight line of the sill's edge. The three plants selected, Cissus, Pellionia and Davallia, all meet these requirements and have the further advantage of continuing the diversification of foliage color, shape, and texture.

The Pellionia contains reddish-purple shades which complement both the reddish brown of the shrimp plant and the slightly lavender hue of the heliotrope. Perhaps this is what led me to add the pale blue African violet in the front border. The window is really too cold for it, but the color is just right, and on cold nights it can easily be moved to a warmer spot.

One of the most engaging characteristics of this garden is the way it responds to its weekly washing. The light and variegated foliage emerges crisp and shining with a freshness reminiscent of an outdoor garden after a spring shower.

The overall effect of this garden is airy and colorful, and this effect will last the entire indoor season without replacement of any of the plants. After a full year of growing, some may get too big; but thoughtful summer care, including both pruning and propagating, will keep the garden in proper size and proportion indefinitely.

A GARDEN WITH ARTIFICIAL LIGHT
(*Fig. 13*)

Small enough to fit underneath kitchen cabinets and large enough for an amazing variety of dwarf tropicals, this artificially lighted garden makes kitchen chores a pleasure for one who would rather be potting than cooking.

Like so many projects, it evolved over a period of several months. The first step was the lights, two four-foot fluorescent tubes in standard commercial "channels" spaced four inches apart. (We had no room for reflectors, but I am sure they would be worth the cost if space were available.) One tube is the daylight type and the other cool white. The two together span a sufficient portion of the visible spectrum—which is the only part of the light that plants use—to serve as an acceptable substitute for the sun. The area eleven inches below the tubes receives about 700 foot-candles of light. I renew the tubes every three or four months to keep them as bright as possible.

Once the lights were in, the garden began to grow. African violets, which had languished flowerless on my kitchen window sill, began blooming within three weeks, and I began to wonder how I had endured that dark kitchen without this cheerful corner. Then the need for extra humidity became apparent, so I made aluminum trays to fit along the counter, filled them with small pebbles, and wet them every time I cooked a meal. (See Fig. 2 for an illustration of how to make these trays.) This improved the situation considerably, but the fifteen-hour artificial day kept the plants growing at such a rate that they still tended to dry out quickly. Also, the chilly drafts from the kitchen door were harmful to the tender tropicals that grow in such a subdued light.

The solution was obvious: a transparent enclosure to retain the moisture and exclude the drafts. A few evenings in the family workshop produced the sliding glass panels visible in the picture, and the beneficial effect on the plants could be noticed almost immediately. Incidentally, if you are tempted to try such a garden, remember that a certain amount of air circulation is helpful. Absolutely tight fitting doors are unnecessary. We leave ours open an inch or two at each end in spring, summer, and fall. In winter, the house air is so dry that we keep them closed all the time; enough fresh air gets in during watering and pebble-wetting.

FIG. 13. A GARDEN WITH ARTIFICIAL LIGHT.

With the acquisition of the glass panels my appetite was whetted still further. I wanted now to be able to maintain the high and relatively constant temperatures that jungle plants need for best growth regardless of chilly nights, open windows, doors ajar, and the other vicissitudes of household existence. So the final step in the development of my fluorescent garden was the installation of a heating system—a six-foot 2½-watt electric cable of the kind sold for heating seed flats and cold frames. It is laid beneath the trays and is turned off and on automatically by a small thermostat sold by the same company that makes the cable.

At 7:30 each morning, as the orange juice is squeezed and the eggs are cooked, the plants' day begins with the erratic blink of the fluorescent tubes and the twist of the thermostat to its daytime setting of 80°. At bedtime each evening the lights are turned off and the thermostat set back to 70°.

Any plant that lives naturally in a place with subdued or filtered light, high temperatures, and a high degree of humidity will grow in this miniature jungle. African violets and gloxinias develop into specimen plants with as many blossoms as those in my greenhouse. Semperflorens begonias also bloom freely, and I was surprised last fall to find *Tillandsia ionantha* in flower there. On the other hand, episcias and Kohlerias grow rampantly but do not bloom. Apparently there is not quite enough light for them.

Other plants that do particularly well here are rex begonias, Crossandra and dwarf caladiums. In early spring, small pots of seeds and cuttings crowd the violets and episcias out onto window sills again, for the combination of mild bottom heat and low illumination is ideal for germinating tiny, tricky seeds and for rooting cuttings.

A HEATED SUNPORCH
(*Fig. 14*)

This is part of my sunporch. By eight o'clock on winter mornings the sun rises over the tall trees across the road and pours in on the plants until the middle of the afternoon. Only this much light could produce flowers of the kind shown here. The plants are so dependent on it that I have to turn each one around every few days so it will look at me instead of at the sun.

The plant benches are a design I have found both practical and decorative. The upper bench is made thirteen inches narrower than the lower one, giving a tiered effect that is not apparent in this picture but shows clearly in Fig. 1. If I have a chance to build another, I will make the upper bench shorter as well, giving the same tiered effect to the ends. The legs are pipe, screwed into metal flanges. This permits adjustment of the height of both benches to suit the proportions of the room. Both upper and lower benches are four inches deep—to hide the bulk of the pots.

The wood is cypress, stained and treated in the same way as the planter box described in the following section. As in the case of the planter box, the bottom slats are spaced a fourth of an inch apart to allow for swelling. The sides have shown a tendency to warp as a result of the damp interior and dry exterior, so the corner joints must be securely fastened to resist the strain. Care taken in joining and finishing benches or planters of this kind is well repaid. A dressy bench gives a finished look to the plant display.

Sun-loving, flowering plants of the kind grown here are prone to wilting—particularly Browallia, Coleus, and the fuchsias. This makes it even more important than usual to set the pots on damp pebbles and to spray the plants periodically with a fog-type sprayer. I have made aluminum trays to fit inside

FIG. 14.   A HEATED SUNPORCH.

the benches and hold the pebbles so I can wet them generously without fear of leakage onto the floor.

My routine is to wet the pebbles, water the plants, and spray thoroughly each morning, and to wet the pebbles and spray again toward sundown. On cold, sunny days, when the relative humidity in the house is low, the pebbles and the most wilt-prone plants often dry out by noon, necessitating an extra round of wetting and spraying and an extra watering for those that need it.

KEY TO FIG. 14:

1. *Stapelia gigantea*
2. *Hoya carnosa variegata*
3. *Kleinia Mandraliscae*
4. *Aloe striata*
5. *Sedum lineare variegata*
6. *Adromischus Cooperii*
7. *Echinopsis* sp.
8. *Kalanchoe globulifera coccinea*
9. *Opuntia microdasys*
10. *Echinocactus* sp.
11. *Crassula falcata*
12. *Kalanchoe uniflora*
13. *Agave striata echinoides*
14. *Echinocereus* sp.
15. *Euphorbia obesa*
16. *Echinocereus* sp.
17. *Chlorophytum comosum*
18. *Opuntia* sp.
19. *Kleinia tomentosa*
20. *Mammillaria elongata*
21. *Astrophytum ornatum*
22. *Cephalocereus senilis*

23. *Cleistocactus* sp.
24. *Begonia macrocarpa*
25. *Browallia speciosa*
26. *Coleus Blumei*
27. *Rivina humilis*
28. *Jacobinia suberecta*
29. *Fuchsia triphylla*
30. *Achimenes* hybrid
31. *Kohleria Lindeniana*
32. *Pelargonium hortorum* 'Ricard'
33. *Philodendron oxycardium*
34. *Asparagus Sprengeri*
35. *Begonia Weltoniensis rosea*
36. *Peperomia incana*
37. *Pellionia pulchra*
38. *Ixora javanica*
39. *Begonia* 'Sachsen'
40. *Begonia acida*
41. *Begonia* 'Abel Carriere'
42. *Rechsteineria cardinalis*
43. *Plectranthus Oertendahelii*
44. *Cissus hypoglauca*
45. *Hedera Helix tortuosa*

The cacti and succulents, of course, are different. They live on the cool glass shelf above the benches without wet pebbles or spraying, and even during excessively dry spells they will go several days without being watered. Note that they are all in standard clay pots. A variety of containers would give a confused effect and distract attention from the plants.

Though the porch is heated by a radiator which runs along one-third of its length, a great deal of the heat is lost on cold nights, and the thermometer I keep there sometimes registers a chilly 55°. This is too cold for tender tropical plants like *Rechsteineria cardinalis*—which I often carry into the living room on winter evenings—but it is fine for the flowering plants from mountains and plains. During the day, as if to make up for the nightly chill, radiator and sun work together, often running the thermometer into the nineties.

These are not ideal conditions, but they are typical of those on most sunporches. They present a challenge and a real reward when plants put on new growth or blooms. I try new plants first in one place and then in another, turning and moving them frequently until each comes to rest in the place that suits it best.

PHILODENDRONS ON A WALL
(Fig. 15)

"Jungle paradise" might well be the title of this garden, which grows against the north wall of my sunporch. In winter the early morning sun shines across the floor and onto the foliage of the ferns and low-growing plants in the box, but no sun ever shines directly on anything above the velvet-leaved philodendrons.

To me, one of the most fascinating things about this garden is the lushness of the highest philodendron leaves. Here the plants enjoy growing upwards as they do in their jungle home, rather than trailing out of a pot or vase as they are so often forced to do. Under these naturalistic conditions they produce larger leaves with every upward thrust. I am also amazed at how the leaves remain on the vines, evergreen and alive, for so long. In two years only about half a dozen have turned yellow.

When this garden was first set up, the philodendrons were planted in pots and the other tropical plants were grouped around them, also in pots and containers of various sizes and shapes. The effect was spotty, a fault common to many indoor gardens. To obtain a neat and unified effect, and at the same time to elevate and protect the plants, we built the box shown in the picture. The original three philodendrons are permanently planted in it. The other plants are still in their own pots, which are sunk in the mixture of peat moss and perlite with which the box is filled. This jungly formula is light and airy, yet stays damp enough that the pots need watering only once every three or four days.

FIG. 15.   PHILODENDRONS ON A WALL.

When the plants (in their pots) are removed for their biweekly bath, the dampness of the mixture is checked and water is added as needed. Since the philodendron cannot be removed for washing, I spray the leaves, stems, and aerial roots daily, although this amenable plant will continue to thrive even if vacation or sickness causes a halt in the man-made dew for a week or more.

Once a week throughout the growing season the philodendron leaves and climbing roots are sprayed with a weak solution of water-soluble fertilizer.

KEY TO FIG. 15:

1. *Philodendron oxycardium*
2. *P. micans*
3. *P. Andreanum*
4. *Codiaeum variegatum*
5. *Adiantum hispidulum*
6. *Scindapsus aureus*
7. *Pellaea viridis*
8. *Anthurium Andraeanum*
9. *Piper ornatum*
10. *Calathea zebrina*
11. *Stenandrium Lindenii*
12. *Dichorisandra thyrsiflora*

Since the few roots that it has below the ground in the planting box are insignificant in comparison to those it has developed in its climb to the ceiling, I have given up applying fertilizer to them. The foliar feeding has produced such fine results that ordinary root feeding seems superfluous.

A brilliant spot of color is supplied by the crimson flowers of the anthurium, which, though it blooms only once or twice a year, holds its blossoms for two or three months. In spring, summer, and fall fancy-leaved caladiums brighten the garden, and on special occasions a small blooming exotic from the greenhouse is added.

The box itself is made of lightly stained cypress, although the other decay-resistant, aromatic woods such as cedar or redwood would do as well and would not require stain. I am reluctant to use ordinary woods with wood preservatives because I have found that most of these compounds tend to be harmful to plants for some months after application.

To provide drainage and also to avoid distortion from swelling, the bottom was made of longitudinal slats set nearly a quarter of an inch apart, with shallow aluminum trays underneath to catch excess water draining through. The wood was coated inside and out with a silicone water repellent, the

FIG. 16.   A RADIATOR GARDEN.

thought being that this would reduce excessive swelling and warping and still allow some passage of moisture; but this treatment has not proven entirely successful. Two cracks have developed, indicating that the inside of the wood is swelling more than the outside.

A RADIATOR GARDEN
(*Fig. 16*)

When your other indoor gardening space is full, it is time to use the radiators. Don't be dissuaded by the frequently repeated warnings that plants will not live in the hot dry air above them. Cacti and succulents will, of course, and so will heat-loving tropical plants—as this picture shows. The trick is to have a buffer between the radiator and the plant tray to cushion the abrupt changes of temperature when the heat goes on and off. In the picture you will see that the tray is supported on blocks, leaving an air space as a buffer.

KEY TO FIG. 16:

1. *Cycas revoluta*
2. *Podocarpus macrophylla*
3. *Calathea Makoyana*
4. *Aeschynanthus Lobbianus*
5. *Scindapsus pictus argyraeus*
6. *Streptocarpus* hybrid
7. *Asparagus asparagoides*
8. *Zebrina pendula*
9. *Episcia lilacena* 'Fanny Haage'
10. *Saintpaulia* hybrids
11. *Begonia leptotricha*
12. *Senecio mikanioides*
13. *Sinningia regina*
14. *Tradescantia multiflora*
15. *Aeschynanthus marmoratus*
16. *Cordyline indivisa*
17. *Sinningia regina*
18. *Peperomia glabella variegata*
19. *Spathiphyllum Clevelandii*
20. *Caladium candidum*
21. *Howea Forsteriana*

This garden is in an east window which gets direct sunlight only in the early morning. It is a good example of the varied and interesting plant material that can be grown in such an exposure, particularly where the humidity as well as the temperature can be kept high.

A radiator garden requires more frequent pebble-wetting and spraying than the usual type, and a lapse in this routine can be fatal. I generally use deeper trays and thicker layers of pebbles to provide a bigger reservoir of moisture, although it happens that the tray shown in the picture is of standard depth. Also, if I am going to be away from home more than a day, I turn off the radiator or move the plants to the floor.

A NORTH WINDOW
(*Fig. 17*)

This cool, sunless north window presents a challenge. Even with an extra pane between the plants and the sash, the temperature near the glass falls as

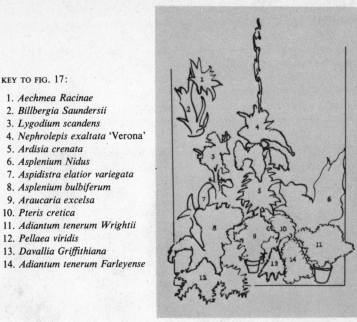

low as 48° on winter nights. This is too cold for the jungle plants—philodendron, peperomia, and the like—which would otherwise be an obvious choice. However, it is not too low for evergreen ferns, which, though natives of the tropics, can withstand considerably cooler nights than foliage plants from the same habitat. So ferns are the mainstays of this group.

Fortunately, ferns present a variety of shapes, shades, and textures. The wide, thick strap leaves of the bird's-nest fern are a striking contrast to the plumes of the mother fern and the lacy delicacy of the maidenhair. The dark, almost bluish green of the Davallia is set off by the light green of the Lygodium twining around a curved cedar branch. This climbing fern, although rarely seen, is neither difficult nor demanding and grows considerably faster than the others in this window. All of them require comparatively little care.

The other plants chosen for the garden are also tough and undemanding. The Norfolk Island pine and the cast iron plant (*Aspidistra*) blend well with the diversified fronds of the ferns, and the sparkling red berries of the Ardisia add a welcome spot of color through the winter. In summer the Ardisia is moved into the outdoor garden, where it blooms and sets its fruit for the following year.

FIG. 17.   A NORTH WINDOW.

Hanging on the left-hand wall of the window niche you will see two bromeliads—an Aechmea and a Billbergia—growing on a piece of cork bark. Any of the epiphytic bromeliads can be grown in this fashion, and the different shapes and colors of their foliage can be arranged in decorative patterns against the rough texture of the cork. The easiest way to attach the plant is to hold it in place by a small concave piece of bark wired to the larger piece. I run the wire medially between the inner and outer surface of the small piece of bark and then through holes in the larger piece, twisting the two ends together behind the latter. The roots of the bromeliad, wrapped with a little

FIG. 18.   A ROCK AND WATER GARDEN.

sphagnum and a generous wad of osmunda, are placed between the two pieces of bark and the wire is then drawn up, compressing the osmunda and holding the plant firmly in place. If you take advantage of the natural depressions and crevices in the bark (occasionally enlarging them with a chisel or gouge), you can achieve a surprisingly graceful effect.

There are many variations in this technique. Driftwood or decorative slabs can be used instead of the basic bark, and other epiphytes—particularly staghorn ferns—can be substituted for bromeliads. The important thing is to

KEY TO FIG. 18:

1. *Begonia rex-cultorum*
2. *Cissus discolor*
3. *Saintpaulia Grotei*
4. *Begonia Bunchii*
5. *Platycerium bifurcatum*
6. *Cyperus alternifolius*
7. *Jussiaea longifolia*
8. *Phlebodium aureum*
9. *Davallia Mariesii*
10. *Colocasia antiquorum illustris*

11. *Acorus gramineus variegatus*
12. *Helxine Soleirolii*
13. *Myrtus communis*
14. *Pistia Stratiotes*
15. *Nymphoides aquatica*
16. *Hydrocleys nymphoides*
17. *Myriophyllum brasiliense*
18. *Adiantum cuneatum*
19. *Caladium 'Red Arrow'*
20. *Asplenium Nidus*

give the plant a good supply of fiber, at least as much as it would have in a pot, and to be sure that water will drain freely through the fiber and will not catch in a crevice. Don't be alarmed if the root system of the bromeliad seems inadequate. In six months or a year it will grip the bark firmly with a new system of holdfast roots and will begin to sucker, giving your planting a look of tropical abundance. Keep its cup full of water at all times, and soak the whole thing in a tub or bucket of water at least once a week.

A ROCK AND WATER GARDEN
(Fig. 18)

This greenhouse pool and the dry stone wall behind it suggest intriguing possibilities for contemporary architects. If I were planning a modern house, I would certainly include a glass-topped entry or enclosed patio where an indoor pool like this could serve as a home for tropical aquatics.

Almost all the available water plants suitable for use indoors are natives of quiet backwaters and ponds where the water is warm and still. They will not grow in cold or running water. To approximate natural conditions, an indoor plant pool should be fifteen to eighteen inches deep, with an inch or two of sandy soil on the bottom. Most of the plants, such as water lilies, cyperus, and taro, must be planted in pots submerged to various depths according to their individual requirements. A few—notably floating heart (*Nymphaea*) and parrot-feather (*Myriophyllum*)—naturalize themselves by putting out floating stems and runners which send roots down to the soil at the bottom of the pool. Others, such as Salvinia and water lettuce (*Pistia*) will float on the surface. Goldfish and snails will help to keep the aquatic life balanced.

Pools like this should look deep and natural, with lush plant growth and mossy edges, so don't paint the inside of your pool and don't change the water more often than absolutely necessary. A bit of murkiness makes it all the more natural.

Two vital necessities for an indoor water garden are sunlight and warm water. If you want to grow water plants indoors, you must provide direct sun through either a skylight or a large window, and you must keep the water temperature above 58°. Because the water is changed so infrequently, a drainage system is less important; indeed, my pool has no drain at all. I siphon the water out with a garden hose.

A dry stone wall around the pool provides niches and crevices where many jungle plants will thrive. It can also be used to create the illusion of a tropical spring by allowing water to seep out between the rocks. Pack osmunda or sphagnum moss behind the wall and in the end of the water line, and let the water drip slowly. The moss will diffuse the water over the rocks, producing a quite natural effect. Remember, however, that a still and silent pool is both appropriate and restful. A constant audible drip does the plants no good and may be irritating to people in the house.

Quite apart from the pool, a dry stone wall is a great asset to any greenhouse or modern indoor garden. There is one in my greenhouse in which I grow begonias, African violets, ferns, peperomias, jungle cactus, anthuriums, and other denizens of the tropical forests. Not only do the plants look well against a background of mossy rocks, but many of them, particularly the begonias, develop into finer specimens than I can grow in pots.

The construction of my wall follows the principles recommended for dry walls outside, the front slanting back and each stone sloping down and back so that water running down the face flows into the wall and packs the soil and plants more firmly. Each crevice in the wall connects with the mass of soil, gravel, and peat moss behind it, enabling the roots of the plants eventually to reach this reservoir of food and moisture. If the ground behind the wall extends outside the foundation of the house or greenhouse, I would recommend a barrier of galvanized screening at the foundation line to keep moles from coming inside when they get hungry in the spring.

A GARDEN UNDER GLASS
(*Fig. 19*)

This ideal indoor garden is a tiny greenhouse, six feet wide and ten feet long, designed as part of the living room it leans against. No door separates it from the room, though some might want folding or sliding glass doors in the wide opening. Even if doors were used, they would unquestionably be open throughout each sunny day; and a person sitting in this living room would feel that he was truly in a garden.

Because of the radiant heat through the glass on sunny days and the corresponding loss at night, a greenhouse like this should have radiation around the exterior walls (the fin type is good), a separate circulating pump, and a special thermostat. And if, as in this case, the greenhouse is not partitioned off, the thermostat must be set at about 65° to avoid chilling the adjacent room, and the gardener must choose jungle plants adapted to high temperatures. The humidity required by these plants is maintained by setting the pots in the ground beds in damp peat moss and those in the benches on wet pebbles, and by spraying not only the plants but the brick walk between the beds and the sand under the benches.

While a prefabricated greenhouse encloses this particular garden, a similar glassed-in space can be incorporated into a contemporary house, using large expanses of plate glass. Regardless of the kind of structure used, the success of the garden will depend on adequate provisions for full winter sunlight, high humidity, separate ventilation, and separately regulated radiation. The plan-

ning and construction of greenhouses—traditional or modern—is highly specialized and usually beyond the competence of the home handyman or neighborhood contractor. Costs can easily get out of hand, and expert advice pays for itself many times over.

If you want a basketful of trailing lantana for winter display (like that shown in the picture), you should start with a small plant in the summer while there is plenty of light for vigorous growth. In a sunny location, bloom will become full in the fall and continue throughout the winter and spring.

This particular lantana is growing in a twelve-inch wire basket. My procedure for basket planting is to fill the basket with fresh sphagnum moss and then to make a hole in the center large enough to receive the root ball of the plant with a half inch or so of potting soil around it. There should be an inch or more of sphagnum moss outside the soil, and epiphytes and jungle plants can get along with no soil at all. The moss keeps the basket reasonably "tight" and dripless, allowing air to reach the roots and at the same time preventing them from drying out too fast. The basket is watered as frequently as any potted plant and, in addition, the entire thing is plunged in a tub or bucket about once a week.

Hanging baskets of various sizes can be purchased from florists or florists' suppliers. You will also find them easy to make yourself out of galvanized screening—chicken wire, for example. The only tools required are a pair of pliers and a small wire cutter. With a little practice, you can obtain a bowl shape like the commercial baskets; or using stiffer wire, you can experiment with other shapes, such as triangles and squares. Don't be upset if your work is rough. The sphagnum moss protruding through the mesh and the plant falling over the edge of the basket will soon hide any irregularities.

From hanging baskets it is an easy step to other kinds of hanging containers. The flexible French salad baskets sold in hardware and cutlery stores are convenient in size and attractive in shape. Coconuts can be used for plants that don't require much space. On page 126 you will see a picture of a columnea growing in a hanging coconut filled with a mixture of perlite and peat moss. The "eyes" in the lower end of the coconut have been punched out for drainage. If you want to prevent dripping from these drainage holes, invert the severed upper end of the nut and hang it like a small saucer half an inch or so below the bottom of the main container.

A BROMELIAD TREE
(*Fig. 20*)

A bromeliad tree—meaning a tree planted with bromeliads—can be a decorative accent in many indoor gardens. While the luxuriant growth on the greenhouse specimen pictured in Fig. 20 can not always be duplicated in the

FIG. 19.   A GARDEN UNDER GLASS.

house, highly satisfactory results can generally be obtained if interesting plants are used on unusually shaped stumps or roots. Driftwood is good for this purpose. Its gray color contrasts with the blue-green of much of the bromeliad foliage, and it can often be found in complicated and twisted shapes with natural cavities for planting.

KEY TO FIG. 20:

1. *Aechmea fasciata*
2. *Tillandsia usneoides*
3. *Billbergia leptopoda*
4. *Cryptobergia Meadii*
5. *Billbergia* hybrid
6. *Aechmea* 'Foster's Favorite'
7. *Anthurium Andraeanum*
8. *Aechmea Racinae*
9. *Aechmea* 'Foster's Favorite'
10. *Billbergia horrida* hybrid
11. *Acanthostachys strobilacea*
12. *Rhaphidophora celatocaulis*
13. *Asplenium Nidus*
14. *Billbergia Lietzi*
15. *Cryptanthus zonatus zebrinus*
16. *Cryptanthus lacerdae*

The tree in the picture was the root of a giant sycamore, uprooted and washed free of soil in the hurricane of 1955. What looks like the trunk is actually the portion of the root nearest the stump, and the branches are the smaller roots that extended outward into the soil. Like the roots of many trees, they fused together as they crisscrossed through the earth, forming intricate loops and occasionally enfolding a rock in their twining grasp. You can see the bottom of such a rock just below and to the right of the center of the mass.

Aechmeas and Billbergias are the most prominent bromeliads on the tree. In addition, if you look closely, you will see less common members of the family like the pendant Acanthostachys on the right and the Spanish moss on the top, and also some other epiphytic plants such as the bird's-nest fern near the bottom. An anthurium which is scarcely visible in the center of the picture has grown well and bloomed several times.

Preparing the tree for planting is a fascinating task. In your mind's eye, picture where the clumps of bromeliads will look best and then search for natural crevices near these spots—knotholes, patches of decay, or crotches

FIG. 20.   A BROMELIAD TREE.

where the tree has branched—which you can enlarge enough to accommodate the plants. I use an augur and a heavy gouge to shape the cavities, and I bore at least a half inch hole from the bottom of each, downwards and out to open air, to provide drainage. Indeed, many of the cavities more nearly resemble tunnels through the tree, tapering slightly so that osmunda fiber can be packed firmly into them. Naturally the dimensions vary. I try to get a space as big as a two-inch pot.

The bromeliads are "planted" by wrapping their roots in sphagnum and osmunda and pressing them firmly into the cavity or crevice. The trick is to use small plants, which take hold faster and grow better, and to apply real pressure to the osmunda around them, anchoring them securely and establishing close contact between the fiber and the roots. If you want a plant at a spot where no cavity can be hollowed out, the wad of osmunda can be held in place with cork bark and wire or with wire alone. Again, be sure that the wire is tight and the anchorage firm.

After several months the bromeliads will fasten themselves in place with a new system of holdfast roots and will begin to put out shoots and offsets, forming the massive clumps shown in the picture. Culture is about the same as for bromeliads in pots, although watering may be needed a bit more frequently if a large proportion of the osmunda is exposed to the air. Because the water must—and will—drain rapidly out of the fiber, the tree should be in a ground bed, or the floor beneath it should be protected from drip.

A CLIFF GARDEN IN A MODERN HOUSE
(*Fig. 21*)

Rock and water are the heart of this indoor garden in a contemporary house built on the side of a high hill overlooking a river valley. A skylight in the ceiling allows the noontime sun to shine on the plants growing near the top of the wall. Those on the bottom get no direct sun, but the illumination is sufficient for ferns, philodendrons, and other plants that grow naturally in light of low intensity.

A thin copper tube with perforations at intervals runs along the top of the wall, and a controlling spigot behind the fireplace allows the gardener to drench the face of the rock, increasing the humidity and watering the roots of the begonias, ferns, and bromeliads growing in the crevices. The fact that the water comes directly from a spring and is only a degree or two above freezing in winter discourages the more delicate tropical plants, but those that do not mind an occasional cold shower have attached themselves firmly to the wall and have grown well in this unusual situation.

Planting a wall such as this is quite similar to planting a bromeliad tree

FIG. 21.   A CLIFF GARDEN IN A MODERN HOUSE.

like that described on page 63. In both it is important to choose only epiphytic or climbing plants with tenacious roots that will cling to every nook and cranny. The next step is to clean all loose dirt from the crevices in the rock, and, if possible, to chisel them out until they will drain freely. Then wrap the plant roots in sphagnum moss and osmunda fiber and stuff them into the cavity, packing in the osmunda with considerable pressure. In my experience small plants are preferable to large ones. They are less apt to fall out of place before their roots take hold, and they seem to attach themselves more quickly and firmly.

The picture of this garden was taken only a short time after the wall was planted. It shows the very small plants that were used—smaller than usual because in this case none of the crevices was as large as a two-inch pot and most of them were totally lacking in drainage. It gives no indication of the growth these same small plants were to make in the ensuing year, growth so luxuriant that today many of them must be pruned regularly to prevent their getting out of scale.

This garden is enjoyed by dinner guests as much as by those who visit in the daytime, for at night three 150-watt spotlights show off the beauty of the rock and the foliage of the tropical plants that cling and clamber over its face. While there are not many sites as dramatic as this, the very fact that a garden will grow in such a place should challenge the imagination of architects.

A SUNNY ALCOVE
(*Fig. 22*)

Perhaps the most unusual features of this alcove are its practical equipment and design. To begin with, the exposure is south, and all the available winter sun shines through the broad expanse of casement windows and the skylight overhead. The ivory painted walls and woodwork reflect the light onto the near side of the plants and into the spaces behind the valance, giving a higher general level of illumination than prevails in most indoor gardens.

Steady, reliable heat is provided by the greenhouse-type pipes running under the windows and controlled by a separate thermostat. This extra radiation, together with the ventilation from the windows, permits excellent temperature control.

Humidity, the other essential of a successful indoor garden, can be maintained by frequent spraying and by wetting the cement floor. The painted woodwork is not harmed by moisture, and a drain in the floor carries off any excess.

Watering, repotting, and all the other gardening jobs are facilitated by the combination sink and workbench tucked into the left-hand end of the alcove, which affords stowage space for soil, sprays, fertilizer, and pots. The plant benches are also sturdy and practical, made of slate and soapstone with galvanized pipe legs.

In such a garden you could grow flowering plants, tropical foliage plants, or cacti and succulents with equal ease. Those shown in the picture are a group of old favorites, gathered through years of house plant collecting. Occasional plants appropriate to the season—like the chrysanthemums

FIG. 22. A SUNNY ALCOVE.   *George M. Cushing Jr.*

shown in Fig. 22—are brought in from a neighbóring greenhouse to brighten
the picture from time to time. The overall result is to make this end of
the dining room a sunny spot of greenery and to enliven every meal that
is eaten here.

AN UNHEATED SUNPORCH
(*Fig. 23*)

A garden in an unheated sunporch can be among the most satisfying of all.
The low temperature makes the care of the plants relatively easy because it
discourages pests and minimizes the task of humidification. And if the porch

gets four or five hours of sun a day, you can grow many flowering plants that would not do well in a warmer, dryer location.

The garden in the picture is a case in point. It gets sunlight from three sides—east, south, and west—and if you look closely you will see Camellia, Cyclamen, Nicotiana, Felicia, and sweet alyssum in bloom, and maturing buds on the kalanchoe in the hanging basket. Later in the season there will be small yellow flowers on the Acacia and white blossoms on the Eurya. The combination of flowering plants and radiant warmth make a porch like this especially pleasant on a sunny winter day.

The temperature in this particular porch—which is located in Philadelphia —drops into the forties on cold nights, but is kept above freezing with a small electric heater. This makes it satisfactory for all the plants shown except the bird of paradise, which suffers when the thermometer goes below 50°. Evaporation from the pebble trays provides ample humidity, as the condensation on the windows shows. Very little washing or spraying of the foliage is required to keep the plants attractive all winter. In summer, all are moved to a partly shaded place outside.

If your porch is sunny but can't be kept above freezing, don't try a winter

KEY TO FIG. 23:

1. *Ophiopogon japonicus*
2. *Kalanchoe Fedtschenkoi*
3. *Strelitzia Reginae*
4. *Camellia japonica*
5. *Rhododendron obtusum*
6. *Citrus taitensis*
7. *Cyclamen persicum*
8. *Nicotiana alata*
9. *Felicia amelloides*
10. *Lobularia maritima*
11. *Eurya ochnacea*
12. *Acacia armata*

FIG. 23.   AN UNHEATED SUNPORCH.

FIG. 24.   A DESERT GARDEN FOR A MODERN HOUSE OR OFFICE.

garden. Instead, pot some hardy shrubs, both evergreen and spring flowering, and the extra warmth and protection of your porch will force them into early bloom.

A DESERT GARDEN FOR A MODERN
HOUSE OR OFFICE
(Fig. 24)

Succulent plants are accustomed to dusty, dry places where the days are hot and the nights are cold. They do well in locations like that in the picture where there are several hours of sun each day. They do not mind if the temperature drops to 50°—as it is apt to do in an office building over week-ends—nor are they hurt by the infrequent watering which is too often the lot of house plants either in an office or at home. In fact, if they are in a box such as that shown here, they will need watering only once every ten days or two weeks. Finally, their furry leaves and stems do not require periodic wiping or spraying and show the dust much less than the patent leather foliage of jungle plants.

The trick with desert gardens is to use good sized plants. Older cacti like those in the picture are much more satisfactory than the smaller ones, which have a tendency to look spotty. Don't be discouraged by the very considerable cost of the larger plants. Cacti are slow growing and can be considered almost a permanent investment. Of the plants shown in the picture, only *Kalanchoe*

KEY TO FIG. 24:

1. *Kalanchoe beharensis*
2. *Cleistocactus Straussii*
3. *Cephalocereus senilis*
4. *Crassula 'Imperialis'*
5. *Haworthia radula*
6. *Mammillaria* sp.
7. *Gasteria hybrida*
8. *Euphorbia lactea cristata*
9. *Sedum dasyphyllum*
10. *Aloe variegata*
11. *Pleiospilos Neilii*
12. *Opuntia* sp.

beharensis will get out of hand. This particular one is a year old and may need replacement before another year has passed.

The succulents in this garden are planted in desert mixture in individual pots, so that casualties can be easily replaced and those that need it can be summered outside. The pots are sunk in perlite—which is light in weight and airy in texture—with a thin layer of white sand on top. The planting box is built of cypress to give a lighter color than redwood or cedar. The bottom is raised nearly an inch above the floor, and a waterproof aluminum tray (hidden by the sides) is suspended beneath it to catch any excess water draining through. The bottom of the tray hangs clear of the floor to prevent an accumulation of condensation under it.

A desert garden like this is practical and easy to maintain. The decorative effects that can be achieved through careful selection and arrangement of bizarre-shaped succulent plants make this kind of garden one of the best for modern interiors.

A GARDEN IN A HARDWARE STORE
(*Fig. 25*)

Today, designers rely increasingly on specimen plants, planters, and ground beds to relieve the austere lines of stores, offices, lobbies, and reception rooms. Indoor gardens can add a welcome note of decoration to such places, but they present a number of problems not commonly encountered in the house.

In the first place, indoor gardens in public places are always on display. You and I can neglect the gardens in our houses for days or even weeks at a time and then spruce them up for an occasion, but every business day is an occasion for a bank or a store, and a garden there should be at its best whenever the public is invited. A dusty, ill-kempt group of plants will give an impression of carelessness. The plants should be replaced, therefore, whenever they begin to look tired or straggly. It is even more important for the businessman than for the house gardener to realize that the plants in an indoor garden are often not a permanent investment.

Secondly, growing conditions in a business garden are often surprisingly rigorous. Temperatures during the business day are kept at a warm 70°, but at night and over weekends and holidays the thermostat is often turned down into the fifties, which may be too cold for some of the tropical plants that would otherwise come to mind for such a location.

Finally, storekeepers and office workers are generally too busy to spend more than a few minutes a day on their plants. Pebble trays, spraying, and other methods of increasing humidity are apt to be neglected, and the garden

FIG. 25.   A GARDEN IN A HARDWARE STORE.

Lloyd P. Wells

designer should avoid plants that need a moist atmosphere. Also, remember that many offices are closed two days a week and even stores that are regularly open on Saturdays take occasional long weekends over holidays. During these periods ventilation is poor and watering is generally omitted. So the plants should be plunged in damp peat moss in a large planter or ground bed or otherwise protected from drying out. Or, plants should be chosen which will stand periods of drought—as in the desert garden pictured in Fig. 24.

The garden shown in Fig. 25 is in a hardware store. It is based on a square pool eight or nine inches deep, which accommodates a number of goldfish. Because the window faces northwest and is shaded by trees, there is too little light for a real water garden. Only the Cyperus and the Chinese evergreen (*Aglaonema*) grow in the pool. The other plants are set on stones and inverted pots several inches above the surface, but they benefit immensely from the evaporation which keeps the air moister around them than elsewhere in the store.

The plants selected for this garden are all tough, long-lasting species that require little care—philodendrons, Boston fern, peperomias, Kentia palm, Cyperus, and Chinese evergreen. The striking foliage in the foreground is the large self-heading philodendron *P. Wendlandii*. The light color of the foliage is a photographic illusion; the leaves are really a dark, leathery green. The hanging basket plant is *Cissus capensis*, the Cape grape, a vigorous grape-leaved vine which thrives in this location.

All the plants shown in the picture have been in this garden for more than a year except the grape, which was pruned heavily in the early summer and spent the following two months outside in a shady place.

A PLANTER GARDEN
(*Fig. 26*)

When decorators call for planters and room dividers, they imagine vigorous growth that brings a sense of life and well-being into the room, and foliage of contrasting shapes and colors which makes the plant group as decorative and attractive to the eye as a painting or a piece of sculpture. All too often the effect is quite the opposite—dull, dusty plants which are either uninteresting or, if they catch the attention, downright depressing.

The secrets of this gardener's success are a good location, with full sun pouring in through a south-facing picture window, and meticulous care, consisting primarily of proper watering, regular spraying, and careful wiping to remove dust from the leaves.

The feature plant is a five-year-old *Dieffenbachia picta*, 'Rudolph Roehrs,' a florists' standby in its small stages but not often seen as large and voluptuous as this. Clockwise around its base are *Lantana camara*, *Episcia cupreata*

FIG. 26.   A PLANTER GARDEN.

'Variegata,' *Tradescantia fluminensis variegata*, *Begonia metallica*, and *B. rex-cultorum*, providing a wide variety of leaf texture and color and a considerable amount of bloom in most months of the year. The bright red foliage of the croton (*Codiaeum* hybrid) in the pottery crock sets off the cream-colored leaves of the dieffenbachia, and the airy graceful fingers of the *Dizygotheca elegantissima* nodding at the top of the arrangement give a change in feeling from the heavier tropical foliage below.

Each plant grows in its own pot and the pots are arranged in the metal-lined planter box. The box is placed at the proper distance from the window so that it is shaded from the high summer sun but receives full benefit from the low winter sun. Most of the plants are kept in their places all year round.

FIG. 27.   A CELLAR WINDOW GARDEN.

The dieffenbachia has been there three years and has never been pruned or put outside.

A CELLAR WINDOW GARDEN
(*Fig. 27*)

An ingenious window garden brightens this cellar game room both day and night. Daylight comes in through the overhead glass sash, which is set at ground level, and at night artificial light shines on the plants from fluorescent fixtures behind the wooden valance. However, the garden receives little, if any, direct winter sunlight; and the comparatively low level of illumination makes it best suited for plants from tropical jungles.

Since the bottom of this garden is a ground bed, many of the plants have been taken out of their pots and are growing in the soil, which has been lightened with humus and peat moss. This method of planting reduces the chore of watering, but complicates pest control because the plants can't be readily removed for washing. On the other hand, the stone and plaster surroundings facilitate spraying with insecticides and for humidification and foliar feeding.

PART THREE

Selection of Plants

Here is a list of the plants I have grown, with a description of where and how each has done best. You will find here not only the common plants grown under glass, but also enough of those generally considered unusual to lend distinction to almost any indoor garden or to keep a collector busy for a considerable time. Being an inveterate collector, I am always trying new plants, so my personal list will never be finished.

Many amateur growers, and even a few professionals, refuse to use the Latin binomials in naming their plants. This is a pity, for there is no other way to be sure what plant you are talking about—a matter of some consequence, particularly when you are buying by mail from a catalogue, which is the only way to get indoor plants in many parts of the country. I have tried to name each listed plant properly, using Bailey's *Manual of Cultivated Plants* and *Hortus II* for my authorities in almost every case, with reference to the Bailey Hortorium at Cornell University in cases of doubt. I have not, however, tried to distinguish between varieties and cultivars, as the taxonomists would do. There are, of course, alternate systems of nomenclature, particularly for the succulents; but I think that anyone who prefers one of those other systems will be able to find his way from this list to another without difficulty.

I have included the family name because I find it interesting to see the similarities in flower structure which have led to the family groupings, and also because there is often a marked similarity in the culture of members of the same family—for instance, bromeliads, gesneriads, aroids, and plants of the various succulent families. If the plant has a well-known alternate name, I have listed this just below its correct name; and if it has an established common name, I have shown that at the upper right-hand corner of the description. You will also find the alternate botanical names and the common names included in the list in alphabetical order, with a reference to the correct botanical name under which the plant is described.

One important key to success in growing house plants lies in knowing the environment in which the particular species developed and in doing your best to duplicate these natural conditions in your house or greenhouse. For this reason I have tried to supply pertinent facts about the native habitats of the plants to help you in selecting the plant for the place or the place for the plant, as the case may be. Speaking very generally indeed, plants suitable for indoor growing may be divided into three groups:

Tropical plants, which grow naturally in the hot, steamy tropics of Central and South America, Africa, and Indonesia—where the light is often filtered through higher layers of foliage, where the temperature and humidity are high and relatively steady, and where the "soil" often consists of a thin layer of spongy, partially decayed vegetation.

Sub-tropical plants, from countries such as India, China, and Japan, the shores of the Mediterranean, the South African veld, Australia, and our own southern states—regions where there is considerably more difference between the seasons, where summer days are warm and sunny and winter is comparatively short with the lowest temperature about 40°, and where there is fairly high humidity and reasonable rainfall, more or less evenly distributed throughout the year.

Desert plants, native to the deserts of the Southwestern United States, Mexico, South America, Africa, the Middle East, and Australia—where the sun shines intensely nearly every day, where it seldom rains, where the humidity is low, and where the temperature is high by day and often drops sharply at night.

You can see how much emphasis I put on knowledge of a plant's habitat, but I warn against concluding that plants will grow only where their native conditions can be reproduced. Actually, it is almost miraculous how plants which have evolved to meet the special conditions of jungle, desert, or plain—or even an isolated group of islands in the middle of the ocean—can adjust to the environment of an American house, where the air is heated and dried in winter and sometimes cooled in summer and the temperature is relatively constant in all but the hottest months. Liberty Hyde Bailey's remark about the ferns can almost serve as a password for entrance to my list: "Some kinds, however, withstand untoward and changing conditions, and these are adapted to window gardens and porches."

ABUTILON   *Malvaceae*   FLOWERING MAPLE

All the abutilons make good flowering house plants. Despite the common name, they are related not to the maple tree but to the hollyhock, a connection which becomes apparent with the first flower. They must be grown in the sun and kept slightly pot bound, otherwise few flowers appear. I use all-purpose soil.

A. hybridum has flowers of white, yellow, pink, or red, shaped like bells, two inches across. The leaves are reminiscent of a sugar maple, though not so large. The plants tend to be leggy, but by pinching them back when they are young you can keep them fairly compact. Start new plants from time to time from seeds or cuttings, as young ones look best. (Fig. 48)

FIG. 28. *Acalypha Wilkesiana Macafeana, Abutilon megapotamicum variegatum, Acalypha hispida, Acanthostachys strobilacea, Acacia Baileyana, A. armata, A. Farnesiana.*

A. megapotamicum is from Brazil; the name means big river and refers to the Amazon. A good plant for a hanging basket or the edge of a sunny window sill or greenhouse bench, it never grows too large. The bell-shaped red flowers can be expected all year round, but are shy about appearing in the fall. The variety *variegatum* has yellow blotches on the leaves. (Fig. 28)

A. striatum from Guatemala has orange flowers with thin red stripes. The leaves of the variety 'Souvenir de Bonn' are variegated with white margins, and those of variety *Thompsonii* have yellow spots. All three are vigorous and free-flowering.

ACACIA   *Leguminosae*   ACACIA

Most acacias sold by house plant dealers are suitable for unheated sunporches but not for the house because they will not stand a hot, dry atmosphere. They need plenty of sun and water and will not thrive in winter temperatures above 50°, preferring a range of 35° to 40°. All bear yellow flowers in early spring, from February to April, and should be pruned after flowering. New plants may be raised from seeds or cuttings.

If you have a cool sunporch, you might try one of the following species:

A. armata, kangaroo thorn, a native of Australia. The small, dark green leaves are thorny, and the whole plant has a stiff appearance. The yellow flowers are about the size of peas. (Fig. 28)

A. Baileyana, a native of New South Wales, with graceful, ferny, blue-gray foliage and large puffs of flowers. Cuttings are very difficult to root, but seeds germinate quite readily. (Fig. 28)

A. Farnesiana is a plant widely grown in the tropics. It adapts well to cool interiors. In his *Cyclopedia of Horticulture,* Liberty Hyde Bailey tells us that it is grown in France for perfumery; the essence is obtained from the flowers.

ACALYPHA   *Euphorbiaceae*

This is the name Hippocrates gave the nettle, and one can easily see the resemblance between these decorative house plants and that unfriendly weed. Both kinds described below refuse to grow except in full sun, but will wilt rapidly in its heat unless the humidity is high, a perversity which makes them difficult to get along with. Both are easily propagated from cuttings and are used as bedding plants in the south.

A. hispida, known as red-hot cat tail or chenille plant, is from the East Indies, where it grows to be a large shrub. It will reach considerable size in a tub or in the ground bed of a conservatory, or can be kept small enough for a window sill by pruning of roots and tops. Its most striking feature is the bright pink flowers, like strings of chenille four to six inches long, which are borne profusely the year round. There is a variety *alba* with white flowers. (Fig. 28)

A. Wilkesiana Macafeana, from the South Sea Islands, has leaves variegated in shades of red and copper, reminiscent of oak leaves in the fall. Its flowers are small and inconspicuous. (Fig. 28)

ACANTHOSTACHYS strobilacea
Bromeliaceae

An epiphyte from Brazil that is quite unlike most of the other bromeliads in my collection. The leaves are slender and spiny, and the red and yellow conical flower is set in unusual fashion on a round stem protruding from one of the leaves. The numerous suckers that grow from the original base will produce a striking hanging basket and one that needs only a minimum of attention in the house. Cultural requirements are about the same as for other bromeliads. (Fig. 28)

ACANTHUS   *Acanthaceae*

Both species described here have whitish flowers opening from a four-sided spike which protrudes from the top of the plant. They will not grow in dark corners, but add an exotic touch to a group of tropicals in a partially sunny place.

A. montanus, the mountain thistle, is from tropical Africa. The large, dark green leaves covered with vicious spines explain the common name. The plant grows to its full height of three or four feet in one year, making it unsuitable

FIG. 29. *Acanthus mollis, A. montanus,* and in front, three small plants of *Acorus gramineus variegatus.*

for your window garden unless it is a roomy one. Cuttings root easily. (Fig. 29)

A. mollis, from southern Italy, is called the architectural plant because its leaf design appears on the capital of Corinthian columns. It is a compact and attractive house plant with no apparent stem, but only a fleshy rhizome from which the rich dark green leaves grow. The plant in the picture grew in a part of my sunporch that received about an hour of sun every morning. It needs a short, semi-dry rest after flowering. Propagate by seed or division of the rhizome. (Fig. 29)

ACHIMENES   *Gesneriaceae*   MAGIC FLOWER

The fact that these gesneriads have a dormant season seems to frighten people away from them, which is unfortunate, for they are easy to grow and well suited to window sills and summer porches. Their modest requirements include good light, a little sun—two or three hours a day is enough—plenty of humidity and moisture, and protection from the cold (their name means "to suffer from cold" in Greek).

The tiny tubers or rhizomes can be planted any time from January on. Put as many as thirty in a bulb pan in African violet soil. When they are about two inches high, transplant a half dozen into a basket or other container. They soon begin to bloom and continue for six or eight months. When they look tired, I water them less often until they are obviously dormant. Then I

FIG. 30. *Achimenes* 'Ambroise Verschaffelt.'

Paul Arnold

clean the soil from the little tubers, which have multiplied prodigiously, and store them in a plastic bag for a few months.

Most achimenes are sold as named varieties, which are hybrids developed from various species including *A. grandiflora, A. longiflora, A. patens, A. coccinea,* and *A. Ehrenbergii,* all native to tropical America. They can be had in bloom at all times during the year when grown under fluorescent lights. While it may take some doing to get the growing recycled from summer to winter, it has been done by resourceful growers.

The gloxinia-like flowers are various shades of pink, blue, lavender, and white. (Fig. 30)

ACORUS gramineus   *Araceae*   CHINESE SWEET FLAG

As members of the Jack-in-the-pulpit family, these tufty little plants have no business calling themselves flags, even though the eight-inch leaves do bear some resemblance to those of the iris. Acorus will grow in water and is one of the few plants that needs "wet feet." It has been cultivated for centuries indoors in the orient, where it is used by both the Chinese and the Japanese for dwarfing. Since Acorus is hardy outdoors, there is no need to worry about keeping it in a warm place; in fact, the cooler the better.

A. gramineus variegatus is pictured in Fig. 29, and is the one usually sold. *A. gramineus pusillus* is already dwarfed by nature. It grows only two or three inches high. Both are propagated by dividing the plants, roots and all.

ADIANTUM   *Polypodiaceae*   MAIDENHAIR FERN

No more decorative foliage can be found than the delicate lacy fronds and dark leaf stalks of the maidenhair ferns. There are a great many species of tropical maidenhairs, only a few of which are available commercially. All require high humidity and a temperature not less than 50°. North, east, and west windows are best, since the ferns are not so apt to dry out there as in a south window. A soil composed largely of humus, such as African violet mix, produces good results.

I cut back all the fronds in the summer time so that the pristine beauty of the new fronds uncurling is not marred by the browning of the old.

A. bellum, the Bermuda maidenhair, is a small and very fluffy species. It never gets more than six or eight inches high.

A. cuneatum is the most commonly grown tropical maidenhair. One is pictured in Fig. 17.

A. decorum 'Pacific Maid' is smaller and more frilly.

A. hispidulum is also small with forked leaves.

A. tenerum Wrightii is another commonly grown species.

ADROMISCHUS   *Crassulaceae*

These low, fleshy South African succulents often have dark spots on their swollen leaves. Being desert plants, they need sun, a well-drained growing medium (desert plant mixture), and careful watering. A good rule is to water thoroughly once a week unless new growth or flowering is in process, at which times your plant can be watered more often. See Fig. 71 for a picture of *Adromischus Cooperi*, plover eggs.

AECHMEA   *Bromeliaceae*   Living Vase Plant

Flowers of most Aechmeas last for many weeks, and the red berries that follow on many species remain attractive for months. The plants grow naturally on the trees of the South American tropics. Under cultivation they do best in osmunda fiber, fir bark, or a mixture of peat moss and sand very well drained. Keep the "living vase" formed by the leaves full of water.

After flowering, the plants send out suckers from around the base. These can be cut off and planted in the same way as the parent plant, which will eventually wither and die. There are many species and varieties. All make good house plants and respond to very little care. Several are growing in the bromeliad tree pictured in Fig. 20. Those described below are a few of my favorites. (See *Bromeliaceae*)

A. caudata is a large bromeliad. Its bright green leaves have cream-colored stripes.

A. fasciata, the urn plant, has powdery blue foliage and pink flower heads which last for an unusually long time.

A. 'Foster's Favorite' is an outstanding hybrid. Its wine-colored leaves are decorative all year round, and its bright red pendant flowers usually appear in winter.

A. Racinae, a small, all-green species, has been given the name "Christmas jewel" because of its accommodating way of producing a drooping string of red flowers with yellow tips at that season of the year.

AEONIUM   *Crassulaceae*

Interesting succulents from the Mediterranean regions and the Canary and Cape Verde Islands. The leaves grow in attractive rosettes, some close to the ground and others on the ends of a stem. Most varieties are semi-dormant in the winter, when they need only enough water to keep the leaves plump. They make good house plants, but must be grown in the sun.

A. arboreum grows eighteen inches or more and looks like a miniature palm. The variety *purpureum* is named to indicate the color of its leaves. Part of a two-year-old plant can be seen in the group of succulents pictured in Fig. 71.

AESCHYNANTHUS   *Gesneriaceae*   LIPSTICK VINE

These are trailing epiphytic gesneriads, not from South America like most, but from the Asiatic tropics. Until recently, when American horticulturists rediscovered the gesneriads, Aeschynanthus was called Trichosporum. It is possible to grow a basketful from a single cutting in a year's time in a warm, sunny window. High humidity must be maintained, and the plants should never be allowed to dry out. African violet soil will suit them, and they need about the same amount of light as gloxinias. The exotic tubular flowers appear in spring, summer, and fall.

A. paruifolius (A. Lobbianus) grows best for me. The mature leaves are green like those of *Hoya carnosa,* and the new growth is a soft, smoky lavender. The flowers which appear in clusters at the tips of the branches, are brilliant red. (Fig. 16)

A number of growers offer other species, generally *A. speciosus, A. marmoratus,* and *A. pulcher.* They do not flower as freely for me, though when it does produce its orange blossoms, *A. speciosus* is quite spectacular. The leaves of *A. marmoratus* are speckled with brown and the flowers are scarcely distinguishable from the leaves. *A. pulcher* is very similar to the first mentioned species.

AFRICAN VIOLET: *Saintpaulia*

Agathaea coelestis: See *Felicia amelloides*

AGAVE   *Amaryllidaceae*   CENTURY PLANT

There are literally hundreds of species of these decorative plants from our American deserts. Their stiff, succulent leaves with spiny points grow in a bristling cone without a stem, and vary in shades of blue, gray, green, and green with white stripes. The common name is a reflection of the fact that potted agaves rarely flower.

Agaves respond to almost any culture, provided they have bright light in spring and summer and are not frozen or drowned in winter. They are not as fast growing and in most cases are handsomer than the South African aloes, which they resemble. If you want big plants, repot them every year. Most species put out suckers or offshoots, which are easy to cut off and root.

A. americana marginata is an old-time favorite. Its green leaves are banded with white or yellow.

A. Victoriae-Reginae is a sculptured curiosity. I have a plant in a five-inch pot which has been there for three years. You can see it in Fig. 71.

AGLAONEMA   *Araceae*   CHINESE EVERGREEN

These denizens of far eastern tropical forests need a minimum of light and a maximum of moisture. Indeed, they will grow directly in water and will survive on unlighted mantle pieces and coffee tables for long periods—although, of course, they do much better in good light. They are among the toughest of house plants. They are also easy to propagate by cutting the stems into pieces with at least two eyes and placing these lengthwise in moist sand, just covered.

A large number of species are grown by collectors, but only a few are generally available. In choosing between species, the important characteristics are the color and marking of the leaves. The flowers are inconspicuous, and some are followed by long-lasting bright red berries.

A. commutatum is very accommodating in the matter of flowers and berries.

A. modestum is the common Chinese evergreen. (Fig. 31)

A. pictum is small and branches freely; it is good for dish gardens. Its dark green leaves are handsomely marked with silver spots.

A. Robelinii, usually called Schismatoglottis, has attractive leaves of blue-green.

A. Treubii has small leaves, bluish with gray splotches. It is the most distinguished one in my collection. (Fig. 31)

AICHRYSON domesticum   *Crassulaceae*   YOUTH AND OLD AGE

A Canary Island succulent with green and white leaves on which a pink cast appears if the plant is grown in the sun, as it should be. New plants are easily propagated by leaf cuttings and old plants get more trailing and attractive each year. (Fig. 31)

FIG. 31.   *Araucaria excelsa, Aichryson domesticum, Allamanda cathartica, Aglao-nema Treubii, A. modestum, Allophyton mexicanum, Aphelandra chamissoniana, A. aurantiaca Roezlii.*

ALGERIAN IVY: *Hedera canariensis variegata*

ALLAMANDA cathartica Hendersonii
Apocynaceae

The five-inch yellow flowers for which this tropical vine from Guiana is grown appear only in spring and summer. This trait, together with its large size and need for full sun, makes it of doubtful value for the average house.

ALLOPHYTON mexicanum
Scrophulariaceae   MEXICAN FOXGLOVE

This plant, often sold as *Tetranema mexicanum*, bears clusters of lavender flowers like tiny snapdragons suspended several inches above the flat, dark green leaves. While it is everblooming in a sunny window and never gets big, it is not an easy plant to grow well. Plant it in the garden in summer, and in August divide the clump for next winter's plants. It can also be grown from seed, which it sets fairly readily. (Fig. 31)

ALOCASIA   *Araceae*

These exotic natives of Borneo, Australia, and southeastern Asia are a temptation to all indoor gardeners because of the dramatic patterns and colors of their foliage. Given plenty of heat (at least 65°) and humidity, they will do very well; but should either be less than they like, they will drop their leaves and sulk. In the summer, if the pots are sunk in damp peat moss under lath or tree shade, Alocasias will grow and send out suckers from the bulb-like rhizomes. A large plant that has not had any of its suckers removed is a striking sight.

If you want more plants, remove the suckers and pot them in a mixture of sand and peat moss until they begin to grow on their own, at which time they can be moved into pure sphagnum moss or African violet soil. Good drainage is very important.

The flowers have the typical Jack-in-the-pulpit shape, but none has special merit. A number of species are offered for sale, and it is hard to choose the best. All are expensive. (Fig. 32)

ALOE   *Liliaceae*

Do not expect many flowers from small aloes grown in the house, for the brilliant yellow, orange, or red spikes of bell-shaped blooms that characterize this genus rarely appear indoors. Most types grown for pot culture are spiny, succulent rosettes, many very handsome and some straggly and not handsome at all. They are South African desert plants, and therefore need as much sun as possible.

A. striata and *A. variegata* are attractive species, generally available. *A. variegata* is shown in Fig. 24 and *A. striati* is pictured in the group in Fig. 50.

ALSOPHILA australis   *Cyatheaceae*   AUSTRALIAN TREE FERN

Tree ferns make good accent plants for an indoor garden if the humidity can be kept high. They grow slowly, eventually filling an eight- or ten-inch tub and getting three to four feet tall. One or two wiltings will kill them, so don't buy one unless you take meticulous care of your house plants.

Alsophila has fluffy, light green, divided fronds and brown, hairy leaf stalks. There is one in the indoor garden pictured in Fig. 21.

ALUMINUM PLANT: *Pilea cadierei*

AMAZON LILY: *Eucharis grandiflora*

FIG. 32.   *Alocasia cuprea* and *A. Korthalsii.*

AMARYLLIS   *Amaryllidaceae*

The large flowered amaryllis you get today is a variety or hybrid developed from *A. vittata* and several other species, all native to South America. *A. vittata* is the one the modern giants most resemble. (Fig. 33)

The large bulbs need a dry rest, not immediately after flowering—for then the leaves are making food to produce new blooms—but when the foliage turns brown, which usually occurs in the fall. After six weeks or two months

FIG. 33. *Amaryllis striata, A. striata fulgida, Amaryllis* hybrid, *Ananas comosus variegatus, Amomum Cardamon.*

of rest, the green tongue of the new flower bud will be seen starting out of the bulb. Then is the time to repot—but only if there is no more room in the pot for the bulb to expand.

When the plant is in active growth, keep it in your sunniest window and later in partial summer sun outside until it is tired again. Some very vigorous bulbs will flower a second time in spring or summer before their dormancy sets in.

If you are sometimes overcome by the size of your hybrid amaryllis, you will be charmed by the diminutive South American amaryllid, *A. striata*. It is evergreen and evergrowing and puts forth one or two tastefully small, apricot-colored, trumpet-shaped flowers every year. Sun, a minimum temperature of 60°, and a pot-bound condition in all-purpose soil are prerequisites. The variety *fulgida* is more sturdy. (Fig. 33)

AMOMUM Cardamon   *Zingiberaceae*   Spicy Ginger Plant

This ginger from the East Indies is the plant which produces the cardamon seeds used to flavor tonics. It will probably never flower in a pot, but the plants are worth growing if you have plenty of room, because the leaves and stems are aromatic when rubbed and crushed. The foliage is dark green and bamboo-like, very similar to Zingiber but better looking. Some growers dry off both this plant and Zingiber at resting time, usually in the autumn; but complete drying out is unnecessary—just don't water copiously if the plant seems dormant. Plenty of water and shade from strong sun are the requirements for the rest of the year, making this plant a candidate for your north window. (Fig. 33)

ANANAS comosus   *Bromeliaceae*   Pineapple

What could be more fun than growing a pineapple at home? It can be done, although unfortunately it is doubtful that the plant will bear fruit. Cut off the top of a pineapple from your grocery store and plant it in sand or perlite, or divide the top and plant the sections. Since pineapples are terrestrial bromeliads native to South America, they do best with some soil added to the usual bromeliad mixture.

A. comosus variegatus is better than the species for indoor decoration; the leaves are beautifully striped with pink, green, and white, whereas the species is a dull gray-green. (Fig. 33)

ANTHURIUM   *Araceae*   Flamingo Flower
                                              Tail Flower

Most anthuriums are from the Central and South American jungles. Unless the developing roots, which appear along the stems, are covered with damp sphagnum, new growth will not be as lush and fine as you would like, and the flowering varieties will stop blooming.

They are climbers by nature, and it is best to make new plants when the old ones start climbing out of their pots. Cut the tops off with a few roots and wrap these in damp sphagnum until they are ready to pot.

For a growing medium I use African violet soil, sphagnum, or sometimes osmunda fiber; I am sure they would also grow in fir bark. Whatever you use, be sure it is well drained and that you water the plant every day. Winter sun will help anthuriums to grow, but spring and summer sun will burn them.

FIG. 34. The large heart-shaped leaves of *Anthurium caribbeum* point down to the smaller strap-shaped ones of a flowering *A. Scherzerianum* and the long exotic leaves of *A. Warocqueanum. Geogenanthus undatus* is in the lower right-hand corner.

A. Andraeanum produces the beautiful red, white, pink, and orange flowers that florists sell. I have had one of these in flower almost continually on my sunporch (Fig. 15). The individual flowers last a month or more.

A. caribbeum is the toughest of my group. It has large, heart-shaped, leathery leaves and does not outgrow its pot too quickly. The flowers are insignificant. (Fig. 34)

A. crystallinum and *A. Forgetii* are very similar. Both have large, velvety, green leaves with white veins. *A. crystallinum* is larger.

A. Scherzerianum, though small, is the best flowering kind for the house. Different plants produce their blooms in all shades of red, pink, and orange. The plants are small and everblooming under favorable conditions. (Fig. 34)

A. Warocqueanum is the most exotic. The heat and humidity of a Philadelphia summer are just what it likes. (Fig. 34)

APHELANDRA   *Acanthaceae*

The showy flowers of the Aphelandras are borne in terminal spikes. The plants are easy to grow, but get leggy if they are not pruned once a year, or better still, replaced by new plants from cuttings. Each plant blooms once or twice a year depending on its environment, which should be as much like its native American tropical forest as possible. The best time to prune and propagate is when new growth is starting, and plants that have bloomed appreciate a semi-dry rest for a few weeks.

A. aurantiaca Roezlii has gray-green leathery leaves. Its flowers are orange at first, becoming a beautiful dark red as they open. Their development takes about a month. (Fig. 31)

A. chamissoniana has a bright yellow flower spike and attractive shiny leaves with white midrib and veins. (Fig. 31)

A. squarrosa Leopoldii and *A. squarrosa Louisae* have distinctive bright foliage; the leaves are large, shiny, and corrugated, and the veins and midrib appear coated with white. The flowers are yellow.

Aralia: See *Dizygotheca, Fatsia* and *Polyscias*

ARAUCARIA excelsa   *Pinaceae*   NORFOLK ISLAND PINE

This wonderful pot plant, shaped like a modernistic Christmas tree, will thrive in a shady north window or in an unheated sunporch, or will grow in a hot, sunny window for months before it starts to protest. It is a permanent plant, not one that needs replacing or cutting back in spring. If its leader is removed, it will lose its tree-like shape and most of its charm. Growers propagate Araucaria by cutting the leader and then taking cuttings from the side shoots. (Fig. 31)

ARCHITECTURAL PLANT: *Acanthus mollis*

ARDISIA crenata   *Myrsinaceae*   CORAL BERRY
(*A. crispa*)

An Ardisia covered with red berries is as nice a Christmas present as one can find. Plants start to flower in their second spring and by the end of the summer, which they like to spend outside in partial shade, the flowers have turned to lustrous berries which will hang on as long as two years. In winter

I bring my Ardisia into a cool north window, where its berries provide a welcome touch of color.

As the plant grows older and loses its lower leaves, it is worth a try at air layering. If your air layer does not take, cut off the top anyway, and new growth will soon appear just below the cut. A season later, flowers will appear and the cycle will begin again. New plants may also be grown from seed, which takes six to eight months to germinate. The genus is native to China. Fig. 17 shows my own north window with *Ardisia crenata* growing in it.

A. japonica has white berries, not as gay.

ARISTOCRAT PLANT: *Haworthia*

ARISTOLOCHIA elegans   *Aristolochiaceae*   CALICO FLOWER

This curiosity from Brazil is not particularly well suited for a window garden because it stands still all winter. In the spring and summer it grows as much as six feet, and bears large, odd, brown flowers with calico spots.

ARRHENATHERUM elatius bulbosum
Gramineae   VARIEGATED OAT GRASS

The green and white striped blades of this Mediterranean grass grow from a string of tiny tubers. Small pots make a pretty edging for a sunny window sill or a greenhouse bench. In the summer they can be cut back, shaken free of soil, and stored in plastic bags. When you want them again, pot an inch or so of beads to a 2½-inch pot and they will soon begin to grow and multiply. They will stand temperatures as low as 30° and perhaps lower, but would never do in a hot, dry apartment. (Fig. 48)

ARROWROOT: *Maranta arundinacea*

ARTILLERY PLANT: *Pilea microphylla*

ASPARAGUS   *Liliaceae*   ASPARAGUS FERN

Many people do not realize that some species of asparagus are twining vines and will clamber up strings, sticks, trellises, or other supports. Being native to South Africa, they like strong light, preferably full sun. Few insects bother these plants, and the common kinds are inexpensive and easy to replace if they fall by the winter wayside. Propagation is from either seeds or cuttings.

A. asparagoides, the small-leaved smilax used by florists, is a fine vine for a window garden. (Fig. 16)

A. plumosus is the ferny foliage you often get with a dozen roses.

A. Sprengeri makes a lovely and house-hardy basket which, in a sunny window, will flower and bear small, round, red fruits. (Fig. 14)

ASPIDISTRA elatior   *Liliaceae*   CAST IRON PLANT

The common name is fully justified. If you have poor light and difficult growing conditions, this is the plant to abuse. In adversity it is not particularly striking in appearance; but the elongated dark leaves, springing in a graceful cluster from the base, can be stunning if the plant is grown under favorable conditions. The variegated forms are particularly attractive. The globular purple-brown flowers appear inconspicuously near the base.

Aspidistras, which are native to China, were the Victorian housewife's standby. They are now so out of style that they are hard to buy, but they deserve an introduction to modern interiors. I grow one in the north window shown in Fig. 17.

ASPLENIUM   *Polypodiaceae*   SPLEENWORT

Many tropical Aspleniums appeared in the ferneries that used to be maintained on English estates. Of these, only a few are commercially available today:

A. bulbiferum, the mother fern, from New Zealand and Australia, derives its name from the baby ferns that appear out of small bulblets along the tops and edges of the fronds in spring and summer. These can be rooted like cuttings. The ferns themselves are good for house culture. One is pictured with some other ferns in Fig. 73.

A. Nidus, the birds nest fern, from Asia and Polynesia, has fronds shaped like leaves and chartreuse in color—quite different from those of other ferns. They spring from a short fibrous "trunk" that looks like a bird's nest, and form a circular wall around an open base, which would be a good place for a nest. Birds nest ferns are easy to raise in the house. They do not need direct sun, but do best with good light. They can be grown on pieces of bark as well as in pots.

For a growing medium, I use damp sphagnum or osmunda or African violet soil. I keep the fronds clean and repot the plant each spring until it reaches the size I want. New plants will appear around the base and can be cut off and potted. A versatile and decorative addition to an indoor garden, it is pictured in Fig. 17.

ASTROPHYTUM   *Cactaceae*   STAR CACTUS

A fairly free-flowering Mexican cactus. The deeply indented trunk and prominent thorns offer a change from the pincushion and barrel types. Full sun in summer and a sunny window in winter are the requirements for flowering. The small pot third from the right-hand end of the shelf pictured in Fig. 14 contains *A. ornatum*. Another common species is *A. Asterias*.

AUCUBA japonica variegata   *Cornaceae*   Gold Dust Tree

This Japanese evergreen is grown for its striking leaves, which are covered with yellow spots of different shades and sizes, depending on the variety. Mature plants in tubs make impressive specimens for a protected breezeway or unheated sunporch, and tiny rooted cuttings often turn up in dish gardens. Large plants bear bright red fruits which hang on for months in a cool place.

Australian Flame Pea: *Chorizema cordatum*

Australian Tree Fern: *Alsophila australis*

Australian Umbrella Tree: *Schefflera actinophylla*

Avocado: *Persea americana*

AZOLLA caroliniana   *Salviniaceae*

Azolla is a Greek word meaning "to destroy by drying"—an apt warning that this tiny plant from tropical America will live only when floating in an aquarium or indoor pool, where its mossy leaves are very decorative. It reproduces by division of its leaves instead of by seeds. In the full sun the plants turn quite brown, but in ordinary light they are bright green.

Babys Tears: *Helxine Soleirolii*

Babys Toes: *Fenestraria rhopalophylla*

BAMBUSA   *Gramineae*   Bamboo

There are many kinds of bamboo, a number of which have botanical names other than Bambusa. Most are handsome, and any of them is worth growing in a pot or tub, at least as an experiment, the hardy kinds being suitable for an unheated porch or sunroom and the tropical kinds being adapted to warmer places.

In the orient, indoor gardeners dwarf the smaller bamboos, particularly *B. nana,* which the Chinese call "The Bamboo of Filial Piety" because the new shoots are said to grow in the center of the clumps in summer and on the perimeter in winter, thereby exposing the older shoots to the refreshing summer breezes and protecting them from the freezing winter winds. Others used for dwarfing are *B. striata, Phyllostachys congesta,* and *Chimono-bambusa quadrangularis.*

Banana: *Musa*

Banana Plant: *Nymphoides aquatica*

Banana Shrub: *Michelia fuscata*

BARREL CACTUS: *Echinocactus*

BASKET GRASS: *Oplismenus compositus vittatus*

BAT PLANT: *Tacca Chantrieri*

BEAUCARNEA recurvata   *Liliaceae*   BOTTLE PLANT
                                                                 PONY TAIL

This unique tree, with graceful strap-like leaves and bulbous base, reaches a height of thirty feet in the deserts of Texas and Mexico. In a pot it grows slowly enough to justify classification as a small plant. The plant is a fine addition to a collection of succulents. (Fig. 35)

FIG. 35.   *Bambusa nana variegata* and *Beaucarnea recurvata.*

BEGONIA   *Begoniaceae*

Of all house plants, no group can equal the begonias for amenability and beauty. Being native to tropical and subtropical countries, they grow best in temperatures of not less than 58°, but as a group they do not require the high humidity that many tropical plants must have. Begonias generally do best in south windows, though some kinds can be kept healthy and attractive in east or west exposures. In spring and summer, all will need protection from the noonday sun.

There are several hundred species, and the varieties run into the thousands. Begonia growers, professional and amateur, have developed countless hybrids, and more varieties are being put into circulation all the time. Begonias, of course, can be propagated vegetatively by leaf or stem cuttings, depending on the type, and the characteristics of any desirable seedling can be perpetuated in this way.

Most reference books classify the species according to the structure of the roots or stems, rather than according to the foliage. The four divisions are bulbous, tuberous-rooted, rhizomatous, and fibrous-rooted. Of these, the fibrous-rooted and the rhizomatous are the kinds most often grown indoors.

The bulbous type started with but one representative, *B. socotrana* from the Indian Ocean island of Socotra. It has been crossed with other types over the years and is the ancestor of the very floriferous begonias sold in florists' shops at Christmas time. 'Lady Mac,' 'Marjorie Gibbs,' 'Melior,' 'Emily Clibran,' and 'Gloire de Lorraine' are members of this group. They do not make good house plants because of their predilection for cooler night temperatures and a high degree of humidity. Best let the florists fuss with them.

Most of the tuberous-rooted types are familiar to all—if not first hand, at least from the advertisements in the garden magazines. They, too, are hybrids developed from species found in the mountains of South America. They are excellent shade plants for the garden or terrace in those parts of the country where summer nights are cool, but because they bloom only in summer and are completely dormant all winter, they are not suitable for the house. In the same group are two semi-tuberous plants that can be grown indoors and are generally referred to as maple leaf begonias, *B. Dregei* and *B. weltoniensis*. These bloom and grow profusely during most of the year, but usually droop and ask for a short rest in early winter. One can be seen in the plant bench shown in Fig. 14.

While some begonias of the rhizomatous group are gigantic, there are a large number of suitable size for a window sill and a few charming dwarfs that would melt any gardener's heart. *Bowerii*, *rotundifolia*, and 'Maphil' are in this diminutive class. More familiar are the large star begonias, *ricinifolia*, *Sunderbruchii* and 'Joe Hayden.' The popular beefsteaks, *erythrophylla* and *Bunchii*, are also in this group.

All rhizomatous begonias have a thick stem or rhizome from which the leaves, flowers, and roots grow. They do not need deep pots, as the root system is never as big as you would expect from the size of the plant. They send up spikes of pink, white, or red flowers from very early spring through early summer. Propagation is easy; simply break off a piece of rhizome, imbed it part way in your cutting box, and wait for roots and leaves to appear. Another method of propagation for many of this group is by leaf cuttings; any main vein, when severed, will produce a new plant. This method is slower, however, and not always so easy for home gardeners.

Many of the colorful rex begonias are also rhizomatous. These are all descended from a plant found in the Indian province of Assam. Many of

FIG. 36.   BEGONIAS COME IN ALL SHAPES AND SIZES.

them are more or less dormant in the winter, and when growing, require a high degree of humidity. For these reasons, they are not the best house plants. Often, however, you will find a variety that adapts itself to your location. I have had great success with small plants under my fluorescent lights in winter, the only difficulty being that they soon outgrow the limited space.

KEY TO FIG. 36:

1. *frondosa*
2. 'Tingley Mallet'
3. *luxurians*
4. 'Abel Carrière'
5. 'calla lily'
6. *Lindleyana*
7. 'Sarabelle'
8. *sanguinea*
9. 'Cuban species'
10. *phyllomaniaca*
11. 'Ricky Minter'
12. 'Stitchleaf'
13. 'Orange Dainty'
14. 'Silver Star'
15. *subvillosa*
16. 'Jinnie May'
17. 'Zeebowman'
18. *Schmidtiana*
19. *speculata*
20. 'Joe Hayden'

The fibrous-rooted begonias may be further divided into four sub-groups: the semperflorens, the cane-stemmed, the small-leaved branching types, and the hirsute or hairy begonias. True to their name, the semperflorens are fine flowering house plants. Many kinds are available, with single or double flowers and leaves of various shades of green and red. Their fibrous roots are more vigorous than those of the rhizomatous types, and repotting may be needed more often.

The cane-stemmed group is familiar to all, for sooner or later everyone seems to have an oversize "angel wing" to cope with. There is no need to let one of these giants crowd you out of the house. They can either be renewed by spring-rooted cuttings or kept down to size by pruning away the old canes and roots in the spring or summer.

The small-leaved branching begonias are becoming legion. They are apt to be everblooming and of manageable size; many have colorful leaves and stems. Two rather new ones hybridized in Germany, 'Preussen' and 'Sachsen,' have bloomed steadily for me for over two years.

The hirsute begonias have large, fuzzy, pink or white flowers and cause more comment than any others in my collection. Their foliage is sometimes hairy too, though some have shining, leathery leaves. They make attractive, fast-growing house plants and are apparently unharmed by low humidity. *B. Scharffii*, a universal favorite, turns up in the ancestry of many of these.

Because of the enthusiasm and success of begonia breeders the world over, many plants have been developed that fit none of these groups exactly. One thing they all have in common is attractiveness. Once you become interested in begonias, all your other house plants are in danger of having their places usurped.

Begonias are a specialty, and there is extensive literature on the subject. Just to list and describe the varieties commercially available would require a large volume, and cultural hints for the difficult kinds would fill another. Fig. 36 shows some of my favorites.

BELOPERONE guttata   *Acanthaceae*   SHRIMP PLANT

The shrimp-colored bracts and white flowers are what give this plant its common name. It is very satisfactory for a sunny window, where it can be depended on for bloom most of the time. Small plants from cuttings will bloom the first year, and mature ones grow to two feet or more in a five-inch pot.

Being native to Mexico, shrimp plants tolerate very warm days, but do better if the nights are cool. They get leggy by March unless they have more sun than is available in most houses. Be sure to prune them back in the summer so as to start the season with a low, bushy specimen. (Fig. 37)

BERMUDA BUTTERCUP: *Oxalis Pes-caprae*

BILLBERGIA   *Bromeliaceae*   PITCHER PLANT

These decorative epiphytic bromeliads from the Brazilian jungles adapt remarkably well to the desert conditions of our living rooms. They are called pitcher plants because most of them hold half a cup or more of water in the rosette of leaves. They absorb the water needed for living functions from this central reservoir rather than through their roots, which function mostly to attach the plant to the crotch of a jungle tree.

Many species are offered by dealers, and all grow well in baskets or attached to cork bark or a piece of cedar. Their main requirement is perfect drainage, such as they enjoy in their native eyrie. The leaves take on added color and the plants flower more freely when grown in the sun, but many will live and flower in east, west, and even north windows. Happily growing plants will sucker freely and eventually make a massive complex, which can be cut into small plants or left to grow in intricate confusion. (Fig. 20)

B. distachya is a fast-growing and free-flowering variety with long, thin, cream-spotted leaves.

B. euphemiae has tubular pitchers of dusty gray-green. It makes an attractive hanging basket plant.

B. horrida, and the hybrid *horrida euphemiae* are both brightly marked with transverse stripes of dark purple.

B. leptopoda is usually listed as the permanent wave plant because of the way the ends of the leaves are curled.

B. Lietzei is a curly, cream-spotted dwarf.

B. nutans is called Queen's tears. It is one of the most floriferous bromeliads.

B. Saundersii hybrids are brightly colored with red, green, and yellow.

BIRD OF PARADISE: *Strelitzia Reginae*

BIRD PEPPER: *Capsicum annuum*

BIRDS EYE BUSH: *Ochna multiflora*

BIRDS NEST FERN: *Asplenium Nidus*

BLACK-EYED SUSAN: *Thunbergia alata*

BLECHNUM gibbum *Polypodiaceae* TREE FERN

This stiff, green tree-like fern from New Caledonia is quite satisfactory for our warm, dry houses, because it does not need the high humidity required by most ferns. If it is watered regularly and afforded good light, it will develop into an impressive specimen. (Fig. 37)

A number of other species are occasionally available and would be worth trying.

BLOOD BERRY: *Rivina humilis*

BLOODLEAF: *Iresine Herbstii*

BLUE CHALK STICKS: *Kleinia Mandraliscae*

BLUE DAISY: *Felicia amelloides*

BOSTON DAISY: *Chrysanthemum frutescens*

BOSTON FERN: *Nephrolepis exaltata bostoniensis*

BOTTLE PLANT: *Beaucarnea recurvata*

BOUGAINVILLEA glabra   *Nyctaginaceae*

These Brazilian vines reach tremendous size if allowed to grow in open beds, and could crowd everything else out of the greenhouse or conservatory. Fortunately, they will also grow in small pots if pruned to bush form or trained on a trellis. (Fig. 37) Bougainvilleas are good for sunny window sills or sunporches, although they will flower there only sporadically and frugally. Varieties with blooms of white, salmon, purple red, and yellow are available.

B. Harrisii has small variegated green and white leaves. It never flowers, but is an attractive trailing plant.

BOWER PLANT: *Pandorea jasminoides*

BOWIEA volubilis   *Liliaceae*   CLIMBING ONION

Bowiea volubilis is an onion-like climber, and peculiar enough to interest almost any curiosity seeker. The thin green shoots growing out of the bulb will twine around a stick or trellis and fit in well with a succulent collection. Stop feeding and watering when growth stops in late summer, and resume attention when new green shoots appear in the winter.

In the wilds of South Africa this oddity grows eight inches across, but potted plants, even in a sunny window, are not apt to crowd you out. One is pictured in Fig. 82.

BROMELIACEAE   BROMELIADS
        BROMELS

Bromeliads are a family of tropical plants native (with the exception of one species in the genus *Pitcairnia*) to Central and South America. Most have stiff leaves which grow in rosettes—some brilliantly marked and others, like the pineapple and Spanish moss, plain dull green or gray. A large number are epiphytic, making their homes high in the trees. The others grow on the ground like ordinary plants.

Many of the epiphytic varieties are peculiarly well suited to house culture because the rosette formed by their leaves holds a supply of water—which seems to protect them from the dry indoor atmosphere. While their shape is not particularly graceful, you can achieve surprisingly elegant effects by using

FIG. 37. *Blechnum gibbum, Browallia speciosa, Bougainvillea glabra, Beloperone guttata, Brunfelsia calycina eximia.*

them in groups and clumps as shown in Fig. 20.

Bromeliad flowers are among the most exotic in shape and color, often combining unusual shades of pink and blue in their complex structures. In bromels of the rosette type the flower appears inside the rosette, remaining half hidden in some varieties and in others emerging startlingly and then drooping over the rim. The duration of the flowers and the attendant bracts varies from a few days to several months, depending on the species.

There are more than 1600 species in at least fifty genera of bromeliads. Those I have grown include Aechmea, Ananas, Billbergia, Cryptanthus, Greigia, Neoregelia, Tillandsia, and Vriesia.

BROWALLIA speciosa   *Solanaceae*

A native of South America that should have a place in every sunny window, where its bright blue flowers will be a pleasure all the year. Browallia also does well in hanging pots and baskets, or drooping over the edge of a plant box or shelf. (Fig. 37)

Both *speciosa* and *americana* grow well in all-purpose soil. While cuttings root easily and new plants can be raised this way, the nicest plants are those grown from seed sown each spring.

BRUNFELSIA calycina eximia   *Solanaceae*   CHAMELEON PLANT

This excellent winter-blooming plant deserves a more impressive name than chameleon, which it is called because its deliciously fragrant flowers change from purple to white in the two or three days they are open. Being a native of Brazil, it enjoys tropical temperatures; don't try it in a cool greenhouse or unheated porch. Although Brunfelsia has a compact habit of growth, it will get too large for the average window unless the roots and tops are pruned each summer. It should be planted in begonia soil and kept slightly pot bound for fullest blooming. It needs full sun in winter. (Fig. 37)

CACTACEAE   *Cacti*   CACTUSES

According to the *Scientific American,* a cactus can live 29 years on its own weight in water. By comparison, a man can live four weeks, a tortoise one year. While these statistics apply to mature plants growing under desert conditions, they make it obvious that watering is one cultural practice that must be done sparingly for desert cactuses grown indoors.

The genus is very large, consisting of over 2,000 species and many hybrids. All are woody plants and are found in the tropics, subtropics and temperate zones of the Western Hemisphere. While some are jungle epiphytes (*Epiphyllum, Schlumbergera, Zygocactus*), most are the thick, fleshy, spiny desert plants we know so well.

Generally speaking, the desert cactus species can be subjected to rather casual winter care. If they are kept in a cold (40°-50°) place, they can be "stored" with little or no light, no water, and without soil at their roots. (Plants shipped from the Southwest will arrive with completely bare roots and can stay that way for several months.) In the spring they can be repotted and gradually brought into the sun. They should have full sun for two or three months.

Cold, dark, winter storage is not necessary, but is often a convenience for the grower. Whatever the conditions, cactuses need little or no water during November, December, January, and February.

CALADIUM   *Araceae*   FANCY-LEAVED CALADIUM

These flashy, large-leaved aroids are increasingly popular. They thrive where it is very hot and grow equally well in sun or shade. I use them in my indoor garden to replace the plants that go outdoors for the summer.

The growing season for caladiums is six to eight months long. By starting them at intervals, you can have one in leaf at all times except the darkest winter months. The flowers are inconspicuous and should be removed so that all the strength of the plants will go to producing foliage.

In the fall the leaves die down and no more new ones are produced, an indication that the dormant season is approaching and that less water should be given. When growth has completely stopped, the tubers can be removed from the pots and stored dry in plastic bags in a warm place for a few months and then repotted.

Begonia soil is right for caladiums; the diameter of the pot should be at least four inches bigger than the diameter of the tuber. To make the dormant tubers start growing, you may have to set the pot for a few days on a radiator (over a wet pebble tray, of course) or in some other really hot spot. The easiest method of propagating is to cut large tubers into pieces, each containing one or two eyes. (Fig. 38)

Most of the numerous named varieties are hybrids and forms of *C. bicolor* and *C. picturatum* from tropical America. The kinds with lance and arrow leaves are smaller than the common hybrids, but are definitely the aristocrats of the group. (Fig. 18)

C. Humboldtii (also listed as *C. argyrites*) is a dwarf. Its leaves are brightly marked with green and white, and the plants are about six to eight inches high and perfect for window gardens. One can be seen growing under lights in Fig. 13.

CALAMONDIN: See Citrus

CALATHEA   *Marantaceae*

Foliage plants, which require not only the heat and high humidity of their native Brazil but also good light. If you can meet these conditions, they are fine house plants. Their leaves emerge directly from the crown, making them well adapted for use as a ground cover between other plants. They need a very loose soil, either African violet or begonia mixture, and plenty of water, which should drain freely. Keep them well washed, as red spider is their worst enemy.

C. argyraea has silver and green leaves with thin straight lines where the veins cross the leaf.

C. Lietzei and *C. Louisae* are very similar. Both are small and subtly

FIG. 38.   *Caladium candidum.*

Misao Matsumoto

marked with maroon and shades of green. One is growing under the fluorescent lights in Fig. 13.

C. Makoyana is the peacock plant. The leaves are held erect like a peacock's tail, displaying an unbelievably intricate meshwork of markings. One is pictured in Fig. 16.

C. micans is a dwarf.

C. Vandenheckei has a broad white stripe on its dark green leaves.

C. zebrina is a large, deep green, velvety plant with darker stripes across its leaves. I grow mine with philodendron on my sunporch. (Fig. 15)

These are but a few of the species cultivated in various collections around the country. They are available commercially, while some of the others you will read about are not.

CALCEOLARIA crenatiflora   *Scrophulariaceae*   POCKETBOOK FLOWER

This is one of the gift plants featured by florists at Easter time. It will not grow in the house, but can be kept in an east or west window for several weeks until it begins to drop its flowers and look unhappy. With a cool greenhouse you can grow new plants each year from seed sown in the summer. The common Calceolarias are hybrids of species originally found in Chile.

CALICO FLOWER: *Aristolochia elegans*

CALIFORNIA GERANIUM: *Senecio Petasitis*

CALIFORNIA PITCHER PLANT: *Darlingtonia californica*

POWDERPUFF
CALLIANDRA   *Leguminoseae*   SAMAN

If you have a craving for a tropical tree, a Calliandra is a good one to buy. It is big enough to warrant classification as a tree, but small enough to live in a tub. The compound leaves resemble locust leaves and the flower puffs are red and large. In the northeastern part of the country their blooming period lasts six to eight weeks in the winter, and the foliage is pretty all year round.

The kinds I have grown are *C. haematocephala, C. inaequilatera* and *C. surinamensis.*

CANTON GINGER: *Zingiber officinale*

CALONYCTION aculeatum   *Convolvulaceae*   MOONFLOWER VINE

If I had a greenhouse adjoining my living room like the one pictured in Fig. 19, I would try to find a corner for the tropical moonflower vine. A seed planted in early summer will grow by September to a thick twining vine which can be trained around a heavy string or stick to display the large, white, fragrant, trumpet-shaped flowers that open only at night. When the blooming season ended, probably in late October, I would uproot the plant, put it on the compost pile, and give the space to something else.

CAMELLIA japonica   *Theaceae*

Many people have success with camellias in the house, but seldom in the living room because camellias come from temperate China and Japan and can't endure dry heat. They need winter temperatures in the high forties or low fifties and good light, though not necessarily direct sun. An unheated sunporch or large, cool bay window is good.

Plants growing outdoors reach heights of forty feet, but pot- and tub-grown specimens can be kept within bounds by pruning in the early spring. Flower buds are set in the summer while the plants are outside, and only those with buds showing in September will bloom that year. If you want large flowers, pinch off all but one bud in each cluster. Camellias need an acid growing medium, such as African violet soil or garden soil mixed half-and-half with peat moss. Use acid-loving plant fertilizer in the spring when the new leaves appear. One can be seen on the sunny porch pictured in Fig. 23.

CAMPANULA   *Campanulaceae*   Star of Bethlehem
Italian Bellflower

The two campanulas I grow indoors come from Italy and are hardy as far north as Wilmington, Delaware. Their most attractive feature is the cascade of blue bell flowers they will produce from March to November. If you supply a cool location throughout the year, you will find them quite easy to bring to bloom. If your summers are hot, you will find them harder to grow, but well worth a little extra trouble.

After flowering is over, I cut the trailing growth away and put the plants in the cold frame for the winter. In March I get them out, shake the old soil off the roots, and repot them in a pot of the same size, or possibly one size larger. New growth appearing at this time provides tips for cuttings, which should be taken promptly, as plants started in early spring will flower by August. They should spend the spring in a sunny window or back in the cold frame—if you are careful to water and ventilate regularly. By May they can be put on the terrace, or back into a sunny window.

C. fragilis, which I have grown from seed, blooms first, starting in early July. I keep it in my sunniest window where it trails over the edge of the sill when most of the other plants are outside.

Fig. 39.   *Campanula isophylla alba.*

Merry Gardens

C. isophylla, with smoky green foliage, is next, coming into flower by the end of July. *C. isophylla alba* has white flowers and plain green foliage. (Fig. 39)

CAPE GRAPE: *Cissus capensis*

CAPE PRIMROSE: *Streptocarpus*

CAPSICUM annuum *Solanaceae* CHILIPIQUIN BIRD PEPPER

The tiny redhot peppers of this South American native give color to a sunny window sill, even if you are too timid to use them for seasoning. The plant holds both fruit and leaves in a hot room better than the Jerusalem cherry. Bird peppers are perennial, but since new ones look best, I grow a pot or two each summer from seeds collected in the winter's harvest.

CARISSA grandiflora *Apocynaceae* NATAL PLUM

Carissa is a tropical shrub from South Africa. In our southern states it is used for a hedge plant, as it withstands frequent shearing. House grown specimens can be trained as topiary or bonsai.

The glossy, green, heart-shaped leaves and long, forked spines are decorative, as are the pure white flowers and luscious red fruit. Flowering, which is not prolific, is most apt to occur in summer. Grow Carissa in a sunny window that is cool at night. (Fig. 40)

CARYOTA mitis *Palmaceae* FISHTAIL PALM

A native of Burma, this palm is well adapted for use in the house, as it stays a reasonable size and forms clumps from suckers around the base. It will stand as much abuse as most potted palms, including lack of light and intermittent watering. The fish-tail leaves will strike you as stylish or ragged, according to your way of looking at them. (Fig. 40)

CAST IRON PLANT: *Aspidistra elatior*

CENTRADENIA floribunda *Melastomaceae*

This small shrub from Mexico has been a delight ever since I bought it. It blooms all winter in a sunny bay window, and in late spring I cut it back and put it outside in a slat-covered cold frame for the summer. My plant is now three years old and less than a foot high and is growing happily in a six-inch bulb pan. I am confident I can maintain its present size and compactness by annual pruning of the roots as well as top, but if it gets too big, I can easily make another, for cuttings root readily. (Fig. 48)

<small>FIG.</small> 40.   *Carissa grandiflora, Citrus taitensis, Chamaedorea adenopodus.*

<small>CENTURY PLANT</small>: *Agave*

CEPHALOCEREUS senilis   *Cactaceae*   <small>OLD MAN CACTUS</small>

The common name of this "venerable cactus"—as one California grower aptly describes it—refers to the long white hairs covering its barrel shape. In the wilds of Mexico, thirty-foot specimens used to be found, but most of these have now been transplanted by collectors. When planted in a pot, it grows much more slowly. (Fig. 24)

CERATOPTERIS thalictroides   *Parkeriaceae*   WATER FERN

A floating fern from the old world tropics suited to water gardens where the water temperature stays above 55°. New plants are formed from buds on the fronds of older plants. I have never bothered to pot mine, though I suspect that if I did so, and sunk the pots just below the surface, I would have larger plants.

CERIMAN: *Monstera deliciosa*

CEROPEGIA Woodii   *Asclepiadaceae*   ROSARY VINE
HEART VINE

The small leaves of this intriguing plant from Natal are shaped like a valentine heart, accounting for one of its common names. Their basic color is dark green, but this is almost obliterated by gray markings on the front of the leaves, which are succulent and of a soft, felt-like texture. The flexible pendant stems grow several feet long, and in spring and summer develop small round tubers—the rosary beads. It is a curious and attractive plant for a sunny window. There are a number of other equally curious species of Ceropegia, but none is as nice as this one. A plant is shown in Fig. 50.

CESTRUM nocturnum   *Solanaceae*   PERFUMED NIGHT JESSAMINE

The inconspicuous, greenish-white flowers of this weedy looking West Indian plant fill the night air with a scent which most people find fragrant, and a few cloying. Flowers are borne off and on throughout the year, provided the plant is afforded sunlight and at least as much humidity as is found in the average indoor garden. Don't let your plant get too large. Small ones bloom as well as big ones, and the less of the undistinguished foliage you have, the better. Cuttings root easily, and old plants do not die even if tops and roots are drastically pruned. (Fig. 41)

CHAMAEDOREA   *Palmae*   PALM

The two species described here are among my favorite indoor plants. Both are clump forming, and neither requires any special care. (See general description under PALM).

C. adenopodus is native to Central and South America. It grows slowly while young, but after being pot grown for six or eight years, it may suddenly put on a great spurt of growth and become, in a short time, a very large clump, up to six feet tall. The fish tail leaves are bright green. (Fig. 40)

C. seifrizii, the grass-leaf parlor palm, is a handsome, small, clump-forming palm with delicate feathery fronds and a striking inflorescence, which appears on orange stalks. Excellent for indoor growing in a sunny place.

CHAMELEON PLANT: *Brunfelsia calycina eximia*

CHENILLE PLANT: *Acalypha hispida*

CHICKEN GIZZARD: *Iresine Herbstii*

CHINESE BANYAN: *Ficus retusa*

CHINESE EVERGREEN: *Aglaonema*

CHINESE SWEET FLAG: *Acorus gramineus*

CHIRITA lavandulacea   *Gesneriaceae*

This unusual Asiatic gesneriad with a Hindustani name is an annual, and is best grown from seed in early spring. Germination is almost guaranteed, and in ten months or less you should have full-sized, flowering plants a foot tall, with clusters of pale blue, gloxinia-like flowers at regular intervals up the stem. While not particularly spectacular or graceful, it is easy to grow on your sunny window sill through the fall and winter months when little else blooms. Like most gesneriads, it prefers night temperatures above 60°. (Fig. 41)

CHLOROPHYTUM   *Liliaceae*   SPIDER PLANT

This is one of my favorite house plants, not only because it is so dependably decorative, but also because it can be neglected for days at a time. It is a hanging plant by nature and sends out pendant runners on which the off-spring form, looking remarkably like spiders. These can be left as an ornament or potted to make more plants. Chlorophytum is native to South Africa.

A. capense (*elatum*) and *A. comosum* and a number of their varieties are sold. They are all very similar, and the names appear confused. To make matters worse, *Chlorophytum* is sometimes called *Anthericum*, which is the proper name of a similar but botanically different plant not in cultivation in this country. (Fig. 41)

CHORIZEMA cordatum   *Leguminosae*   AUSTRALIAN FLAME PEA

A small climbing shrub with holly-like leaves and diminutive orange-red flowers, which appear in the early spring when the plant is grown in full sun. Though beautiful in flower, this plant is too fussy for my window garden. The cool nights it prefers can be provided more easily in a cool greenhouse. Also, like many natives of Australia, where the soil is poor and the plants are used to a starvation diet, it is harmed by what we consider an ordinary amount of fertilizer.

CHRISTMAS CACTUS: *Zygocactus truncatus*

FIG. 41. *Cestrum nocturnum, Chlorophytum capense, Chamaedorea erumpens, Chrysanthemum frutescens, Chirita lavandulacea.*

CHRYSALIDOCARPUS lutescens   *Palmae*   ARECA PALM

   This graceful, clump-forming, feather palm is grown in all parts of the world. It has arching, pale green leaves and, when mature, beautiful grey-green striped stems. Native to Madagascar, it should be grown at normal house temperatures. A location near a window which receives strong light (though not necessarily sun) throughout the day suits the Areca palm well.

CHRYSANTHEMUM frutescens   *Compositae*   Boston Daisy

Boston daisies will flower all year round, though the yellow or white blooms are few and far between during short winter days. Cuttings for winter plants should be made early in August; if taken later, they will be hard to root. To obtain spring plants, keep one of your winter plants growing in a back window until March. Cuttings taken then should flower by early May and can be put out in the summer garden. (Fig. 41)

Cineraria: *Senecio cruentus*

CISSUS   *Vitaceae*

All of these tendril-climbing vines will grow in windows with any exposure, and except for *C. discolor*, will stand a wide range of temperatures. All do well in hanging baskets.

C. adenopodus, from South America, has velvety, trifoliate leaves which lose their red color as they age. Frequent pruning encourages the production of colorful new growth. (Fig. 42)

C. antarctica, the durable kangaroo vine from Australia, is a hotel lobby plant. *C. antarctica minima* is a more attractive dwarf variety. The leaves have a fresher green color and are not so large.

C. capensis, the Cape grape from South Africa, is a rampant grower with large, grape-like leaves. The new growth has a fuzzy appearance. (Fig. 42)

C. discolor, from Java, is aptly called the rex begonia vine. It has long, pointed, velvety green leaves covered with silver markings, and its stems and tendrils and the backs and margins of its leaves are deep wine red. Like all jungle plants, it needs high humidity and protection from temperatures below 60°. If your *Cissus discolor* languishes in winter, check the temperature; it may need to be moved back from the window glass. (Fig. 42)

C. rhombifolia, also from South America, looks for all the world like poison ivy. It is an indestructible house plant and I should not make fun of it, for I use it in impossible places. Its common name is grape ivy. (Fig. 42)

C. striata, from South America, is the baby of the group. It is like a tiny Virginia creeper with neat little five-fingered leaves. (Fig. 42)

CITRUS   *Rutaceae*   Orange and Lemon Trees

The tubbed lemon tree which grew for years on my grandmother's sunporch and now grows happily on mine causes more comment than all my other plants put together; and little wonder, for it always has some lemons that are good enough to eat.

The green branches and twigs of both orange and lemon trees can be pruned into ornamental patterns. The flowers, which usually appear about

FIG. 42.   *Cissus discolor, C. capensis, C. hypoglauca, C. striata, C. rhombifolia, C. adenopodus.*

February and then again through most of the summer, are very fragrant. In winter we pollinate the blooms with a camel's hair paint brush and generally manage to achieve a few fruits. In summer, insect pollination will set as much fruit as the tree can bear. The only time I have ever seen my orange tree lose its ripened fruit in less than six months was when one of my children could no longer resist the temptation. Fortunately for future fruit, it tasted terrible.

Culture is simple. Use the same soil as for begonias or African violets, water copiously when plants are in fruit or flower, and grow them in the sun in as cool a place as you can. Plants grown from the seeds in your orange juice or lemonade may never flower. Those grown from cuttings of fruit-bearing plants will.

C. mitis, the calamondin is the small fruited plant which is sold by the thousands each year. It is much more difficult to grow than any other citrus in my collection.

C. ponderosa, the American wonder lemon, bears lemons the size of a grapefruit when it is two years old. A three-year-old plant with a half-ripe lemon can be seen in Fig. 12.

C. taitensis, the Otaheite dwarf orange, has smaller leaves and fruit than the lemon. (Fig. 40)

CLEISTOCACTUS Straussii   *Cactaceae*   SILVER TORCH

I am fond of my white woolly Cleistocactus. Bought five years ago in a 2¼-inch pot and grown since then in full sun summer and winter, it is now eighteen inches tall, very decorative, and little or no trouble to keep. It is watered thoroughly once a week in winter and more often when it is outside in summer. This cactus grows to tremendous size in the mountainous deserts of Bolivia. One is pictured in the cactus garden shown in Fig. 24.

CLERODENDRUM   *Verbenaceae*   CLERODENDRON

The vining types of clerodendron are as decorative as any plants you can grow in your greenhouse or sunny window. They bloom in all but a few of the winter months, when they are dormant and often lose all their leaves. At the beginning of their resting season the stems can be pruned severely; and as long as they are dormant, the plants should be watered only enough to prevent drying out. If you train your clerodendron on a trellis attached to its pot rather than to the wall, you can put the dormant plant in some cool place where it can't be seen until growth starts again. Cuttings root easily and will bloom the first year. Clerodendrons do well in any soil mixture; I use an all-purpose one.

C. Thompsoniae, the glory bower, from West Africa, is at the height of its bloom in the summer and fall. White bracts are evident for three or four weeks before the small, blood-red flowers appear, much resembling bleeding hearts. The shoots twine energetically and need something to climb around.

C. speciosum is a hybrid between *C. splendens* and *C. Thompsoniae*. It has the same kind of flowers as *Thompsoniae*, but the bracts, instead of being strikingly white, are dull red. However, it is very floriferous and has a shorter dormancy. (Fig. 48)

FIG. 43. *Clivia miniata, Citrus* sp., *Philodendron Wendlandii.*

CLIFF-BRAKE FERN: *Pellaea*

CLIMBING FERN: *Lygodium scandens*

CLIMBING ONION: *Bowiea volubilis*

CLIVIA miniata   *Amaryllidaceae*   KAFIR LILY

During the months when I have to find a frost-free place for nonblooming Clivias, I feel like throwing them away. The dark green strap leaves are thicker and less graceful than those of other members of the amaryllis family and take up much more room. But when the orange clusters of flowers begin to push out between these heavy leaves, I am glad to rescue the plant from the garage or workroom and put it on the sunporch while the blooms last.

Clivias grow in all-purpose soil and seldom need repotting, perhaps once in five years if the pot doesn't burst meanwhile. (Fig. 43)

CODIAEUM variegatum   *Euphorbiaceae*   CROTON

The brilliant and decorative foliage of the crotons makes artificial copies of them favorites for shops and restaurants. The living plants require high humidity and high temperatures. Crotons may be allowed to develop into large specimens, or kept at moderate size by summer pruning. While they will grow in a north window, the coloring of the leaves will be brighter if they see the sun.

There are countless varieties, differing in the color and, to a lesser degree, in the shape of their leaves. The name is thought to be derived from the Greek word for head, indicating that the leaves were used for crowns. The original species are native to the Old World tropics. (Fig. 26)

COFFEA Arabica   *Rubiaceae*   COFFEE TREE

We all have an urge to grow food plants indoors—oranges, lemons, alligator pears, and of course, coffee. It is a fast-growing tree, native to tropical Africa and not particularly graceful. However, with careful pruning and shaping it can be coaxed into an interesting shape. Its leathery dark green leaves are probably helpful in making it resistant to the damaging effect of dry, indoor air.

Winter sun and night temperatures no lower than 60° are desirable. In spring and summer, fragrant white flowers will produce bright red coffee beans.

COLEUS Blumei   *Labiatae*

Here is a plant that anyone can grow. The game is to see who can find the most striking variety (a packet of seeds will produce a hundred different kinds) and who can grow the bushiest plant. The traditional rules obtain: exposure to the sun, ruthless pinching, and regular watering and fertilizing.

COLLINIA elegans   *Palmae*   <small>PARLOR PALM</small>
(*Neanthe bella, Chamaedorea elegans*)   <small>DWARF PALM</small>

This is the palm you are apt to find in dish gardens. Regardless of which name you use, it is easy to buy, for commercial growers produce them from

<small>FIG. 44.</small> An attractive dish garden planted with *Polyscias Balfouriana, Collinia elegans, Serissa foetida*, and *Pellionia pulchra*.

seed by the thousands. It is easy to grow in sun or shade, with or without attention, and it never gets too big. (Fig. 44)

COLOCASIA antiquorum   *Araceae*   <small>TARO</small>

The starchy roots of the taros are used for food in the tropics of the Pacific, and you and I can use the foliage for decorative effect in water gardens, where they should be planted in pots with the crown of the plant at or slightly above the water level. They will also grow well with the pot completely out of water if kept quite moist. What appear to be stems are actually the leaf petioles, which sometimes need help in holding up the enormous elephant-ear leaves. If the water temperature falls below 60°, growth will stop, but the plant will be revived by the heat of the spring and summer sun.

The species has plain green velvety leaves. The East Indian variety *illustris*, called black caladium or imperial taro, has purple petioles and ornate purple markings on the leaves. (Fig. 18)

FIG. 45.   TOP ROW, LEFT TO RIGHT: *Columnea hirta, C. Allenii, C. gloriosa, C. arguta, C. Banksii.* BOTTOM ROW: *C. sanguinea, C. tulae* 'Flava.'

COLUMNEA   *Gesneriaceae*

These trailing epiphytes from the jungles of Central and South America are fascinating for indoor gardeners who are willing to expend a little extra care for something unusual. Warmth, winter sun, and high humidity are the main requirements; spectacular tubular flowers, starting in winter and continuing off and on throughout the spring, and graceful growth at all seasons are the rewards.

I have had good results with columneas in my sunniest windows, where I sometimes place them on the pebbles and sometimes hang them above the other plants. Either African violet soil or epiphyte mixture suits Columneas, provided the container is very well drained.

C. Allenii, gloriosa, and *hirta* have small leaves covered with downy red fuzz and brilliant red or orange flowers. Others, such as *arguta* and *Banksii,* have shiny, fleshy leaves. *C. tulae* 'Flava' has yellow flowers. (Fig. 45)

CONFEDERATE JASMINE: *Trachelospermum jasminoides*

CONVOLVULUS Cneorum
Convolvulaceae   SILVER BUSH MORNING GLORY

Don't let the weedy connotation of the common name frighten you away from this attractive plant from the sunny shores of the Mediterranean. The small, elongated leaves, silver-blue in color and silky in texture, are what make Convolvulus worth growing. The white morning-glory flowers, which cover the plants in spring and summer, are insignificant by comparison. This is a plant for a sunny situation with cool nights. All-purpose soil and summer pruning are the cultural requirements. (Fig. 48)

COMMON FIG: *Ficus carica*

COPPER LEAF: *Acalypha Wilkesiana Macafeana*

CORAL BERRY: *Ardisia crenata*

CORDYLINE   *Liliaceae*   TI PLANT
DRACENA

Commonly called dracena and almost always confused with the genus *Dracaena,* which they closely resemble. As a general rule, if the plant has brightly colored foliage with shades of red, pink, or copper, it is apt to be a Cordyline rather than one of the Dracaenas. The apparently lifeless Hawaiian log which comes to life in a dish of water is also a Cordyline.

They need good light and preferably some sun to keep their bright colors. In other respects they are tough and able to withstand all manner of abuse. When they grow too tall, they can be air layered or simply cut off; new growth will soon appear below the cut.

C. indivisa, from New Zealand, is a thin, green-leaved type. (Fig. 16)

C. marginata, from Madagascar, is a slow-growing dish garden favorite. Its leaves are grayish with purple edges.

C. terminalis, from eastern Asia, has many brilliantly colored forms and varieties. This species is usually called ti plant.

CORN PLANT: *Dracaena*

COTYLEDON   *Crassulaceae*

Succulents from the deserts of South Africa and the Mediterranean region, resembling their American counterparts, Echeverias and Pachyphytums. *C. undulata* is in the picture in Fig. 50, growing on a sunny shelf in desert soil

FIG. 46.   *Crassula perforata, C. argentea, C. deceptrix, C. falcata, C. Triebneri, C. argentea variegata, C. rupestris.*

mixture. Like other members of this family, Cotyledons can be easily propagated from leaf cuttings.

CRAB CACTUS: *Zygocactus* or *Schlumbergera*

CRASSULA   *Crassulaceae*

Twenty or more kinds of crassula are offered for sale and all make good house plants. The succulent leaves and stems they developed in their native South Africa enable them to withstand lack of moisture in air and soil. Gray or blue crassulas need sun to keep their light color, but the darker green ones will survive without sunlight for months at a time. In the winter when little or no growth is taking place, care must be taken not to overwater; too much at this time will cause unattractive, spindly growth. (Fig. 46)

CREEPING CHARLIE: *Pilea nummulariaefolia*

CREEPING FIG: *Ficus pumila*

CROSSANDRA infundibuliformis   *Acanthaceae*

Somewhere along the line, the species name of this flowering plant from India got changed from *undulaefolia* to the tongue twister above. The plant is as exacting to grow as its name is to pronounce. Heat (70°), humidity, and plenty of winter sun are the main requirements; and Crossandras seem to do best in African violet soil. Spikes of orange flowers and shining dark green leaves are the rewards of success. New plants can be raised from seed, which germinates slowly and erratically, or from cuttings. (Fig. 47)

CROTON: *Codiaeum variegatum*

CROWN OF THORNS: *Euphorbia Milii*

CRYPTANTHUS   *Bromeliaceae*   EARTH STARS

The typical cryptanthus is a flat, brightly colored rosette found on the

FIG. 47. *Cryptanthus zonatus zebrinus, Crossandra infundibuliformis, Cuphea hyssopifolia, Ctenanthe Oppenheimiana tricolor, Cyanotis somaliensis, Ctenanthe Oppenheimiana.*

jungle floor in Brazil. All of them are admirably suited to use in indoor gardens and will not suffer from long periods of neglect. When placed on a bed of peat moss or grown in a pot, they multiply rapidly by off-shoots.

C. acaulis and *C. bivittatus* are very common. *C. lacerdae*, not as frequently encountered, has particularly attractive green and white markings on its leaves. *C. zonatus zebrinus* makes a striking specimen after two or three years of undisturbed growing. (Fig. 47) (See Bromeliaceae)

CTENANTHE Oppenheimiana   *Marantaceae*

Pronounce this "tenanthy," and buy one if you find it for sale. It is a house-hardy foliage plant from South America. The leaves have the shape and markings which characterize the Maranta family, but are stiffer and more upright than most. They do well in all-purpose soil in any location with strong light.

The variety *tricolor* has pink, white, and green leaves. It does not grow as vigorously as the species. Both the species and the variety can be propagated by dividing the clump with a sharp knife. (Fig. 47)

CUPHEA hyssopifolia   *Lythraceae*   ELFIN HERB

The only reason for growing this small Mexican plant is the fun of finding the tiny lavender flowers, which appear frequently but are almost too small to see. Mature Cupheas are only six to eight inches tall and can be accommodated in a three-inch pot. The most favorable location is a cool, sunny window. Propagate by seeds or cuttings. (Fig. 47)

CYANOTIS somaliensis   *Commelinaceae*   PUSSY EARS

This small trailing plant grows quite slowly and can be pruned into a neat compact shape. The common name refers to the soft white hairs covering its leaves. The flowers are blue and appear in spring if the plant has been grown in a sunny window, but you can also grow pussy ears as a non-blooming foliage plant in a north window. It comes from tropical Africa and likes to be kept warm. (Fig. 47)

CYCAS revoluta   *Cycadaceae*   CYCAD
SAGO PALM

Cycads are primitive plants, the forebears of which flourished in the carboniferous age 200 million years ago. They are slowly vanishing from the earth—which is hard to believe if one has grown a cycad, for they seem practically indestructible. Given sun out of doors for four or five months of the year, they can survive the rest of the year indoors under almost any conditions. (Fig. 16)

CYCLAMEN persicum   *Primulaceae*

Recipients of cyclamens from the florist's are often disappointed because the plants soon go into a decline and have to be thrown out. The change from a cool greenhouse to the dry heat of the average house is too much for them. People with unheated sunporches or cool sunny windows can have blooming cyclamens for six months as the mainstay of their winter gardens. Those without such cool situations must be reconciled to enjoying their plants for only a few weeks. The cool sunporch in Fig. 23 is a perfect location.

All growth on cyclamens comes from the corm, which carries the plant through its summer dormancy and can be dried and revived if you are both careful and lucky. The most attractive plants are one to two years old, the age of those the florists sell at Christmas time. They grow naturally in Greece and along the eastern shores of the Mediterranean.

CYMBALARIA muralis   *Scrophulariaceae*   KENILWORTH IVY

Incredible as it may seem, this garden weed makes a dainty trailing plant for a sunny place indoors, with fresh-looking light green leaves no larger than a quarter and tiny purple flowers that appear throughout most of the year. Hold-fast roots form along the stems; it might be interesting to train Kenilworth ivy on a totem pole.

CYPERUS   *Cyperaceae*   SEDGE

These are among the most satisfactory water plants—adaptable and attractive both indoors in winter and outdoors in summer. They need no sun and are easily propagated from seed by dividing the clumps, or by cutting the heads and rooting them in damp sand or peat.

Though they grow naturally in the swamps of tropical America and Africa and therefore enjoy "wet feet," they will do as well in pots not immersed in water, provided they never dry out.

C. alternifolius, the umbrella plant, from Madagascar, is the most common. It will continue to grow in water temperatures as low as 50°—which most other tropical water plants cannot stand (Fig. 18). The variety *gracilis* is smaller in every dimension.

C. diffusus is much more compact than *C. alternifolius*, though the leaves are larger. It does better out of water than in.

C. Papyrus (*Papyrus antiquorum*) is the Egyptian paper plant, interesting as a curiosity, but not in a class with the other three for decoration.

CYPHOMANDRA betacea   *Solanaceae*   TREE TOMATO

Before you try this indoors, note the common name. The plant is indeed a small South American tree, and it grows like Jack's beanstalk. I have one in my greenhouse ten feet tall with heart-shaped leaves a foot long that grew to this size from seed in eighteen months. It bloomed and bore bitter but edible fruit its second summer.

CYRTOMIUM falcatum   *Polypodiaceae*   HOLLY FERN

A sturdy, leathery fern, and one of the best for the house because it will withstand abuse. It can be grown under any indoor conditions, light or dark, cool or warm. Be sure to keep the leaflets clean to get the most out of its appearance and to control scale, its only indoor enemy. The species is native to several widely separated regions, including South Africa, Polynesia, Japan, and Asia. It is closely allied to *Aspidium* and *Polystichum* and is sometimes listed as either of these.

The variety *Rochefordianum* is smaller with more leaflets and is generally more attractive. One is pictured with some other ferns in Fig. 73.

DAVALLIA   *Polypodiaceae*

These ferns have finely divided fronds and creeping rhizomes which greatly resemble the fuzzy paws of a small animal. Like most plants with thick rhizomes, they have insignificant roots and need comparatively little root room. Grow them in pans in a light soil mixture, on sphagnum poles, or in hanging baskets filled with sphagnum so that the rhizomes can creep along the outside.

D. Mariesii (*bullata*), the squirrel's foot fern, is found in northern India and Japan. It used to be sold as fern balls, apparently lifeless with no green fronds. When the ball was watered, the fern came to life and made an attractive decoration to hang in a window, where it would grow for months. (Fig. 48)

D. fejeensis plumosa, the rabbits foot fern, from the Fiji Islands, has the fluffiest fronds of the group. (Fig. 48)

D. Griffithiana, from India and south China, has gray feet and bluish fronds. (Fig. 48)

D. solida, from Malaya, is sometimes called the leather leaf fern. The shiny, stiff fronds are a fresh, bright green. The rhizomes do not travel as much as those of the other species. (Fig. 48)

DEVILS IVY: *Scindapsus aureus*

DEW FLOWER: *Drosanthemum speciosum*

DUMB CANE: *Dieffenbachia*

DICHORISANDRA   *Commelinaceae*

Upright South American cousins of the wandering Jew, and good candi-

FIG. 48.   TOP: *Arrhenatherum elatius bulbosum.* MIDDLE: *Clerodendrum speciosum, Nepeta hederacea variegata, Schizocentron elegans, Abutilon hybridum.* BOTTOM: *Davallia solida, D. Griffithiana, D. fejeensis, Convolvulus Cneorum.* FLOOR: *Davallia Mariesii, Centradenia floribunda.*

dates for indoor gardens with poor light. They should bear blue flowers in the spring and summer, but not all mine have done so. If they are repotted from time to time they will make tall clumps.

All three species described below are apt to go through a winter dormant period. During this period you can either cut them back or leave them to rest as they are, but in either event water them very sparingly. New growth will start in spring. Another procedure is to remove the potato-like tubers from the roots, use them to form new plants, and discard the old one. The tubers may be stored (wrapped in polyethylene) in a warm dry place for a month or two before they are planted.

D. Reginae has the smallest leaves of the three, with purple and silver markings. It never grows more than about a foot high. Young plants have much more vividly colored leaves than old, large ones.

D. thyrsiflora reaches a height of two or three feet, and the plain, dark green leaves grow six to eight inches long and two inches wide. Its brilliant blue flowers, which appear in summer and fall in the northern part of the country, are long lasting. One is pictured in Fig. 15.

D. Warceswiczii has a silver streak down the middle of the leaves, which are midway between those of the other two in size.

Dichorisandra undatus: See *Geogenanthus undatus*

DIEFFENBACHIA   *Araceae*   DUMB CANE

The large, splotchy leaves of mature dieffenbachias are familiar to all house plant fanciers. The plant is so tough that it will grow almost anywhere indoors. Its common name, dumb cane, is derived from the paralyzing irritation of the mouth and throat produced by calcium oxalate in the stem if it is chewed. Once you know the significance of dumb cane, the implications of the other name, mother-in-law plant, are obvious.

Dieffenbachias do well in light or shade, but lose their leaves and die at temperatures below those found in their native Brazil. When your plant gets too tall, cut it off at the ground and it will sprout anew.

D. maculata (*D. picta*) is the common species. It has a number of varieties, 'Rudolph Roehrs' being a particularly bright one. A beautifully grown specimen is pictured in the planter in Fig. 26.

D. Bausei is one of my favorites because of the bluish cast to its variegation.

D. Oerstedii is all green and *Oerstedii variegata* is green with a single white line down the main vein.

These are but a choice few of the many species, varieties, and hybrids available.

DIOSMA ericoides   *Rutaceae*   BREATH OF HEAVEN

The name Diosma can be translated as breath of heaven, or more accurately as divine fragrance. The fragrance is there, but only when you rub the feathery leaves. Diosma is said to be a winter bloomer, but has not proved to be such for me. A few very pale pink flowers in the spring were all I could achieve in my sunniest window.

Use all-purpose soil for this native of South Africa, and prune it in summer to produce a bushy plant for next winter. (Fig. 49)

DIPLACUS puniceus *Scrophulariaceae*
(*Mimulus*)

The shiny, dark green leaves and stems of this shrubby plant from Southern California are hairy and sticky and only reasonably attractive through the winter; but in May, plants that have been grown in the sun and have survived the heat and dryness become covered with dark orange flowers, which continue throughout the summer. One plant of Diplacus will dress up a sunporch for the spring and early summer, making it seem less bare after the bulk of its regular occupants have moved outside. In the fall, when the blooming is done, the plant can be cut back and rested behind something more decorative until growth begins again in early spring. Then it should be revived by having the old soil knocked away from its roots and being repotted in fresh all-purpose mixture.

DIZYGOTHECA elegantissima *Araliaceae* Finger Aralia

The slender leaflets growing in flat palmate fans give this woody plant from the Pacific Islands its common name, and their airy grace is a welcome change from the heaviness of most tropical plants. If deprived of light and humidity, it will lose its leaves, particularly the lower ones, and there is no way to restore the loss. All you can do is to cut the plant back in the summer, put it outside in a shady place, and wait for new growth to appear. This species does not branch, but plants with several stems may be obtained by cutting the main stem close to the ground. The cuttings obained from this operation can be rooted and grown to a height of ten feet in three years. (Fig. 49)

The ferny leaves are juvenile; after two or three years the plants produce much larger foliage—also attractive, but quite different. When the plants are cut back, a recommended procedure when they have gotten too tall, the newly emerging buds will produce the juvenile form of leaves for a number of months.

DRACAENA *Liliaceae* Dracena

Dracenas are popular house plants because of their ability to survive under adverse conditions. In winter they need good light but don't require direct sun. Some species, particularly those with brightly colored leaves, are extremely decorative. The more common kinds are scarcely worthy of space in the house. All are African natives.

D. *deremensis Longii* is a slow-growing, non-branching type, with vividly striped green and white leaves (Fig. 49). D. *deremensis Warneckii* is much more usually grown. Its gray-green striped leaves make it an effective accent plant.

FIG. 49.   *Dracaena deremensis Longii, Dizygotheca elegantissima, Drosanthemum speciosum, Diosma ericoides.*

D. *fragrans Massangeana* has the descriptive common name, corn plant. If it is cut off near the ground level when it grows too big, a new plant will sprout from the roots.

D. *Godseffiana* and D. *Goldieana*, from Upper Guinea in Africa, have a lower habit of growth, and their leaves are wider in proportion to their length. The former has yellow-spattered green leaves and is a dish garden favorite. The latter is a collector's item because it is difficult to propagate. Its leaves have transverse white stripes instead of the longitudinal stripes common to the corn plant types.

D. *Sanderiana* is a smaller species often used in dish gardens.

FIG. 50.   A GROUP OF SUCCULENTS.

DROSANTHEMUM speciosum   *Aizoaceae*   DEW FLOWER

This blue-gray succulent from South Africa belongs to a large group formerly called *Mesembryanthemum*. It likes a sunny exposure and cool night temperatures such as generally prevail close to the window pane. The small, orange, daisy-like flowers appear in the spring and continue all summer if the plants are put out in the sun. They are easily propagated by cuttings, of which you should have a good supply each summer when you prune your parent plant. (Fig. 49)

KEY TO FIG. 50:

1. *Stapelia variegata*
2. *Ceropegia Woodii*
3. *Oscularia deltoides*
4. *Echeveria pulvinata*
5. *Kleinia Haworthii*
6. *Pachyveria* hybrid
7. *Cotyledon undulata*
8. *Senecio scaposus*
9. *Pachyphytum* 'Moonstone'
10. *Bowiea volubilis*
11. *Aloe striata*
12. *Echeveria* 'Doris Taylor'
13. *Crassula falcata*
14. *Echeveria candida*
15. *Gasteria hybrida*
16. *Kleinia Mandraliscae*
17. *Echeveria pulvinata*

DWARF LILY TURF: *Ophiopogon japonicus*

EARTH STARS: *Cryptanthus*

EASTER CACTUS: *Schlumbergera Bridgesii*

EASTER LILY CACTUS: *Echinopsis*

ECCREMOCARPUS scaber   *Bignoniaceae*   GLORY FLOWER

The common name is a little grand for this dainty tendril climber. In its native Chile it climbs as high as twelve feet, but in a pot it can easily be kept under control. It is of doubtful value for the house, since it blooms in summer and fall, but it is a good summer-blooming vine for a sun room. The flowers are small orange trumpets, which are born the first year on plants raised from seeds sown in the spring.

ECHEVERIA   *Crassulaceae*

These Mexican succulents attract attention by reason of their beautiful leaf rosettes, waxy in some species and hairy in others. Small plants can be made at any season by cutting off and potting a rosette with a little stem attached, or from single leaf cuttings. All the echeverias need full winter sun to keep their color and compactness. Grow them in desert soil mixture and take care not to overwater them in winter. They do not need fertilizer as often as leafy plants—once a month from March to September is enough. Most species bear orange or red tubular flowers continuously throughout the spring and summer. Several kinds can be seen in Figs. 50 and 71.

ECHINOCACTUS	*Cactaceae*	BARREL CACTUS
ECHINOCEREUS	*Cactaceae*	HEDGEHOG CACTUS
ECHINOPSIS	*Cactaceae*	EASTER LILY CACTUS

These three genera are typical of the cultivated cacti of North and South America. They will survive the winter wherever they get at least a little sun and are protected from freezing. During the summer many will flower once or even twice if put outside in full sun. If they are also repotted—or better still, planted directly in a well drained garden bed—and given water and fertilizer regularly, they will grow rapidly into impressive and decorative specimens. Be careful not to overwater them in the winter. (Fig. 14)

EGYPTIAN PAPER PLANT: *Cyperus Papyrus*

ELEPHANT BUSH: *Portulacaria afra*

ELFIN HERB: *Cuphea hyssopifolia*

EMPRESS FLOWER: *Tibouchina semidecandra*

ENGLISH HEDGE FERN: *Polystichum setiferum*

ENGLISH IVY: *Hedera Helix*

EPIPHYLLUM	*Cactaceae*	ORCHID CACTUS

Neither the common name nor the family gives any clue to the cultural requirements of these large epiphytic cousins of the common cactus. Being big and droopy, they must have either support or room to hang; and as natives of the rain forests of Central and South America, they need warmth and a loose, well-drained growing medium.

The problem with epiphyllums is what to do with them all winter when they are at their enormous worst and still must be watered occasionally and kept at 50° or warmer. If you resist the inclination to throw them out, you will reap a worthwhile reward in the flowers, which are born on last year's leaves over a period of several weeks in the summer. In general, the individual flowers mature and wilt in a twenty-four-hour period.

If you have an old epiphyllum that has big, white, night-blooming flowers, it is probably *E. oxypetalum*. (Fig. 51) If you have a new plant, it is probably one of the 3,000 named hybrids developed over the past decade. These have flowers in all shades of pink, red, purple, and white—never yellow or

FIG. 51.   *Epiphyllum oxypetalum.*

Marjorie Wihtol

blue (there are no blue cactus flowers). Some are day-blooming, and some have an upright rather than a drooping habit of growth.

EPISCIA   *Gesneriaceae*

If you have a warm place in your house that gets three or four hours of winter sun a day, and where the atmosphere can be kept humid, try an episcia (pronounced ee-piss′-ee-ya), an epiphyte from the South American jungles. The plush-textured leaves, with rich, dark colors and decorative markings, and the distinctive habit of growth, with vigorous laterals extending at right angles from the trailing stems, make the episcias among the most decorative house plants. Unlike many gesneriads, they have no leafless dormant period, and if conditions are right, will hold their lush foliage all year round. Don't expect flowers except in the spring and summer.

Episcias need warmth, copious watering, and a well-drained growing medium; and they are good for hanging baskets. If they look straggly in winter, cut back the runners, and soon fresh growth will appear. Cuttings taken from the leaves, stems, or offshoots all root easily.

E. cupreata, from Nicaragua, appears in a number of named varieties. Both this species and *E. reptans*, often misnamed *E. coccinea* and formerly named *E. fulgida*, are commonly called red flame violet—to the horror of botanists, because while the plants are in the same family as African violets, their red tubular flowers bear no resemblance to the pink, blue, and white ones of the Saintpaulias.

E. lilacena is so named because of its blue flowers. (Fig. 16)

E. dianthiflora is quite different from the three first mentioned. It has small, green, velvety leaves on trailing stems, making flat mounds when grown in a pot, and a small compact cluster when grown in a basket. In spring and summer it nearly always has a few tufted white flowers, not unlike garden pinks or *Dianthus*, from which it gets its name.

E. punctata is the least desirable of the group. Its trailing stems get quite woody, its leaves are undistinguished, and its purple-spotted flowers, although the most profuse of the group, tend to hide under the leaves.

A number of growers are hybridizing episcias. New hybrids and cultivars keep appearing in the catalogs and are worth trying.

ERANTHEMUM nervosum   *Acanthaceae*

This is one of the few plants that will produce really blue flowers almost all winter. Mature plants grow two feet tall and need an eight-inch pot, but can be kept to six-inch pot size by pruning. Full sun and regular trips to the kitchen sink to ward off red spider are important. Propagate from cuttings in spring and summer, for small plants flower as profusely as large ones.

Eranthemum is native to India and can be grown at any temperature between 50° and 70°. Use all-purpose soil. (Fig. 52)

EUCHARIS grandiflora   *Amaryllidaceae*   AMAZON LILY

This evergreen bulb deserves a place on your sunny window sill, if only for the distinctive long, heavy leaves. The fragrant, white, star-like lilies, born in groups of five or six on each umbel, are an extra. A well-growing plant flowers once or twice a year. Following the flowering period, keep it on the dry side for a few weeks. It should be kept in the same pot longer than most bulbs. Since repotting sets it back, this is best done at the end of the drying-off time. (Fig. 52)

EUGENIA uniflora   *Myrtaceae*   SURINAM CHERRY

The new foliage of this small, slow-growing tree from Brazil is like shiny burnt sienna. Surinam cherry bears edible fruit, brilliant, loud pink, which forms after the small whitish flowers fade away. The foliage is dark green; the new leaves are an attractive red color. It needs sun, and night temperatures between 55° and 65°. When it grows too large for the window sill, it is worth keeping as a tub plant on a sunporch or in front of a large picture window. (Fig. 52)

EUONYMUS japonicus   *Celastraceae*

An upright evergreen much used in florists' dish gardens. In their native Japan the plants reach a height of eight feet, and even under the adverse conditions of most houses they are apt to grow out of their dishes. When this

FIG. 52.   *Eranthemum nervosum, Eucharis grandiflora, Eugenia uniflora.*

happens, they can be potted, pruned, and kept bushy for many more years. They look best when grown in cool conditions, but will develop into a compact and house-hardy plant at higher temperatures if given good light.

There are numerous varieties on the market, and the species is almost never seen. 'Silver Queen' has white variegation and 'Golden Queen' has yellow. *E. japonicus microphyllus variegatus* is a tiny green and white dwarf. (Fig. 53)

FIG. 53. *Euonymus japonicus* 'Silver Queen,' *Euonymus japonicus microphyllus variegatus, Euphorbia grandicornis, E. lophogona, Eurya japonica, Exacum affine, Euphorbia lactea cristata, E. Milii, E.* hybrid.

EUPHORBIA   *Euphorbiaceae*

Although many members of the family come from other parts of the world, the largest group of euphorbias constitute the South African equivalent of our American cactus and are at least as varied in appearance. Most of the group are succulent plants with insignificant flowers and often with curious tortured shapes. Other euphorbias, like the crown of thorns and the familiar poinsettia, are noteworthy for their brightly colored inflorescences. About the only generalities that apply to the genus are that all species have milky juice and almost all make good house plants for sunny places.

E. pulcherrima, from Mexico, is the poinsettia. It is practically impossible for you to raise a perfectly proportioned, leafy plant such as the florist sells for Christmas, but there is no reason why satisfactory poinsettias cannot be raised at home if your standard is a little lower than perfection. When your

Christmas plant is no longer attractive, put it in a frost-free place and water it once a month if you think of it. In May, cut the dried stalks back to a height of two inches, shake the soil off the roots, repot in the same size pot using all-purpose soil, and plunge it outside in the full sun. Early in September bring it in to a warm sunny place. If you live near 42° north latitude, your poinsettias will flower around Christmas time. Farther south, the bloom will be later. Any artificial light, no matter how indirect, which makes the day longer will delay flowering.

E. Milii (usually listed as *E. splendens*), from Madagascar, is called the crown of thorns. I am partial to it because it was one of my first house plants. As the stems grow, they can be twisted around one another to keep the overall size under control. The small, bright red bracts surrounding the little yellow flowers are ever-present, although too many dark days in December will cause their number to dwindle (Fig. 53). *E. Milii Hislopii* is a dwarf form.

E. lactea, *E. lactea cristata* (Fig. 24), and *E. grandicornis* are decorative desert species (Fig. 53). *E. obesa* looks like a beautiful round stone. Don't overwater these succulent ones in winter.

EURYA japonica   *Theaceae*

If you have success with camellias, try Eurya, an Himalayan evergreen related to camellias and grown in the same way. Pot plants of Eurya cannot be relied on to flower until they are two or three years old, but the dark, red-tinged leaves make them excellent foliage plants. When blossoms appear, they will be clusters of small white flowers and will be followed by black berries. (Fig. 53)

A very similar plant, *E. ochnacea* (*Cleyera japonica*), has larger flowers, white and very fragrant, and its berries are red. One is shown on the cool sunporch in Fig. 23.

EXACUM affine   *Gentianaceae*   GERMAN VIOLET

Small, fragrant, blue flowers with bright yellow eyes cover the shiny green leaves of this little biennial from the island of Socotra in the Indian Ocean. Seeds are sown in March, and the new plants should be cut back hard in August. Flowering begins in September, slackens sometimes in November and December, and grows more profuse as the days lengthen in January. Like so many flowering plants, Exacum needs all the sun it can get and likes cool temperatures (50°) at night. (Fig. 53)

FAIRY PRIMROSE: *Primula malacoides*

Farfugium: See *Ligularia*

FATSHEDERA Lizei   *Araliaceae*   TREE IVY
FRENCH IVY

An English ivy (*Hedera Helix hibernica*) and an aralia (*Fatsia japonica Moseri*) were crossed to produce *Fatshedera* ("fats—hedera"), an excellent plant for the house. The vining characteristics of the ivy parent are reflected in the offspring's stem, which, although thicker than ivy, is not self-supporting and apparently will extend itself indefinitely. The shape of the hybrid's leaves

FIG. 54. *Fatsia japonica, Hedera Helix* 'Ruffled,' *H. canariensis variegata, H. Helix* 'Garland,' *Fatshedera Lizei.* BASKET: *Plectranthus australis.*

is midway between those of its parents, but the large size is inherited from Fatsia. Two or three plants in a tub can be used to brighten a hallway or bare corner. If the place is so dark that the leaves eventually fall, don't be alarmed. A summer in a shady spot outside will usually revive the plant, which will throw out new growth on top and along its stem. (Fig. 54)

F. Lizei variegata is temperamental and slow-growing.

FATSIA japonica   *Araliaceae*   ARALIA

This Japanese parent of Fatshedera produces a large bold effect for the indoor decorator and will survive adverse conditions and lack of attention. It grows slowly, and a single plant will last for years without getting too big for the house. The new leaves, generally appearing in late winter, are covered with a thick, gray felt that gradually disappears as they grow older. Mature leaves need dusting as regularly as the furniture around them. New plants are usually raised from seed. (Fig. 54)

FAUCARIA tigrina   *Aizoaceae*   TIGER JAWS

A small African succulent deriving its common name from the "teeth" along the edges of the fat, light green leaves. They look vicious, but are soft to the touch. On plants grown in sunny windows, yellow daisy-like flowers appear now and then, starting in spring and continuing through the fall.

FELICIA amelloides   *Compositae*   KINGFISHER DAISY
(*Agathaea coelestis*)   BLUE DAISY

This small blue daisy from South Africa will bloom all winter if given sunny days and cool nights. Most houses are too warm for it, so I recommend it only for cool porches. Make new plants each spring from seeds or cuttings, and any you have to spare can go into the garden where they will bloom all summer. Two plants are growing in the sunporch garden pictured in Fig. 23.

FENESTRARIA rhopalophylla   *Aizoaceae*   BABYS TOES

This low, compact, South African succulent is one of the so-called "window plants," as the generic name suggests. The toes referred to in its common name are the leaves, which curve upwards from the ground without stem or petiole and never get bigger than their namesake. The windows are the greener spots on the ends of the toes. They let light into the interior of the leaves, where photosynthesis takes place. The plant will multiply in winter on a sunny window sill if kept quite dry. If you put it outside in full sun in summer, it may bear its white daisy-like flowers by September—but only if you remember to water it very sparingly.

FERNS: *Adiantum, Alsophila, Asplenium, Blechnum, Ceratopteris, Cyrtomium, Davallia, Lygodium, Nephrolepis, Pellaea, Phlebodium, Phyllitis, Platycerium, Polystichum, Pteris, Selaginella, Stenochleana, Woodwardia*

FICUS   *Moraceae*   FIG
                                                      RUBBER PLANT

The genus *Ficus* includes many different species, and every one I have had has proved a perfect house plant, willing to live in subdued light and needing nothing more unusual than all-purpose potting soil.

F. carica, the common fig, is native to the Mediterranean regions. It is known to all for its fig leaves and should be equally well known for its delicious edible fruit. I leave mine outside until the leaves have dropped; then I put it where its bare twigs will add a decorative pattern to my window garden. In January the buds begin to swell, and soon the leaves burst out, a fascinating process to study in the dead of winter. You can let it grow into a large tub plant or prune it small enough for a four-inch pot. (Fig. 55)

F. diversifolia, commonly called mistletoe fig, has small heart-shaped leaves and bears pea-sized figs in profusion. It is an excellent selection for indoor bonsai. (Fig. 55)

F. elastica, the India rubber plant, is one of the commonest house plants. Large specimens that have branched are interesting if you have room; they ask little more. They are trees in their tropical Asian home, and their trunks have no leaves once the juvenile stage is past. The variety *decora* is more compact and slow-growing and is gaining in popularity. (Fig. 55) Other nice varieties are *Doescheri,* with cream, white, and gray-green variegation; *variegata* with white variegation; and *rubra* with a reddish cast to its leaves.

F. lyrata (*pandurata*), the fiddle-leaved fig from tropical Africa, has enormous dark leathery leaves shaped as its name implies. It is a big tough plant. One can be seen growing well at the base of the cliff garden, Fig. 21.

F. pumila, also called *repens,* from China and Japan, is the familiar creeping fig which is generally trained up slabs of cedar bark. The leaves are about one

FIG. 55. On floor: *Ficus decora, F. lyrata, F. carica, F. pumila.* On table: *F. pumila minima* and *F. diversifolia.*

FIG. 56.   *Ficus pumila, F. pumila minima, F. radicans variegata, Fittonia Verschaffeltii argyroneura.*

inch long—the new ones light green and the old quite dark. If encouraged with daily spraying on the leaves, stems, and hold-fast roots, this vine will stick to almost any surface, including glass. Start with a small plant and be patient; once it gets going, it will take care of itself. Variety *minima* has leaves one-half inch long and is slower growing. (Figs. 55 and 56)

F. radicans variegata is like *pumila*, but with larger leaves splashed with white. It makes an interesting basket for a north or west window. (Fig. 56)

F. retusa, the Chinese banyan, from India and Malaya, is my favorite species of fig. It is slow-growing and tree-like, with small, dark green leaves reminiscent of mountain laurel. (Fig. 55)

FITTONIA Verschaffeltii   *Acanthaceae*

This low creeper from the Peruvian jungles is an excellent camouflage for pots on a window sill or along the edge of a planter. Because it needs no sun, it is also recommended as a ground cover under greenhouse benches; but in my experience this use is impracticable because the leaves are so attractive to slugs.

The dark green foliage is veined with pink in the species and with white in the variety *argyroneura,* producing an almost artificial appearance. (Fig. 56)

Fittonias are very sensitive to cold and quickly lose their leaves if the temperature drops below 55°.

FLOATING FERN: *Ceratopteris thalictroides*

FLOATING HEART: *Nymphoides indica*

FLOWERING MAPLE: *Abutilon*

FLOWERING OLIVE: *Osmanthus fragrans*

FLOWERING TOBACCO: *Nicotiana alata*

FORTUNELLA hindsi   *Rutaceae*   FORTUNELLA KUMQUAT

The tiny fruit, like marble-sized oranges, are upright rather than pendulous as is the case with most other citrus fruits. They make Fortunella a tempting miniature for indoor bonsai or just plain pot growing. However, no kumquats are easy to grow in containers. They progress satisfactorily for a year, or two, or three, then, suddenly, they may die. Meanwhile, the requisites are cool nights, sun, and all-purpose soil.

FUCHSIA   *Onagraceae*

Fuchsias need night temperatures below 65° to set flower buds. They generally become dormant in the fall, although a few gardeners with cool porches succeed in keeping them in bloom through the winter. The only exception to the general rule that I know is the *F. triphylla* hybrid 'Gartenmeister Bohnstedt,' sold as *F. Bohnstedtii.* Grown in a cool sunny window in all-purpose soil, it bears pendant orange-red flowers almost continuously. A two-year-old specimen is blooming in the plant bench shown in Fig. 14.

GARDENIA jasminoides   *Rubiaceae*   CAPE JASMINE

The name Cape jasmine, which no one uses except in books, was given the gardenia when it was thought to have come from the Cape of Good Hope, a long way from its actual home in China. Many have tried gardenia plants indoors unsuccessfully. With perseverance, however, it is possible to produce small but fragrant gardenia blossoms off and on all winter long. Start with a new plant from the florist. The first year it will probably lose its buds and many of its leaves as a result of the change from the greenhouse to the house, but don't be discouraged. Put it outside in semi-shade for the summer, and in the fall bring it inside to a warm, sunny place where a reasonable degree of humidity can be maintained.

Gardenias often develop chlorotic leaves as a result of their constitutional inability to absorb iron from the soil when grown at temperatures below 60°. To make iron more readily available, spray the foliage with a commercial preparation containing iron chelates, following the directions carefully.

G. jasminoides radicans is a compact dwarf form, more suitable for a window sill than the species. Both have shiny dark green leaves.

GASTERIA   *Liliaceae*

Stiff South African succulents, most of them with white wart-like spots on the large, flat leaves—which are more interesting than beautiful. However, being quite indestructible, they may be just the thing for a rigorous situation like the one pictured in the desert garden in Fig. 24. Flowers appear on the end of a long stalk in spring and summer and are curious rather than ornamental. Gasterias are desert dwellers and require some sun and scanty watering in winter. Unless you want an immense plant, repot only when the need is acute.

Numerous hybrids and species are sold by cactus and succulent growers.

GESNERIACEAE   GESNERIADS

This is a family that has attracted tremendous interest in recent years. Two large plant societies have been organized to specialize in gesneriads, and publications on the subject are proliferating. Botanists have identified about 125 genera and more than 2,000 species, most of them tropical, but only some 300 are in cultivation. The great majority of these have been introduced since World War II.

The tropical species, on the whole, are well adapted for indoor growing. They are also easy to propagate—in many cases by leaf cuttings—and easy to hybridize. The propagation and hybridization of these plants is a fast-spreading and rewarding hobby.

Some gesneriads (*Saintpaulia, Streptocarpus, Episcia, Nautilocalyx, Chirita*) are terrestrial plants with fibrous roots; some (*Gloxinia, Rechsteineria*) have tubers; some (*Achimenes, Kohleria, Smithiantha*) have scaly rhizomes; and some (*Aeschynanthus, Columnea, Hypocyrta*) are epiphytic trailers.

With the exception of *Streptocarpus*, all those I grow require warm night temperatures, 60° to 70°.

GEOGENANTHUS undatus   *Commelinaceae*   SEERSUCKER PLANT

This member of the spiderwort family comes from Peru and Brazil, where it grows in crevices beside the streams that rush from the mountains to the Amazon. Its leathery, heart-shaped leaves of olive green with purple backs have a crinkled surface which suggests cloth and accounts for the common name. Like most members of this family, it will grow without direct sun, but it needs good light to keep it compact and low.

You may have bought this plant under the name *Dichorisandra mosaica undata.* If so, by all means make a new label. The experts say that that particular *Dichorisandra* is a different plant, not available commercially and almost unknown even in botanical collections.

GERANIUM: *Pelargonium*

GERMAN IVY: *Senecio mikanioides*

GERMAN VIOLET: *Exacum affine*

GHOST TREE IVY: *Hedera canariensis viridis*

GLORY BOWER: *Clerodendrum Thompsoniae*

GLORY FLOWER: *Eccremocarpus scaber*

GLOXINERA rosea   *Gesneriaceae*

This plant is an intergeneric hybrid whose parents are *Sinningia eumorpha* and *Rechsteineria cyclophylla.* It is a combination of the best characteristics of both. The plants grow from gloxinia-like tubers and produce delicate pink, trumpet-shaped flowers in great profusion for months on end. A short dry rest may then be in order, after which your plant will resume growth and put out new leaves from its tuber.

Gloxinia: See also *Sinningia*

GOLD DUST TREE: *Aucuba japonica*

GOLDEN BALL: *Notocactus Leninghausii*

GRAPE IVY: *Cissus rhombifolia*

GRAPTOPETALUM paraguayense
                    Crassulaceae   MOTHER OF PEARL PLANT

The foliage of this succulent from the deserts of Mexico looks as though it has been powdered with blue-gray talc, with occasional traces of pink.

FIG. 57. *Gloxinera* 'Bernice'   *Paul Arnold*

Mature plants bear their rosettes of leaves on upright stems, an unusual habit of growth in this family. Sun and desert soil are the chief cultural requirements. Some small Graptopetalums can be seen in Fig. 71.

GREIGIA sphacelata   *Bromeliaceae*

A green-leaved bromeliad from Chile, which grew happily for me for two years as an epiphyte before I learned that it is actually terrestrial. Like most bromeliads, it asks only that the place where it grows be well drained. While Greigia is not as spectacular as some of the cryptanthus or ananas (pineapple) species it resembles, it is neat and decorative and one of my pets. (Fig. 58)

GREVILLEA robusta   *Proteaceae*   SILK OAK

Of all my house plants, this is almost the most satisfactory. It grows fast, and its fern-like foliage adds a graceful note to my window garden. If you want to raise a house plant from seed, this is the one to try. The seeds are large, they germinate quickly, and in one year the seedling may reach a height of three feet.

FIG. 58. *Haworthia* hybrid, *Grevillea robusta*, two *Gymnocalycium* species, *Gynura aurantiaca, Greigia sphacelata, Hebe Andersonii.*

In their native New South Wales, silk oaks are big flowering trees, and in California they are used for street trees. Here in the East, where they must spend the winter indoors, they can be grown as handsome tubbed trees. (Fig. 58)

Another species, *G. Wilsonii*, from Western Australia, has small needle-like leaves and red flowers, which appear in winter if the plant is grown in full sun.

GYMNOCALYCIUM   *Cactaceae*   BARREL CACTUS

These globular cacti from Argentina are considered among the easiest to bring into bloom indoors. They have flowered freely for me outside in summer, and I am sure they would have done the same if I had left them in their sunny window. Small plants will grow remarkably in the warm months if they are removed from their pots and planted directly in a sunny garden bed. Water them freely during the growing season but very sparingly in the short dark days of winter. (Fig. 58)

GYNURA aurantiaca   *Compositae*   ROYAL VELVET PLANT

The velvet leaves are a regal purple, a much deeper shade when the plants are grown in the sun. Under favorable conditions Gynura will crowd out all its neighbors; so if you want its color in your indoor garden, make new plants from cuttings each summer. All-purpose soil, large pots, high temperatures, and frequent watering suit it well. It is a native of Java. (Fig. 58)

HARES-FOOT FERN: *Phlebodium aureum*

HARTS-TONGUE FERN: *Phyllitis Scolopendrium*

HAWORTHIA   *Liliaceae*   ARISTOCRAT PLANT

These stiff plants, with leaves arranged in tight pointed rosettes, are among the few succulents that will grow in the shade. On the arid South African plains where they are found, they make their home under larger bushes. All the Haworthias I know are dark in color—brown, green, or purple-brown—and all have white, warty spots on the leaves. (Fig. 58)

HEART VINE: *Ceropegia Woodii*

HEBE Andersonii   *Scrophulariaceae*

Formerly called and usually listed as *Veronica*, this shrubby evergreen from New Zealand is a good plant for a sunporch. It needs some sun each day or it will lose its attractive compactness. Blue flowers cover the ends of the branches in summer, at which time it will enjoy full sun on your terrace or in the garden.

Californians are using several species for hedges and foundation planting. Any species of this genus would be worth trying for indoor use. (Fig. 58)

HEDERA   *Araliaceae*   IVY

Given good light and a weekly shower in the kitchen sink, ivy can be as attractive as any foliage plant; but if either of these cultural requisites is omitted, red spider and aphids soon take over and plants become stringy.

Don't try to grow ivy at all if your indoor garden is a warm one. It likes to be cool.

H. canariensis is called Algerian ivy. The variety *variegata* is the only kind I have seen grown indoors. It is recognizable by its large, leathery leaves variegated with creamy white. It is never bushy, even when meticulously pinched, but the almost pure white leaves are useful for brightening a group of all-green plants. Because variegated leaves are deficient in chlorophyll, this ivy needs all possible light. The plant is native to the Canary Islands and is not hardy in the northern half of the United States. (Fig. 54)

H. canariensis viridis, called ghost tree ivy, is an aborescent sport of Algerian ivy. Californians have grown impressive tub specimens ten feet high, but here in the East one seldom sees such giants.

H. Helix, English ivy, has countless varieties, some named and some anonymous. My favorites are a small trifoliate one called 'Shamrock,' a loose-growing one called 'Ruffled,' and 'Garland.' (Fig. 54)

HEDGEHOG CACTUS: *Echinocereus*

HELIOTROPIUM arborescens   *Boraginaceae*   HELIOTROPE

If your sunny window is cool at night, you can enjoy the fragrant blue flowers of Peruvian heliotrope from January until summer, when your plants will be due for replacement. I train mine to a standard, as it takes less room that way. It is one of the best plants I have for late winter flowers. One is growing in the sunny window pictured in Fig. 12.

HELXINE Soleirolii   *Utricaceae*   BABYS TEARS

The common name suggests the delicacy of this Corsican plant, which covers large sections of the ground under my greenhouse benches. In a pot its kelly-green leaves make a pretty mound, dripping over the edges and spreading to any nearby soil if not restrained. Babys tears likes good light, though not necessarily full sun. Moisture and humidity are vital to its existence; it will wither away overnight if allowed to dry out. In the house it is a good practice to set the pot directly in a saucer of water, for the plant will also grow in the water and is not bothered by "wet feet." (Fig. 59)

HEMIGRAPHIS colorata   *Acanthaceae*   RED FLAME IVY

Neither red nor an ivy, Hemigraphis has been recently revived because of its suitability for a house plant. The shining foliage is olive green, with purple veins and a purple underside. The plant is a native of Java and needs heat and moisture. Though it will grow in either sun or shade, the leaf colors are more vivid in a sunny place. Cuttings are easy to root, and five or six planted in a basket will soon make a fine cascade. (Fig. 59)

FIG. 59. *Hereroa Neilii, Hibiscus Rosa-sinensis Cooperii, Helxine Soleirolii, Hibiscus Rosa-sinensis, Hemigraphis colorata.*

HEREROA Neilii   *Aizoaceae*

This small, pale, South American succulent can be relied on to bear diminutive, yellow, daisy-like flowers from May through September if it gets plenty of sun. Though the flowers last only a day, they are constantly replaced by new ones. Those on the plant pictured came out the day before the picture was taken. (Fig. 59)

HIBISCUS Rosa-sinensis   *Malvaceae*   ROSE OF CHINA

My hibiscus plants flower sporadically through the fall and winter and quite regularly in spring and summer. Attention to watering and a pot or tub large enough to provide plenty of room for the roots help keep the flower buds on the bush.

Even a small hibiscus can easily outgrow a sunny window in a year, but they can be pruned to a reasonable size, or new plants can be made from spring-rooted cuttings. Varieties are available in all shades of white, pink, peach, yellow, red, and orange—with single or double flowers. For a sunroom, a large hibiscus is an ornamental plant, even without its flowers. (Fig. 59)

HOFFMANIA   *Rubiaceae*

Plants from the jungle section of Mexico, grown for their velvety foliage. The top surface of the leaves is a mixture of green and dark red. The underside is the color of red wine. Hoffmanias will grow in a sunless window, provided it is a warm one.

H. Ghiesbreghtii is a tall growing plant. (Fig. 60)

H. refulgens, commonly called the corduroy plant, has the same handsome coloring, but is much more compact. (Fig. 60)

HOLLY FERN: *Cyrtomium falcatum*

HOMALOCLADIUM platycladum

Polygonaceae   RIBBON BUSH

(*Muehlenbeckia platyclados*)   CENTIPEDE PLANT

The "ribbons" are the flattened stems of this curious plant. In full sun they are a vivid light green and nearly two feet long, making the plant interesting but not particularly decorative. Cuttings root readily, and the plant grows well in all-purpose soil in either cool or warm places. It is a native of the Solomon Islands. (Fig. 60)

HOMALOMENA Wallisii   *Araceae*

This aroid from the jungles of Colombia has attractive yellowish blotches on its large, leathery leaves. It will not grow without very high humidity and tropical temperatures, and even in the greenhouse it simply marks time until the summer sun sends the thermometer over 70°. This propensity for suspended animation prevents the plant from growing big and leggy like most other tropical aroids. The small plant pictured is over a year old. (Fig. 60)

HONEY BELLS: *Mahernia verticillata*

HOUSE IRIS: *Neomarica*

HOWEA Forsteriana   *Palmaceae*   KENTIA PALM

Named for their native Lord Howe Islands, these slow-growing and indestructible plants are the original "potted palms." Palms should be fed only two or three times a year, in spring and summer. Their only serious enemies are scale insects, which can be kept at bay by wiping the leaves with a damp cloth about every two weeks. (Fig. 16)

HOYA carnosa   *Asclepiadaceae*   WAX PLANT

A thick-leaved, twining vine from Australia, this is near the top of my list of indispensable house plants. Hoyas can be trained over and around a trellis or along the border of a window, or they can be kept bushy by careful prun-

FIG. 60. *Homalocladium platy-cladum, Homalomena Wallisii, Hoffmania refulgens, H. Ghies-breghtii.*

ing. Whether they are grown in north or south light, the waxy leaves are crisp and decorative. Another advantage is their winter dormant period, when they keep the same appearance but require much less water and attention.

The common name would be appropriate for the foliage, but is even more descriptive of the artificial-looking clusters of fragrant pink flowers which mature sun-grown plants bear from June through September on little spurs at six-inch intervals along last year's stems. When blooms appear, water the plant copiously every day until the flowering is definitely over.

H. bella, the midget wax plant from India, is one of my favorites. It blooms periodically on my bathroom window sill from March until October.

H. carnosa variegata has both white and red in the leaves. Like many variegated plants, it is slower growing than the species, and it seldom blooms. I have read that it can be persuaded to flower if grown in pure coal ashes. (Fig. 14)

There is a considerable difference of opinion about the culture of wax plants. I have grown them in pure sphagnum moss, in African violet soil, and in all-purpose soil and have noticed little difference in their behavior. Rest in winter and plenty of water in summer seem to be the two essentials.

HYDROCLEYS nymphoides   *Butomaceae*   WATER POPPY

This diminutive aquatic from Brazil, with small, bright green lily pads, is in scale with most aquariums and indoor pools. The cold water and lack of sunlight characterizing such locations in winter merely keep water poppies under control. In spring and summer they propagate so prolifically along their floating stems that they need thinning every week or so. Water poppies are said to be continuous bloomers, but this cannot be relied on in the latitude of Philadelphia, where the bright yellow flowers are apt to appear only in spring and summer. Two or three, planted in soil in a five-inch bulb pan and set four or five inches below the surface of the water, will be all you need for an indoor pool. (Fig. 18)

HYLOCEREUS undatus   *Cactaceae*   NIGHT-BLOOMING CEREUS

Another jungle cactus called "night-blooming cereus," and the one with probably the best claim to the name. Hylocereus is a climber and will cling to the greenhouse or conservatory wall. It is ungainly and undemanding, worth growing only if you have plenty of room and patience to wait for the summer night when it bears its tremendous white flowers, sometimes a foot across.

HYPOCYRTA   *Gesneriaceae*

Like so many Central and South American gesneriads, Hypocyrta needs winter sun and summer shade and will do best with warm, moist air. The two trailing species listed here do well in epiphytic mixture and should be put in hanging baskets or grown in some place where they can trail. Both have curious flowers shaped like tiny money bags with yellow drawstrings.

H. nummularia has small, green leaves covered with reddish hairs and red flowers. After blooming, it loses its leaves and rests for a few weeks. (Fig. 61)

H. radicans has glossy, dark-green succulent leaves and large orange flowers.

HYPOESTIS sanguinolenta   *Acanthaceae*   PINK POLKADOT PLANT

The common name comes from the tiny pink spots on the dull green leaves. The plant grows rapidly and soon becomes weedy without proper attention. It should be grown in all-purpose soil in good light and should be cut back frequently to force growth at the base, making a pretty pink and green mat. It is a native of Madagascar. (Fig. 61)

FIG. 61.   *Impatiens platypetala aurantiaca, Iboza riparia, Hypocyrta Nummularia,
Impatiens Oliveri, I. Holstii, Hypoestis sanguinolenta.*

IBOZA riparia   *Labiatae*

Iboza leaves impart a pungent odor to your hands; one catalog says they
are used by the natives of Africa as a moth repellant. Plants receiving plenty
of sun bear small, spikey, white flowers through most of the winter. There is
nothing glamorous about Iboza except possibly its aroma, but it is a traditional favorite of many indoor gardeners. (Fig. 61)

IMPATIENS Holstii   *Balsaminaceae*   PATIENCE PLANT

The botanical name refers to the seed pods, which if touched when ripe, burst "impatiently." The common name, "patience," is doubtless a corruption. The plant is native to tropical Africa and will flower well in a shady outdoor garden in summer or in a sunny indoor garden in winter. Small plants are the best and can be started in the spring either from seed or cuttings potted in all-purpose soil. The color of the species flower is orange-red, but hybrids and varieties have been produced with colors in all shades of white, pink, red, and purple. (Fig. 61)

I. Oliveri is a large plant with leaves up to four inches long and pale lavender flowers two inches across. (Fig. 61)

I. platypetala aurantiaca has a dark yellow flower with a small red eye. (Fig. 61)

INCH PLANT: *Setcreasea, Tradescantia* and *Zebrina pendula*

INDIA RUBBER PLANT: *Ficus elastica*

INDOOR OAK: *Nicodemia diversifolia*

IRESINE Herbstii   *Amarantaceae*   CHICKEN GIZZARD
BLOODLEAF

The sanguinary common names of this South American plant are by no means descriptive. The leaves are not blood red, let alone the color of a gizzard, but are such a vivid magenta that juxtaposition with any other color than green gives a displeasing effect. The plants grow well in a sunny window in all-purpose soil.

I. Lindenii, from Ecuador, is called Achyranthes by gardeners and is used by the thousands for summer bedding in parks and public gardens. It is a more upright growing plant than *I. Herbstii* and is a better color—more red and less magenta.

Isoloma: See *Kohleria*

ITALIAN BELLFLOWER: *Campanula isophylla*

IVY: *Hedera*

IVY ARUM: *Scindapsus aureus*

IXORA   *Rubiaceae*   JUNGLE FLAME

These two tender evergreen shrubs from the East Indies make sturdy-looking house plants with decorative foliage and attractive flowers. They need sunlight and will not tolerate cold. Six-inch pots will accommodate mature Ixoras; if this is too big for you, spring cuttings root readily and will make nice small plants for the following winter. The stiff, dark green leaves are quite red when they first unfold, and the flower clusters, which open weeks after the buds first appear, are like small red bouquets. Even the smallest plants flower outside in a shady place in summer and off and on inside throughout the fall and winter.

I. coccinea is the commoner species.

I. javanica has longer leaves and larger flower clusters. A small plant is growing on the plant bench pictured in Fig. 14.

FIG. 62. *Jacobinia carnea, Hypocyrta Nummularia, Jacobinia suberecta, Jacaranda acutifolia.*

JACARANDA acutifolia   *Bignoniaceae*
(*J. mimosifolia*)

This mimosa-like tree from Brazil would be a good selection for your tropical tree. It can be kept at reasonable size, and its feathery leaves will not cast too heavy a shade on the plants below. It is not suitable for a window sill, but might be worked into a sunny ground bed in a modern house. The flowering time is spring, but if conditions do not exactly suit your plant, it may wait until summer to bloom. (Fig. 62)

JACOBINIA suberecta   *Acanthaceae*

The downy, gray leaves and compact growth of this Uruguayan plant put it on the list of desirable house plants. In spring the flower-bearing stems protrude above the rest of the foliage and are soon topped by clusters of orange blooms, which are renewed for several months. I am so fond of the foliage that I usually cut off these flowering stems after a month or so, for they are inclined to get a worn-out look. (Fig. 62)

J. carnea, the kings crown, from Brazil, is much more common and not nearly so attractive. The "crown" of flowers is fluffy, pink, and decorative, but scarcely justifies the considerable space the plant takes on your sunny window sill, since it blooms only in summer. (Fig. 62)

Both *J. suberecta* and *J. carnea* can easily be renewed by spring cuttings.

JADE PLANT: *Crassula argentea*

JASMINUM   *Oleaceae*   JASMINE

The fragrance of a single small jasmine plant will perfume a window garden during the whole flowering season from January to November. Plants grown in cool, sunny places flower best; but some of the smaller kinds do well in a window garden if placed close to the cool glass. The large, faster-growing kinds need replacing now and then, and this can be accomplished by making spring cuttings which will bloom the same season.

J. humile, from tropical Asia, has large yellow flowers. Its stems, which need support, grow several feet in a season; it is usually best to keep them cut and have the plants bushy. This species is too large for most houses, but fine for a cool porch or greenhouse.

J. officinale, from Persia, with white flowers, and *J. Mesnyii* (*primulinum*) from China, with yellow, are smaller in every dimension and better for the house. The white flowers of *J. officinale grandiflorum* (*J. magnificum*) seem the most fragrant to me. Though the leaves are large, the plants do not seem to grow as rampantly as the three species already described.

J. Parkeri is a slow-growing midget from the Himalayas with tiny leaves and tiny yellow flowers. (Fig. 63)

J. Sambac is from India but is called Arabian jasmine. It has round leaves and white flowers and tends to be more shrubby. Its flowers are used for flavoring jasmine tea. (Fig. 63)

JERUSALEM CHERRY: *Solanum pseudo-capsicum*

JUNGLE FLAME: *Ixora*

JUSSIAEA longifolia   *Onagraceae*   PRIMROSE WILLOW

An attractive Brazilian aquatic plant for greenhouse pools or sunny indoor water gardens. The leaves and long, upright stems are reminiscent of willows, and the primroses look like small yellow poppies. Each bloom lasts only a day or so, but once the plant starts to flower in the spring and summer, they are born quite freely.

These plants are annuals and are best renewed each year, either by cuttings or by seed if you can find it. The pots containing the seeds or cuttings should be almost wholly immersed in water. As the plants grow, the pots can be sunk further until the surface of the soil is about two inches below water level. (Fig. 18)

FIG. 63. *Jasminum Sambac, J. officinale, J. Mesynii, J. Parkeri.*

KAEMPFERA Roscoeana   *Zingiberaceae*

The elegantly marked leaves of this tropical ginger grow in pairs directly out of the fleshy roots. The lavender flowers appear once or twice a week from late spring until fall, but each flower lasts only a day. When blooming and growth stop, the foliage dies back and four or five months of dormancy set in, during which time the roots should be stored in plastic bags in a warm place. In April take them out of storage and pot them in three- or four-inch pots in African violet soil. They can be put outside in summer if protected from direct sun, but by September they should be moved to a sunny window sill indoors. The leaves are often mistaken for those of a maranta or calathea. (Fig. 64)

KAFIR LILY: *Clivia miniata*

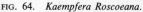

FIG. 64.   *Kaempfera Roscoeana.*

KALANCHOE   *Crassulaceae*

If I had to pick a single plant to take to a city apartment, it would probably be a kalanchoe (pronounced ka-lan'-kow-ee) because they adapt to so many indoor situations, flower in the dead of winter, and are decorative the year round. Succulent leaves and stems render them immune to low humidity.

Taxonomists differ as to the classification, some placing some or all in the genus *Bryophyllum;* and certain kalanchoes, like the bryophyllums, will produce new plantlets along margins of their leaves. They need sunny situations, but temperature seems to be immaterial. Most are native to Madagascar or northern Africa.

K. beharensis is the largest of the kalanchoes I have grown; a rooted cutting needed a six-inch pot by the end of the year. The leaves are covered with brown fuzz on top, gray beneath. An interesting, ugly plant. You will see a specimen in the desert garden pictured in Fig. 24.

K. Blossfeldiana is the familiar Tom Thumb, covered with bright red flowers in midwinter. Flowering is stimulated by the shortness of the winter days and will be delayed if the plant is subjected to artificial light after sundown.

K. Daigremontiana is one that is forever forming leaf plantlets, which drop off and root in almost any medium on which they fall. A group planted together in a pot looks like a clump of miniature desert palms.

K. Fedtschenkoi is the one I would take to my city apartment. The leaves are a powdery blue with rosy margins, and after Christmas the new flower buds open to reveal delicate, nodding, apricot blooms. Highly recommended if you want an easy, attractive basket like the one pictured in Fig. 23. This particular basket has gone two weeks at a time without water.

K. globulifera coccinea bears its red flowers over a relatively long period, but tends to get leggy. One may be seen on the succulent shelf in Fig. 14.

K. marmorata, also a leggy plant, has large light-colored leaves with purple speckles. Its flowers are white.

K. tomentosa, the panda plant, has gray-green fuzzy leaves with brown spots and is indestructible.

K. tubiflora resembles *Daigremontiana*, but with tubular rather than flat leaves. (Fig. 71)

K. uniflora (*Kitchingia*) is a small, prostrate, and charming species from Madagascar. Given sun and a place to trail, it will bear its inch-long pink bell-flowers from late winter through spring. The round flat leaves are ornamental the rest of the year. These plants can be propagated easily from sections of the stem, which throws out roots at every joint. (Fig. 14)

Cactus and succulent fanciers have other varieties, and I would try any new one that came my way.

KANGAROO THORN: *Acacia armata*

KANGAROO VINE: *Cissus antarctica*

KENILWORTH IVY: *Cymbalaria muralis*

KENTIA PALM: *Howea Forsteriana*

KINGFISHER DAISY: *Felicia amelloides*

KINGS CROWN: *Jacobinia carnea*

Kitchingia: See *Kalanchoe uniflora*

KLEINIA   *Compositae*

This group of plants has only recently acquired its own generic name. They were previously included in the genus *Senecio*. All are South African succulents which are grown for the pale colors of their fleshy leaves.

K. articulata, the candle plant, has thick blue upright stems. When it begins to grow in early spring, blue leaves poke out at the ends of the candles.

K. Haworthii and *K. Mandraliscae* make excellent plants for succulent dish gardens when small, and striking specimens when large. *Haworthii* (also called *tomentosa*) has white, felt-like leaves and stems. *Mandraliscae*, appropriately called blue chalk sticks, is powder blue all over. A number of plants of the same species planted in a bulb pan produces a decorative effect. (Figs. 50 and 71)

KOHLERIA   *Gesneriaceae*

Kin to African violets, kohlerias are almost as easy to grow. Most were called *Isoloma* before a recent juggling of names and are probably still being brought and grown under that appellation.

Kohlerias grow from segmented underground rhizomes, which branch and spread as the plant matures. The segments can be potted separately to make new plants, or left in place to make a bushy specimen; or if not to be used at once, they can be stored temporarily in plastic bags. When the rhizomes are in pots and no active growth is taking place, they should not be watered more than once a week.

While kohlerias will grow in a north or west window, the poor light in such exposures during winter will result in a minimum of bloom and will make the plant unattractively leggy. In fact, it would be hard to give them too much sun from November to March.

K. amabilis tends to stay small and compact. Its leaves are velvety green with shades of purple along the veins, and its flowers are dark pink with purple dots. The flowers of variety 'Cecilia' are a delicate pink, one of the most charming colors in all the gesneriad group. (Fig. 92)

K. bogotensis has speckled leaves and red and yellow spotted flowers.

K. eriantha is the most vigorous of this group, as well as the most floriferous. It grows two feet high if conditions are favorable and bears bright red tubular flowers along the length of its stems.

K. Lindeniana is quite different from the others, having blue and white flowers instead of the usual red or purple. Its velvety green foliage with silver veins and maroon edges and its compact habit of growth make it worth growing in spite of its reluctance to flower. There is a two-year-old clump in a four-inch bulb pot on the plant bench in Fig. 14—also a small plant just to the left of the thermometer under the fluorescent lights in Fig. 13.

There is a large and growing number of kohleria hybrids, which can be divided into groups according to which of the species is prominent in their ancestry.

I have grown kohlerias in plain sphagnum moss, a mixture of peat moss and sand, and straight leafmold, well decayed. If the growing plants are fertilized regularly, any of these is satisfactory. African violet soil will also produce good results. Since kohlerias are native to the tropical parts of South America, they need night temperatures of at least 60° and reasonably high humidity.

LADY PALM: *Rhapis excelsa*

LAMPRANTHUS emarginatus   *Aizoaceae*

This gray-green succulent from South Africa is one of the hundreds that used to be included in the genus *Mesembryanthemum*, and may still be offered under that name. It is easily grown in a sunny window either in a hanging

FIG. 65.   *Lippia citriodora, Ligularia tussilaginea aureo-maculata, Lemaireocereus marginatus, Ligularia tussilaginea argentea, Lantana montevidensis, Licuala grandis, Lantana camara.*

basket or on a hot, dry shelf. In spring and summer it will have small, lavender, daisy-like flowers. A plant is pictured in Fig. 71.

LANTANA   *Verbenaceae*

Native to tropical America but naturalized in many tropics of the world, lantana will adapt itself well to hot, sunny window sills, and given three or four hours of sun a day, can honestly claim to be everblooming. The weeping lavender lantana (*L. montevidensis*) is one of the best flowering plants I have seen for a hanging basket. No matter how bad the weather, it blooms all winter long. Plants grown in the house need frequent watering and plenty of sun for maximum production of flowers.

Dwarf varieties of *L. camara*, the garden lantana, are well suited for use among other plants on a sunny window sill, while the taller-growing kinds can be trained as standards and grown in large pots or tubs. All-purpose soil suits them best, but they will grow in almost anything if the root ball is kept from drying out. Small plants need repotting at least once during the indoor gardening year and also require one or two severe prunings. (Fig. 65)

LEMAIREOCEREUS marginatus
Cactaceae   ORGAN PIPE CACTUS

There are people who don't like cacti because, they say, these plants never do anything. Even such skeptics should be satisfied by the remarkable growth and bizarre flowers that this columnar, base-branching cactus from Mexico will show if given cautious watering in winter and a summer out of doors in full sun. (Fig. 65)

LEMON: *Citrus*

LEMON VERBENA: *Lippia citriodora*

LEMON VINE: *Pereskia*

LIGULARIA tussilaginea   *Compositae*   LEOPARD PLANT

Grown for decades in houses and greenhouses under the names *Farfugium*, *Senecio*, and *Ligularia*, this Japanese foliage plant is now seldom seen. Until very recently it was called *L. Kaempferi*, and it is still sold under that name.

Two varieties are available. They are showy and will grow in north light and cold places. *L. tussilaginea aureo-maculata* has golden flecks on its large round green leaves, and *L. tussilaginea argentea*, which is much harder to grow, has white leaf margins. Both can be propagated by dividing the clump of underground stem and roots and repotting the divisions in all-purpose soil. (Fig. 65)

LIPPIA citriodora   *Verbenaceae*   LEMON VERBENA

This traditional favorite from Argentina and Chile owes its popularity to the spicy fragrance of the sandpapery leaves. Lemon verbena does best with a fall rest. In September, after the very tender plants are settled indoors, move your lemon verbena to a cool, protected place such as a garage or cold frame, cut back the top and all the side branches, and water about once a week. After Christmas shake the soil off the roots, repot the plant in the same size pot in all-purpose soil, and put it in your sunniest window. In no time new growth will appear and the leaves will delight your touch and smell. (Fig. 65)

Lipstick Vine: *Aeschynanthus lobbianus*

Little Pickles: *Othonna capensis*

LOBULARIA maritima   *Cruciferae*   Sweet Alyssum

This gay little summer standby from the shores of the Mediterranean will bloom all winter in cool, sunny places indoors. In early September dig up a plant from the garden, cut it back as far as you dare, prune the roots, and pot it in all-purpose soil in a three-inch pot. It can then be left outside, plunged in a garden bed, for two or three weeks until new growth breaks out. When this happens, bring the plant inside and wait for the flowers—which will be sparse in the fall but profuse from January on. Alyssum is not for hot, dry houses, but is well worth the room it takes if night temperatures are as low as 55° and there is reasonable humidity. (Fig. 66)

LOTUS   *Leguminosae*

Two species of these feathery gray trailing plants are grown under glass, but since neither can tolerate a hot, dry atmosphere, they are not strictly house plants. They will grow on a porch or in a sunroom that is cool at night and sunny by day. They are not related to the water plants called lotus, whose Latin name is *Nelumbium*.

L. Berthelotii, from the Cape Verde and Canary Islands, has needle-thin leaves and procumbent stems. Plants put out in a rock garden or on a sunny wall in spring will soon be covered with scarlet, pea-like flowers. (Fig. 66)

L. mascaensis is a silvery shrub from Tenerife, with slightly larger leaves. It flowers freely in early spring in my greenhouse, where it grows in a hanging basket. The pea-shaped flowers are canary yellow, and the blossoming lasts three or four weeks.

LYGODIUM scandens   *Schizaeaceae*   Climbing Fern

From Southeast Asia comes this intriguing fern, whose twining stems (botanically, leaf petioles) will wind around any convenient support, covering it with a lacy network of feathery light green fronds. In spite of its delicate appearance, Lygodium appears to be surprisingly house-hardy. One I keep in a cool north window grows with remarkable vigor throughout the year. (Fig. 66)

Madagascar Jasmine: *Stephanotis floribunda*

Magic Flower: *Achimenes*

Maidenhair Fern: *Adiantum*

FIG. 66.   TOP: *Lotus Berthelotii*. MIDDLE: *Manettia bicolor, Mahernia verticillata*. BOTTOM: *Lobularia maritima, Malpighia coccigera*. FLOOR: *Lygodium scandens*.

MAIDENHAIR VINE: *Muehlenbeckia complexa*

MAHERNIA verticillata   *Sterculiaceae*   HONEY BELLS

The tiny, yellow, fragrant honey bells are the only excuse for struggling with this straggly plant from South Africa. Full sun with cool temperatures and high humidity may induce house grown plants to bloom in spring, though it is not to be counted on. In a greenhouse or cool sunny porch, a hanging basket of blooming honey bells brightens many a dreary winter day. New plants are made from spring-rooted cuttings. (Fig. 66)

MALPIGHIA coccigera   *Malpighiaceae*   MINIATURE HOLLY

A diminutive West Indian evergreen with small, dark green leaves reminiscent of English holly. A Malpighia grown in a reasonably sunny window will be bright and perky all winter and will bear small, fluffy, pale pink flowers from spring through most of the summer. The culture of this plant is not complicated by special do's and don'ts, and it is always a decorative asset. Spring-rooted cuttings will make nice small Christmas presents. (Fig. 66)

MAMMILLARIA   *Cactaceae*   PINCUSHION CACTUS

This is a very large genus of Mexican cacti, most of which are appropriate for a window garden, since they tend to stay small and to flower when very young. Culture is the same as for other cactus plants—little water in winter, regular watering and some fertilizer in summer, and full sun at all seasons. Grow succulents in as small a pot as will support the plant without tipping over.

MANETTIA bicolor   *Rubiaceae*   MEXICAN FIRECRACKER

Called Mexican by most growers, this small Brazilian vine will bloom continuously in a sunny window. The flowers are more like yellow and orange party candies than firecrackers; but whatever you call them, they are ever-present. Train the twining stems up strings or a small trellis, or keep them cut back for a bushy effect. Young plants are the best, so plan an annual replacement—easily accomplished by cuttings which root quickly in the spring. Potted in all-purpose soil and pinched through the summer, they will make fine three-inch-pot size plants to start off with in the fall. (Fig. 66)

MARANTA   *Marantaceae*   PRAYER PLANT

The four South American marantas I have grown indoors are among my favorite house plants. Their culture is easy and they do not need a place in the crowded sunny window to produce their beautiful iridescent leaves. When their resting time arrives, generally in the fall, it is best to cut away the old leaves, leaving nothing but the more recent growth close to the pot, and to water the plants only when the soil appears quite dry. In January give them a little extra light, either artificial or natural. Soon the tightly rolled new leaves will appear right out of the soil, and your plant can resume its place in your east or west window garden. I use African violet or begonia soil and find that the marantas don't do well unless it is warm, never less than 65°

M. arundinacea, the arrowroot, is the plant from whose roots tapioca is made. Its slender leaves and petioles are erect and reedy, but it lacks the lovely coloring of most of the *Marantaceae*. (Fig. 67)

M. arundinacea variegata is larger and has cream-edged leaves. (Fig. 67)

M. leuconeura Kerchoveana is the well-known prayer plant, so named because of its habit of folding up its leaves at night to funnel the dew and moisture down to its roots. The variety *Massangeana* is smaller and more decoratively marked. (Fig. 67)

FIG. 67.   *Maranta arundinacea, M. arundinacea variegata, M. leuconeura Massangeana, M. leuconeura Kerchoveana.*

MEDINILLA magnifica   *Melastomaceae*

Victorian is the word for this handsome, large-leaved plant from the Philippine Islands. The dark, curving leaves growing in pairs along the branching stems and the foot-long clusters of pink flowers like oversize ornaments on a small Christmas tree suggest the "gingerbread era."

Medinilla's thick stems and foliage make it resistant to dry air, and its preference for filtered sunlight makes it eligible for many places where more demanding plants can't be used. However, the location must be spacious and warm and must receive some sunlight each day. Don't count on flowers. House-grown plants may go for years without blooming. (Fig. 68)

Mesembryanthemum: See *Lampranthus, Hereroa, Oscularia*

MEXICAN FIRECRACKER: *Manettia bicolor*

MEXICAN FLAME VINE: *Senecio confusus*

MEXICAN FOXGLOVE: *Allophyton mexicanum*

MICHELIA fuscata   *Magnoliaceae*   BANANA SHRUB

This broad-leaved evergreen from China is also called the banana mag-
nolia because of its close botanical relationship to the magnolias and the
banana-like fragrance of its brown-yellow flowers. These should appear in
the spring, but whether or not your banana shrub flowers, it is an attractive
plant for a cool sunroom or porch. Flowering plants are at least two feet tall,
and a tubbed plant would be a good investment for any situation where
camellias or azaleas do well.

MIMOSA pudica   *Leguminosae*   SENSITIVE PLANT

When you touch the feathery foliage of this silly little plant it folds its
leaves as though in pain. To live through the winter, it needs more humidity
than prevails in most houses; but plants can be easily raised from spring-
sown seed and grown on your window sill for a few months in the fall, during
which time they will attract much attention and stroking.

Both *Acacia* and *Albizzia* are called Mimosa, but this plant is the only one
of the three with a botanical right to the name.

Mimulus: See *Diplacus*

MINIATURE HOLLY: *Malpighia coccigera*

MISTLETOE CACTUS: *Rhipsalis cassutha*

MONDO GRASS: *Ophiopogon japonicus*

MONSTERA deliciosa   *Araceae*   SWISS CHEESE PLANT
                                              CERIMAN

Frequently sold as *Philodendron pertusum* and aptly called "the monster"
by my family, this is no plant for a small house. Its habit of growth is climbing, and its size is large—the leaves are as much as two feet in each dimension.
It climbs the tropical trees in Mexico and Central America, holding fast with
long aerial roots and getting larger and stronger the higher it goes.

If you are being evicted by one of these giants, do not hesitate to cut it back
to within a foot of the pot rim. In a short time it will resume growth. Like
most tropical aroids, it needs little or no soil around its roots and is best
potted in epiphyte mixture or African violet soil in pots or tubs just large
enough to be stable.

MOSES-IN-A-BOAT: *Rhoeo spathacea*

MOTHER FERN: *Asplenium bulbiferum*

MOTHER-IN-LAW PLANT: *Dieffenbachia picta*

MOUNTAIN THISTLE: *Acanthus montanus*

MUEHLENBECKIA: See also *Homalocladium*

FIG. 68. *Musa nana, Muehlenbeckia complexa, Medinilla magnifica.*

MUEHLENBECKIA complexa   *Polygonaceae*   MAIDENHAIR VINE

In New Zealand this vine clambers over rocks, bushes, and even roofs. In the indoor garden it will in time wind around whatever appears in its way, forming a tight mat of dark, wiry stems and small round leaves. It makes an effective hanging basket. Sun is needed for growth, and overwatering is harmful. Tip cuttings root easily. (Fig. 68)

MUSA   *Musaceae*   BANANA

At least two species of small bananas are available for indoor culture. While fruit should not be expected in window gardens, greenhouse plants occasionally flower and bear tiny decorative bananas. I have *M. nana*, from South China, and *M. velutina*, from the Indian province of Assam, with pinkish stems and petioles. Both sucker freely, producing three or four new stalks each year, which can be left to make a clump or cut off with a little root and potted in all-purpose soil to make a new plant. Give them winter sun and summer shade, water them frequently, and feed them weekly from February through October. Neither gets more than three feet high. (Fig. 68)

MYRIOPHYLLUM brasiliense

Haloragidaceae   PARROTS FEATHER

This rampant aquatic from Chile and Uruguay is ideal for any indoor pool that gets a little sun each day. The feathery stems and leaves rise four to six inches out of the water and make a pleasing contrast to the round, flat pads of water poppies and lilies. Each September I put eight or ten rooted cuttings in a five-inch bulb pan with its rim two inches below the surface of the water, and by Christmas my little pool is so full of parrots feather that it has to be drastically cut back. Parrots feather is one of the few tropical aquatics that does not seem to mind water below 58°. (Fig. 18)

MYRTUS communis   *Myrtaceae*   CLASSIC MYRTLE

A dainty, aromatic shrub from the Mediterranean, this makes a charming pot plant which never gets out of hand, because like English box—to which it bears a close resemblance—it can be sheared to any shape or size. Small plants can be grown in windows with a reasonable amount of sun, and larger plants can winter over in sunporches or even unheated garages, provided they are not allowed to freeze. Cuttings root easily in spring, and while small plants do not flower, it is the foliage, not the flower, that smells so good. The shrub planted in front of the pool pictured in Fig. 18 is myrtle.

Naegelia: See *Smithiantha*

NARCISSUS   *Amaryllidaceae*   DAFFODIL

Few sights are more cheerful on a dreary winter day than a pot of golden daffodils. Be sure to order a few top size bulbs each year for forcing, as it is not hard to do and well worth the effort. The flower bud is already formed inside the bulb when you buy it; your task is simply to persuade it to come out.

'King Alfred,' an old-time yellow trumpet, is a good variety for your first try. Buy bulbs from a reliable source and pot as many in each bulb pan (shallow pot) as will fit, imbedding the lower two-thirds of the bulb in the soil. The composition of the soil is unimportant, but whatever is used must not be packed too tight. At least eight weeks' stay in a dark, cool place is necessary for root formation, without which no amount of coaxing will produce flowers. This means that potting should be done in October or November for bloom in the first part of the next year.

During the root formation period, the planted bulb pans can be buried in the garden or stored in a cool garage, barn, or root cellar—or even in the family refrigerator. A temperature of 40° is ideal. If you decide to bury them, dig a trench or hole a foot deep, put the pots in, and cover them with sand or cinders (not soil) and leaves. This will make them easier to dig up. Barn or garage storage is much more convenient. Be sure to water the pots regularly— say, once every two weeks.

After ten or twelve weeks your pots of daffodils can be brought out one by one and forced into bloom. The first week or ten days should be spent in as cool and bright a place as you have—a cool porch or an attic window. Then they can be put in your window garden where they will bloom for a week or more.

Paperwhite narcissus (*N. Tazetta*) are tender bulbs and need no cold storage. They can be brought into flower most effectively by "planting" them in bowls of pebbles filled with water to the level of the top pebble layer. Some authorities recommend putting the planted bowls in a cool, dark place for two or three weeks until the roots are formed, but I have not seen any difference between plants treated this way and those put directly into a sunny window. I know that they do not like temperatures below 50° at any time either before or after being planted.

Once the flowers are out, they will last longer if they are moved to a north or west window. Paperwhites that have been forced are worthless and should be thrown out. *N. Tazetta*, as its common name indicates, has fragrant white flowers. The variety *orientalis*, Chinese sacred lily, has yellow flowers.

A number of other hardy bulbs can be forced—particularly tulips and hyacinths. Good tulip varieties for this purpose are 'Princess Margaret Rose,' 'Smiling Queen,' 'Albino,' 'Carrara,' 'Golden Harvest,' and 'Golden Measure.' Although different procedures are sometimes recommended for different kinds of bulbs, I have obtained satisfactory results with all of them by following the procedure for daffodils described above. Remember, however, that tulips, unlike daffodils, must be protected from mice.

NATAL PLUM: *Carissa grandiflora*

NAUTILOCALYX   *Gesneriaceae*

Attractive, upright growing gesneriads from South America, grown primarily for their foliage and amazingly tolerant of the average indoor conditions—low light intensity, high temperatures and low relative humidity.

N. bullatus (*Episcia tesselata*) has large, shiny, muddy-green leaves, red on the back, with characteristic bumps (*bullatus* is Latin for blistered).

N. forgettii, named for the man who found it in the Peruvian jungles, has handsome bright-green leaves, with dark-brown markings along the veins.

N. lynchii has shiny maroon leaves.

All three species will grow up to two feet and eventually require five- to six-inch pots. Grow each of them in east, west or south windows in African violet soil. Cuttings root easily, and I suggest you make new plants every year or so.

Neanthe bella: See *Collinia elegans*

NEOMARICA   *Iridaceae*   HOUSE IRIS

Also called twelve apostles; guaranteed to grow, bloom, and provide a neat accent plant in any window in your house. The flat green leaves, apparently impervious to insects, grow in a fan from the underground stems and in late winter put forth blue and white iris-like flowers, each of which last only a day. After flowering, the leaves on which the flowers were born flop over, and if they touch a damp pebble tray or the soil of a neighboring pot, give birth to a new plant from the place where the flower grew.

There are two species, *N. gracilis* and *N. Northiana.* They are both from Brazil and very similar, *Northiana* being larger with more fragrant flowers. (Fig. 69)

NEOREGELIA   *Bromeliaceae*

These epiphytic bromeliads from Brazil will grow in sunny or sunless windows and in cool or warm temperatures, asking only that the "pitcher" formed by the rosette of leaves be filled with water every day. The flowers of Neoregelia appear near the bottom of the pitcher and are not as ornamental as the brightly marked and colored leaves, particularly those of *N. spectabilis,* the painted fingernail, whose leaf tips are gaily painted a deep pink. Growers offer several other interesting and decorative species and hybrids. For more information about these plants, refer to *Bromeliaceae.*

NEPETA hederacea variegata   *Labiatae*   GROUND IVY

The small round leaves edged with white and the trailing, prostrate stems make this small plant quite acceptable indoors, though it is considered a weed outside. The stems must be frequently cut back to keep the plants in neat mats; or it may be grown as a basket plant, allowing the hanging stems to receive the full benefit from all the available light, since the other cultural necessity is sun. (Fig. 48)

NEPHROLEPIS exaltata bostoniensis

Polypodiaceae   BOSTON FERN

The Boston fern survives undaunted by any sort of adverse condition. Numerous varieties have appeared among the thousands propagated each year, and some of these are more fluffy, graceful, and desirable than the original Boston fern (which came from Africa), while every bit as tough and undemanding.

All are easily propagated from the runners that emerge from the base of healthy plants during spring and summer. A new plant grows at the end of each runner and ferns plunged in shady places outdoors will have a good number of offspring by the end of summer. One is hanging in the north window pictured in Fig. 17.

NERIUM oleander   *Apocynaceae*   OLEANDER

These indispensable, summer-blooming, terrace tub plants can be put into cool winter storage in a frost-free place or wintered indoors where they will

FIG. 69.   *Nerium oleander, Nicotiana alata, Notocactus Leninghausii, Neomarica Northiana, Nicodemia diversifolia.*

retain their leaves and require practically no care except occasional watering. In March or April new growth will start and some plants may even flower. Repotting may then be in order; if not, fresh soil should be added and the plants should be fertilized. They can go outside in the first week of May or as soon as danger of frost is past, and will begin to flower almost immediately.

Plants wintered in the garage or cellar will take a little longer to get started, for flowering takes place on the new wood after the plant has been outside a while; but the final effect will be just as nice. Different varieties have flowers in various shades of pink, red, buff, and white; and the blooms may be either single or double. They came originally from the countries around the Mediterranean. Prune your plant by cutting away at least one-third of the growth on all stems when you take it in for the winter. (Fig. 69)

NICODEMIA diversifolia   *Loganiaceae*   INDOOR OAK

The leaves of this attractive, shrubby plant from the Mascaren Islands have the same shape as those of an English oak, hence its common name. They are also characterized by a metallic blue cast which makes the plant stand out from among the others in my cool southwest window. I pot mine in all-purpose soil and prune it each spring. Cuttings root readily and new plants grow quickly. (Fig. 69)

NICOTIANA alata   *Solanaceae*   FLOWERING TOBACCO

The dwarf varieties of Nicotiana, the deliciously fragrant flowering tobacco from Brazil, can be grown indoors in pots, and will flower off and on through the winter if the night temperature is reasonably cool and they receive several hours of sun each day.

June-sown seeds will usually be ready for four-inch pots by August or September and should start blooming about that time. As an alternative, garden plants dug up, cut back, and potted in the fall will flower in January or February. (Fig. 69)

NIGHT-BLOOMING CEREUS: *Epiphyllum, Hylocereus, Selenicereus*

NORFOLK ISLAND PINE: *Araucaria excelsa*

NOTOCACTUS   *Cactaceae*   BALL CACTUS

These small South American cacti are good for the start of a collection; they flower quite freely in spring and summer when still very small. To me, the flowering of a cactus is one of the marvels of indoor gardening—something I can't quite believe will actually happen as I watch the plants, inert and changeless, during the long months of winter. When my little 'Golden Ball' (*Notocactus Leninghausii*) puts out a yellow flower from the top of its fat column, it seems to be laughing at me for being so skeptical. (Fig. 69)

NOTONIA pendula   *Compositae*   <small>INCH WORM</small>
(*Kleinia pendula*)

The inch worm is an ugly succulent from Arabia, interesting only because of its curious, prostrate, rooting stems. It is a member of the prolific daisy family and occasionally bears large red flowers. (Fig. 71)

NYMPHAEA Daubeniana   *Nymphaeaceae*   <small>PIGMY WATER LILY, DAUBEN</small>

No doubt there are other species of tropical water lily suitable for indoor pools, but Dauben has done so well for me that I have not tried any other. As long as there is a little sun and the water temperature does not drop below 58°, I have one or two pale blue water lilies from the three plants in my tiny greenhouse pool, even in winter. During spells of dark winter weather, the water gets cold and both leaves and flowers stop appearing, but the plants remain alive and speedily resume their growth when warmth and sun return. The five-inch bulb pot in which each lily is planted is set with its rim about two inches below the surface.

NYMPHOIDES aquatica   *Gentianaceae*   <small>WATER SNOWFLAKE
BANANA PLANT</small>

This small aquatic plant is generally encountered under one of its common names. It is a great favorite for aquariums—where it is frequently set afloat to reveal the clusters of tubers which look for all the world like bunches of bananas. Unfortunately, the plants cannot live indefinitely in this condition; their roots must be planted in soil or sand to produce the pretty heart-shaped leaves. In spring and summer, established plants whose leaves have reached the surface of the pond may bear tiny white flowers—the snowflakes. Full sun is a prerequisite; so plants in indoor pools, which are generally shaded at this time of year, are not apt to flower much.

Nymphoides aquatica can stand quite cold water, though it will not put out much new growth when the temperature is below 58°.

Another species, *N. indica*, is called floating heart. It looks and acts exactly the same except that the flowers are yellow. (Fig. 18)

OCHNA multiflora   *Ochnaceae*   <small>BIRDS-EYE BUSH</small>

A small woody shrub from tropical Africa. In its native habitat it grows four- to five-feet high, but when confined in a pot, the shrub can be kept below 15 inches. Ochna has leathery leaves which are a yellowy bronze color when they open and gradually become dark green. Its bark is a speckled gray. The plant goes through an extraordinary development from flower to fruit, which takes about nine months.

In late winter, deep, yellow, primrose-like flowers appear in profusion along the year-old twigs. Each lasts a week or two. After the petals have fallen, the five green sepals (the leaflike parts which appear outside of, and just below, the petals) turn red, and soon fleshy, black seeds develop on the receptacle to which the red sepals are attached. This fruit persists for two or three months. When it falls off, the seed inside is ready to germinate. This is the best source of new plants.

Grow ochna in a cool, sunny window in all-purpose soil.

OLD MAN CACTUS: *Cephalocereus senilis*

OLEANDER: *Nerium Oleander*

OPHIOPOGON japonicus   *Liliaceae*   MONDO GRASS
                                                    DWARF LILY TURF

Sold as a ground cover in the southern United States and hardy as far north as Philadelphia, mondo grass is also a useful pot plant for cool porches and sunrooms. The slender dark green blades are about ten inches long, and fall over the edges of hanging pots or baskets in an airy, graceful way. Mondo grass spreads rapidly by underground stolons and soon makes a tight mass which can be divided in spring. Three small potsfull are growing on the cool sunporch shown in Fig. 23.

OPLISMENUS compositus   *Gramineae*   BASKET GRASS

This weedy-looking tropical plant is often used for hanging baskets, perhaps because the owner doesn't realize how many other plants are better suited to the purpose. The variety *vittatus* is much gayer, with pink and white stripes on its green leaves. Like all grasses, Oplismenus will not grow without sun. (Fig. 70)

OPUNTIA   *Cactaceae*   PRICKLY PEAR
                                              BUNNY EARS

There are a great many species of opuntia. All are native to the two American continents, but many have become naturalized in other warm parts of the world, where they grow so vigorously that they are used for forage and hedges and sometimes are even considered weeds. Their ungainly, flat, floppy pads and the vicious spines of some species limit their usefulness indoors, but if you have a spot (like the desert garden shown in Fig. 24), you will be hard put to find a tougher house plant. The small species are commonly found in cactus and succulent collections, and a large prickly pear can be a striking specimen.

ORANGE: *Citrus*

ORANGE BROWALLIA: *Streptosolen Jamesonii*

ORCHIDACEAE

People who take up growing orchids often end by getting rid of their other plants and becoming orchid specialists. Because I have been determined to avoid this transformation, I have grown very few indoors. However, I have seen enough collections of house-grown orchids to be convinced that it can be done by any competent and conscientious indoor gardener.

The procedures for growing orchids in the house are the same as those recommended in this book for tropical plants generally. They need winter sun, and the epiphytic varieties (most fall into this category) are generally grown in osmunda fiber or fir bark.

Their only unusual feature is their leaves. These have large pores (called stomata) through which they lose water rapidly in a dry atmosphere. They also have a stiff structure so that the loss of water does not cause wilting and is apt to go unnoticed. This means that you should use every means at your disposal to keep the relative humidity above the 40% level, and you should also water promptly whenever the growing mediums begin to dry out.

The family is enormous. There are some 30,000 species to choose from, not to mention countless hybrids. Those more commonly grown are mentioned in the following excerpt from an article by Thomas Powell in the *House Plants* handbook, Vol. 18, No. 3, published by the Brooklyn Botanic Garden.

"Cattleya species recommended for beginners are *C. mossiae, C. gaskelliana, C. labiata, C. percivalliana,* and *C. trianaei.* There are many others, of course, as well as thousands of hybrids that often boast more gorgeous blooms and greater vigor. The commercial grower from whom you buy your plants will be glad to suggest plants for a succession of bloom throughout the year.

"Three other genera are especially well suited to home growing. *Laelias,* with starry-shaped flowers in many hues, are often found in their native habitat growing in windswept places where the days are hot and nights cool. Thus they are tolerant of the drastic changes in temperature and drafts encountered in the home. *Laelia anceps, L. autumnalis,* and *L. rubescens* are good choices.

"*Oncidiums,* the delightful 'dancing ladies' of the orchid world, have white or yellow flowers marked with brown and red. Some are miniature plants, others bear flower sprays several feet long. *O. cheirophorum* is a fragrant yellow-flowered miniature. *O. ornithorhynchum* bears dainty sprays of fragrant rose-purple blooms. *O. papilio,* the bright and unusual 'butterfly orchid,' often blooms almost all year long. *O. splendidum* produces heavy sprays of comparatively large flowers.

"*Epidendrums,* too, come in all shapes and sizes and are very tolerant plants. One of the best is *E. tampense,* a native of Florida, which bears numerous short spikes of chartreuse blooms in spring.

"You will soon want to get some of the dependable home bloomers, such as *Cypripedium maudiae,* the waxy green and white lady-slipper orchid. *Brassavola nodosa,* the white 'lady of the night,' is very fragrant after dark, and is one of the easiest to grow. *Cycnoches chlorochilon* has large fragrant swan-shaped flowers. Another beauty is *Odontoglossum grande,* the striped 'tiger orchid.' *Dendrobium nobile* bears lovely purple-spotted flowers in spring.

"These are only a few of the popular orchids amenable to home culture. Dozens of other genera—*Phalaenopsis, Miltonia, Catasetum, Lockhartia, Maxillaria* and others—have proven their worth. Today multigeneric hybridizing is producing some spectacular plants that are wonderfully easy to grow. Crosses of *Epidendrum-Cattleya, Vandia-Angraecum* and *Sophronitis-Brassavola-Laelia-Cattleya* are some of these marvels of the plant breeder's art."

I know one good indoor gardener who has an extensive collection of orchids grown entirely under lights in his basement. His collection of blue ribbons and trophies attests to the success of such a method.

OSMANTHUS fragrans   *Oleaceae*   FLOWERING OLIVE

This Asian evergreen is one of the most satisfactory flowering house plants. Not only is the dark green foliage easy to keep shining and clean, but central heat does not dry out the flower buds, and pot-bound plants bear their small fragrant white flowers through most of the year. Use all-purpose soil, grow Osmanthus in a sunny window, and move it outside to semi-shade in summer. (Fig. 70)

O. ilicifolius, both variegated and plain, is frequently used in dish gardens. It has small spiny leaves very like those of the English holly, but I have never seen it bloom in the winter in a house.

OTAHEITE DWARF ORANGE: *Citrus taitensis*

OTHONNA capensis   *Compositae*   LITTLE PICKLES

An old-time favorite from South Africa, called little pickles because of the shape of its small succulent leaves. When grown in the sun, it trails prettily and bears small yellow daisies throughout the year, though few will be seen in winter.

OXALIS   *Oxalidaceae*   WOOD SORREL

A number of evergreen and non-evergreen bulbous oxalises are suitable for sunny winter windows, and a few are among my standbys, for they are profuse bloomers and require a minimum of attention. They grow in all-

FIG. 70. *Oplismenus compositus vittatus, Oxypetalum caeruleum, Osmanthus fragrans, Oxalis crassipes, O. Henrei, O. Regnellii, O. 'Firefern,' O. peduncularis, Ophiopogon japonicus.*

purpose soil, and those that rest in summer do so in plastic bags. They close up both their clover-like leaves and their flowers at night and on sunless days, and tend to act in the same shy fashion if the sun is too hot in summer, or if they are allowed to become too dry.

O. crassipes has small purply-pink flowers. It is evergreen and virtually everblooming.

O. Henrei, also evergreen and everblooming, has tubular stems, small leaves, and small yellow flowers.

O. lasiandra is a large-leaved summer and fall bloomer with purple flowers.

O. lobata comes to life in the fall and bears yellow flowers all through that season.

O. melanosticta is dormant in the spring and summer. It starts to grow in the fall, putting forth gray tomentose leaves and yellow flowers.

O. Ortgiesii, a non-bulbous, upright-growing species, has very dark ever-green leaves with purple backs and everblooming yellow flowers.

O. peduncularis is a larger plant than any of these others. Non-bulbous, evergreen, and everblooming, it has large orange flowers which combine well in a winter window with browallia.

O. Pes-caprae (*O. cernua*), the Bermuda buttercup, has the largest, brightest yellow flowers of all. Bulbs planted in the fall start to bloom soon after the first of the year and make a fine show in either baskets or pots for two or three months. Then they gradually dwindle to nothing and have to be put to rest for five or six months.

O. Regnellii (*rubra alba*) and *O. rosea* are bulbous, evergreen, and ever-blooming. (Fig. 70)

A new red-leaved species, *O. hedysaroides*, is just appearing on the market. It is called Firefern by some growers.

OXYPETALUM caeruleum   *Asclepiadaceae*

This small twining plant from Argentina, often grown outdoors in summer, can also be used in sunny winter window gardens where it may bear its un-usual, ice-blue flowers—not in any profusion, but in sufficient numbers to make it worthwhile. Use new plants each year, renewed by seeds or cuttings and potted in all-purpose soil. A bushier effect can be achieved by judicious fall pinching. (Fig. 70)

PACHYPHYTUM bracteosum   *Crassulaceae*

This succulent from the sunny, arid part of Mexico has glamorous decora-tive rosettes. It will soon lose color and character if not afforded plenty of sun.

Pachyphytum 'Moonstone' is shown in Fig. 50.

PACHYVERIA   *Crassulaceae*

This is a new name for hybrids between *Pachyphytum* and *Echeveria*, two genera of succulents from the Mexican deserts. In Figs. 50 and 71 you will see two handsome white-leaved varieties.

PAINTED FINGERNAIL: *Neoregelia spectabilis*

PALM: *Chamaedorea adenopodus, Chamaedorea seifrizii, Chrysalidocarpus lutescens, Collinia elegans, Howea Forsteriana, Phoenix Roebelenii, Rhapsis excelsa.*
Potted palms, though much maligned, make good plants for indoor grow-ing. They are generally tolerant of dry air, high temperatures and low light intensity. Most species have a colorful inflorescence, which is both interest-ing and attractive.

Palms are monocotyledons, a great subdivision of the plant kingdom, which comprises, among others, all the grasses, cereal grains, orchids, aroids and irids. They and bananas are the only monocots which have evolved into arboreal growth. However, they do not branch, and if the terminal is injured or removed, the stem will eventually die.

Some palms develop shoots from stolons running just beneath the soil surface; others sprout from the base of the bole, just above the ground. These kinds are called clump forming. Others, often the more familiar, are single stemmed.

FIG. 71.   SUCCULENTS ARE GOOD FOR DRY ROOMS.

KEY TO FIG. 71:

1. *Echeveria pulvinata*
2. *Gasteria hybrida*
3. *Kleinia Mandraliscae*
4. *Pachyveria* hybrid
5. *Kleinia* sp.
6. *Haworthia* hybrid
7. *Aichryson domesticum*
8. *Aloe Beguinii*
9. *Lampranthus emarginatus*
10. *Notonia pendula*
11. *Pachyveria* hybrid
12. *Echeveria elegans*
13. *Agave Victoriae-Reginae*
14. *Aeonium arboreum atropurpureum*
15. *Echeveria* hybrid
16. *Graptopetalum paraguayense*
17. *Kalanchoe tubiflora*
18. *Agave striata echinoides*
19. *Adromischus Cooperii*

Because of the lack of branches, the leaf area of a single palm stem never increases to any great degree after the plant passes the seedling stage. As a new frond is produced at the top, the lowest and oldest frond yellows and dies so that there is no net addition to the leaf area. This means that, with periodic root pruning, the plant can be kept in the same size container indefinitely. Clump-forming palms may need dividing from time to time.

PANAMIGA: *Pilea involucrata*

PANDANUS   *Pandanaceae*   SCREW PINE

These spiny and durable foliage plants, often found in houses and in hotel lobbies, are called screw pines because of the spiral arrangement of the leaves. A carefully tended plant can be striking, but too often the vicious teeth along the margins of the leaves discourage the gardener from caring for his plants, and they become a cobwebby mass of leaves, aerial roots, and dust that might best be relegated to the compost pile.

The two species grown commercially are *P. Veitchii* (Fig. 72), from Polynesia, with variegated leaves, and *P. utilis*, from Madagascar, with all-green leaves. Both need warm temperatures, plenty of moisture at the roots, good drainage, and good light—but not necessarily sun.

PANDOREA jasminoides *Bignoniaceae* BOWER PLANT

The shining, compound, evergreen leaves of this Australian twiner are outstandingly decorative; and even though my plant flowers only in the summer, I feel it is worth having because it looks well all the year and is not a prey to bugs and mites. When the pink-throated white flowers do appear, they are profuse and fragrant. It can be used as a green frame for a sunny window in the house.

Papyrus antiquorum: See *Cyperus Papyrus*

PARLOR IVY: *Senecio mikanioides*

PARLOR PALM: *Collinia elegans*

PARODIA aureispina *Cactaceae* TOM THUMB CACTUS

One of a group of small round cacti from Argentina, desirable because it really does flower in the early spring while still in its sunny winter quarters. This cannot be said for many other kinds.

PARROTS FEATHER: *Myriophyllum brasiliense*

PASSIFLORA *Passifloraceae* PASSION VINE

The first Spaniards to travel through the forests of Brazil saw in the complex structure of the passion vine flowers the story of the crucifixion and took it as an exhortation to convert the Indians to Christianity. Rare is the modern gardener who can resist growing a passion vine or two, letting them twine their tendrils over everything in sight, and watching bud after bud fall unopened in the winter—all for the pleasure, when summer comes, of seeing the intricate flowers unfold.

The five sepals and five petals are said to represent the ten apostles present at the crucifixion; the circle of colored filaments is the crown of thorns; the stamens are the five wounds; and the pistils are the three nails.

From a practical point of view, the passion vine is only fairly satisfactory as a house plant, because late spring and summer are the blooming seasons and vines big enough to bloom soon become overpoweringly large. It can, however, be trained along the bars of a greenhouse to provide summer shade and then be cut back and repotted in the fall when shade is no longer needed. Cuttings taken in late summer will make blooming-size plants for the following spring. All passifloras need full sun.

P. alata has stylish, five-fingered leaves and winged stems. (Fig. 72)

P. caerulea is the most commonly grown. Its distinguishing characteristic is a marked blue in the ring of the flower filament.

FIG. 72. TOP: *Passiflora alata, Stephanotis floribunda.* BOTTOM: *Pteris tremula, Plumbago capensis, Pandanus Veitchii, Pentas lanceolata, Asparagus plumosus.*

P. coriacea has unusual leaves shaped like a butterfly wing and mottled with light green. Its flowers are very small.

P. edulis is the purple granadilla of Queensland and New South Wales, where its fruit is used for dessert. Indoors, the plants are not apt to set fruit, even with hand pollination.

P. racemosa has red flowers.

P. trifasciata has leaves marked with purple and green. While its flowers are insignificant, its foliage makes it one of the most worthwhile passion vines.

PASSION VINE: *Passiflora*

PATIENCE PLANT: *Impatiens Holstii*

PEDILANTHUS tithymaloides   *Euphorbiaceae*   REDBIRD CACTUS

This Central American succulent is seldom cultivated indoors, though it is commonly seen outdoors in the far south. In the house it may bear its rather showy red or purple flowers in late winter if grown in a warm sunny place. The variety *variegatus* has white and pink coloring in its leaves and is brighter and more desirable.

PELARGONIUM hortorum   *Geraniaceae*   GERANIUM

South Africa is to be thanked for the geraniums that brighten our terraces in summer and will grace a sunny window in winter. However, not even a geranium should be expected to put on a twelve-month show, and the best plan is to have two sets—one for summer and one for winter. The winter plants should be propagated from four-inch cuttings in July. By October they will be ready for three-inch pots, having been pinched and brought indoors in September. Blooms will be sparse until January, when the plants will begin to flower in earnest, though never as abundantly as in summer. Toward the end of February, cuttings can be made for summer plants.

I have found the pale pinks—'Mrs. Lawrence,' 'California Beauty,' and 'Enchantress'—to be good winter bloomers. The reds do not bloom as well indoors; the salmons only fairly well; and fancy-leaved kinds, while growing satisfactorily, seldom flower.

In contrast, the scented geraniums, since they are not expected to bloom, do not lead to disappointment. Of the scented group my favorite is *P. tomentosum*, the peppermint geranium, because it is both good looking and fragrant. Sun and constant pinching are the secrets of producing compact plants. Other scented varieties include:

P. crispum, the lemon geranium, used in finger bowls.

P. denticulatum, with the odor of pine.

P. fragrans—dainty and smelling like nutmeg.

P. graveolens and *P. fulgidum*, both reminiscent of roses.

P. domesticum is the 'Lady Washington' pelargonium which florists have in bloom at Easter. They are scarcely worth the space they take up in the house because yours will never be half as fine as those you buy. The trick is the temperature, which must be below 60° for the formation of flower buds and must be kept at about this level for three months before the buds open. Hardly practical for a living room!

P. peltatum, the ivy geranium, is a fine trailing plant for a very sunny place. It flowers from March to October.

P. quercifolium is a robust rose-scented type.

PELLAEA   *Polypodiaceae*   CLIFF-BRAKE FERN

The name is derived from the Greek *pellos*, meaning "dusky," and refers to the dark leaf stalks like those of the maidenhairs.

FIG. 73.   *Phyllitis Scolopendrium, Pellaea rotundifolia, P. viridis, Cyrtomium falcatum Rochefordianum* (Back), *Asplenium bulbiferum.*

P. rotundifolia, from New Zealand, is small and low-growing, with round, dark leaves—very unlike a fern. It is one of my favorite plants. (Fig. 73)

P. viridis from South Africa, also called *Pteris adiantoides,* has larger, greener leaflets. (Figs. 17 and 73)

P. hastata is a small, refined version of *viridis.*

All three species grow well in either African violet or all-purpose soil in a north window where it is cool and moist.

PELLIONIA   *Urticaceae*

These two small flat creepers from tropical Asia are good edging plants for window gardens because they do not need sunlight, and the edges of window sills are apt to be shady.

P. Daveauana has leaves one and one-half to two inches long of a dark chocolate color with light green down the middle. There is some growing in the window garden shown in Fig. 12.

P. pulchra, has smaller, more velvety leaves of dark olive green, with purple along the veins and on the undersides. See the upper shelf of the bench in Fig. 14 for a picture of this one.

PENTAS lanceolata   *Rubiaceae*   STAR CLUSTERS

This Arabian shrub grows vigorously. In the greenhouse it bears its pink or lavender flowers from time to time regardless of season, but indoors it is not so prolific. Small plants, which are easily made from cuttings, bloom as well as large ones and are better for the house because they can be kept with other plants on pebble trays, where there may be enough humidity to keep the buds from drying up. The flowers are showy umbels like those of their relative Bouvardia, but the foliage is weedy. (Fig. 72)

There is a variety, *alba*.

PEPEROMIA   *Piperaceae*

These foliage plants from the tropics of South America should be awarded a blue ribbon for outstanding performance on window sills and coffee tables. In their jungle homes, many grow as epiphytes, and others sprawl and crawl over stumps and roots on the jungle floor. Still others live an almost xerophytic life akin to that of succulent plants. Under domestication, they adapt to almost any indoor situation, provided they are not overwatered or asked to grow in too dark a place. African violet or begonia soil makes the best potting mixture.

Fifteen species and varieties are pictured here, and as many more are offered by various growers. The white spikes above the leaves are the flowers. Peperomias grow rapidly and can be propagated from leaf petioles like African violets. (Fig. 74)

PERESKIA aculeata   *Cactaceae*   LEMON VINE

A vine-like cactus from the warm, wet parts of Mexico, with lemon scented, creamy blossoms and shiny succulent leaves—quite unlike what we generally think of as a cactus. It does have spines, however, which are painfully in evidence when I wash the shiny leaves or prune my plant. I grow it with a group of cacti in a sunny window as a welcome change from barrels and pincushions. It tends to lose its leaves in winter, and the flowers appear in the spring or when it goes outside in the summer.

P. corrugata has red flowers and suggestions of red on the veins and on the new growth of its light green leaves. It is not yet available commercially but

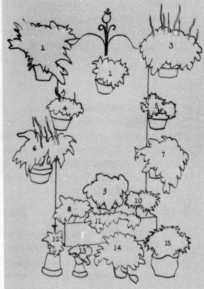

KEY TO FIG. 74:

1. *obtusifolia* 'Silver Edge'
2. 'Astrid' or 'Pixie'
3. *hederifolia*
4. 'Little Fantasy'
5. *rubella*
6. 'Sweetheart'
7. *glabella*
8. *Sandersii*
9. 'Blackie'
10. *verticillata*
11. *glabella variegata*
12. *Fosteriana*
13. 'Moneywort'
14. 'Emerald Ripple'
15. *metallica*

surely will be soon, as it is easily propagated from cuttings and requires no special care.

PERFUMED NIGHT JESSAMINE: *Cestrum nocturnum*

PERISTROPHE salicifolia aureo-variegata
Acanthaceae

The only Peristrophe I have grown is the variegated kind *aureo-variegata*. The leaves of this attractive, low-growing, small-leaved plant are gold, with a decorative border of green. In winter, spring, and summer it bears small lavender flowers which add nothing to its looks. Since variegated plants are deficient in chlorophyll and need all the light they can get, this is a candidate for a sunny window. It can stand a cool place, but being from Java, it does better where the temperature is high. (Fig. 90)

PERSEA americana   *Lauraceae*   AVOCADO

Growing avocados from seeds discarded after the salad is prepared is irresistible. The sprouting end is usually obvious. If not, put the flatter of the two ends down—in water, damp sand, perlite, soil or what have you—and wait. A large-leaved, quite ungainly plant will soon develop. With full sun and periodic pruning, you can produce an acceptable specimen. However, in spite of the ridiculous ease of propagation, the exercise is recommended only for children and shut-ins. Growing an avocado falls within the scope of a newly named avocation—horto-therapy!

PETREA volubilis   *Verbenaceae*   QUEENS WREATH
                                                    PURPLE WREATH

A truly exotic plant from Central America, actually a twining vine. The blue flowers, somewhat resembling lilacs, appear in early spring and often again in summer and are well worth waiting for. While the plant is too big for a window sill, it can be used in a sunny conservatory as a tub plant. Petreas must be two or three years old before they bloom properly, so plan on accommodating something big (eight-inch to ten-inch pot) as a more or less permanent acquisition.

PHILODENDRON   *Araceae*

We would all be hard put to it if we had to garden indoors without this most versatile group of vines from Central and South America, for philodendrons can go for weeks without water or sun; and when they do get good light and regular watering, their exuberant health is a pleasant contrast to the frail condition of many house plants.

The name philodendron means tree-loving and was given because in their jungle home vining philodendrons climb the trunks of the tropical trees, reaching for the light that filters through the foliage above. Their long aerial roots serve both as holdfasts and as a means of absorbing moisture and nutrients from the trunks they climb and from the humid jungle air. There are also self-heading species in which the stem is only a few inches long and the leaves grow in a compact clump.

Florida growers have a good many species and hybrids to offer, and plant explorers are constantly searching for new varieties suitable for use in the house. No one has space large enough to grow all the varieties offered. Those that I have tried and found worthwhile, either in my own house or in the houses of friends, are described below. They all have superficial ground roots and need a pot only large enough to support the plant—and its totem or trellis if it is a vining variety.

Though they will grow in water, they do best in epiphyte or African violet mixture in a well-drained pot that allows the roots to get the air they need. When the vining types get too big or lose their lower leaves, as they are bound to do sooner or later, have no hesitation about cutting them back. This will stimulate new growth to replace the old. My plant of *P. laciniatum* has been growing on the same piece of cork bark in the same pot for seven

FIG. 75. SOME OF THE BEST PHILO-
DENDRONS. TOP: *hastatum, laciniatum.* MIDDLE: *panduraeforme,
squamiferum, Sodiroi.* BOTTOM:
Wendlandii, micans (on totem),
cannaefolium.

years and has developed a sizeable trunk. Each spring I cut off its top, and
each summer the remaining growth gets fuller and the plant grows more attractive. Several years are required before a self-heading philodendron will
grow a full rosette of leaves to make a handsome, round specimen plant.

P. Andreanum is a vining type with very dark green, almost black, velvety
leaves set off by light green veins. It likes high heat and humidity. In summer
it grows magnificently and some of the leaves get ten inches long, but I have
trouble keeping it alive during the winter. One is pictured in the planting
shown in Fig. 15.

P. cannaefolium is a very slow-growing plant of the self-heading type,
excellent for the house. Its large fleshy leaf petioles are unlike those of most
other philodendrons. The plant pictured is four years old and has been
repotted only once. (Fig. 75)

P. erubescens is a large-leaved, vining type with handsome, shiny, dark
green leaves, red petioles, and reddish veins. The new leaves are quite coppery
and are set fairly close together on the stems.

P. guttiferum is a small-leaved climber and is generally sold already started up a totem pole. As in the case of most climbing philodendrons, when it grows past the top of the totem and no longer has any support, its leaves become smaller and farther apart on the stems.

P. hastatum is a popular climber with large green arrow-shaped leaves. There is also a variegated cultivar. (Fig. 75)

P. laciniatum also climbs; its bright green leaves are deeply cut. (Fig. 75)

P. 'Lynette' is self-heading, but has enough stem so that the tip growth can sometimes be removed, causing it to break out at another place and thus get more bushy.

P. Mandaianum is a hybrid of *erubescens* and *hastatum*, its leaves having the red color of the former and the arrow shape of the latter.

P. Melinoni, another attractive self-heading type with oblong leaves, is suitable only for very roomy situations like the top of a grand piano.

P. McNeilianum is a self-heading hybrid. It grew out of my size range in two years, by which time it had developed a six-foot spread. Until this happened, I prized it as a bold and handsome plant. It is one of the few that can withstand low temperatures.

P. micans is a small climber with dark brown velvety leaves shaped like those of the ordinary *P. cordatum*. It insists on high temperatures and humidity. We have solved some of its problems by drilling a well down its tree-fern totem, which is then filled with perlite. (Vermiculite would do as well.) A slight depression is left in the top, and this is where the plant is watered each day. Thus, the totem stays damp and the roots cling to it readily. (Fig. 75)

P. Orlando is a semi-self-heading hybrid with large arrow-shaped leaves and red petioles. The leaves are close together on the stem, and it grows slowly. The flower is a gorgeous Jack-in-the-pulpit, with the outside of the pulpit bright red and the inside pure white. Jack is red.

P. oxycardium, better but not properly known as *cordatum*, is the one that everyone knows. A wonderful display of this versatile plant may be seen in Fig. 15.

P. panduraeforme is a fiddle-leaved climber with pale, olive-green leaves, each just a little different from the others. Well-grown plants develop leaves up to a foot long. It appears to be just as tough as *oxycardium*. (Fig. 75)

P. Selloum is a fast-growing self-header with very deeply cut leaves. It is said to be able to withstand freezing temperatures.

P. Sodiroi has two distinct vining types, one with small leaves and one with very large leaves. Both are slow-growing, and both have heart-shaped leaves mottled with silver-blue lines and blotches. (Fig. 75)

P. squamiferum, a vining type, is finicky. I lost one by exposing it to fifty-degree temperatures. It has dark green lobed leaves with red fuzz on the petioles and grows slowly enough to keep track of. (Fig. 75)

P. Wendlandii is a house plant par excellence. Its broad, flat leaves fan out from a central head but have fairly short petioles, so that mature plants are small enough for a normal sized house. This is my favorite self-heading philodendron. (Fig. 75)

PHLEBODIUM aureum   *Polypodiaceae*   HARES-FOOT FERN
(*Polypodium aureum*)

Because of its toughness, this tropical American fern is commonly grown indoors. The thick, brown, hairy rhizomes give it its common name; and its large, deeply cut, blue-green fronds give it its distinctive charm. The rhizomes lie on the surface of the soil and often grow over the edges of the pots, which need not be deeper than bulb pans, since the root system is very shallow. Use African violet or begonia soil, and make new plants by imbedding a piece of rhizome in your cutting box. (Fig. 18)

PHOENIX Roebelenii   *Palmaceae*   MINIATURE DATE PALM

It would take years for this small feathery palm to outgrow a window sill, and meanwhile it would be a graceful addition to any collection. Because it is such a slow grower, great care must be exercised to avoid overwatering it. Use all-purpose soil, make sure the drainage is perfect, and fertilize once in the spring and once in summer.

PHYLLITIS Scolopendrium   *Polypodiaceae*   HARTS-TONGUE FERN

The fronds of the harts-tongue combine an attractive bright green, leathery texture with an unusual broad "strap" shape. While deciduous and hardy outdoors, they stay evergreen indoors provided they are grown in a cool, humid place. There are over fifty varieties in cultivation and in the wild. My plant can be seen in Fig. 73.

PIGGY-BACK PLANT: *Tolmiea Menziesii*

PIGMY WATER LILY: *Nymphaea Daubeniana*

PILEA   *Urticaceae*

As a group, pileas are among the most useful for the house. While they flower freely, the blooms are so inconspicuous that the plants are generally grown only for their foliage. All need good light, but not necessarily full sun. Grow them in small pots and pinch frequently to encourage bushiness. Cuttings root easily at any time of year.

P. cadierei, from Indo-China, is called the aluminum plant because of the silvery air pockets on its green leaves.

P. involucrata is the Panamiga, so named to promote friendship between

FIG. 76.   *Pilea involucrata, P. nummulariaefolia, P. pubescens* 'Black-leaf,' *P. pubescens* 'Silver-leaf,' *P. cadierei, P. microphylla.*

the American countries, including its native Peru. It has small, rough-textured, brown leaves and an attractive bushy growth habit.

P. microphylla is called the Mexican artillery plant because of the explosive way it discharges its ripe pollen into the air if touched at the proper time. There is a nice unnamed variety of this species with such tiny leaves as almost to resemble a fern.

P. nummulariaefolia from the West Indies has the delightful name Creeping Charlie. It will not grow except in very good light, but given this, it makes a charming flat green mat.

There are at least two varieties of *P. pubescens* from South America—'Black-leaf' and 'Silver-leaf.' They grow flat and low in good light, and make pretty baskets or trailing plants. (Fig. 76)

PINEAPPLE: *Ananas comosus*

PINK POLKADOT PLANT: *Hypoestis sanguinolenta*

PIPER ornatum   *Piperaceae*   CLIMBING PEPPER

I like this shiny climber from the Celebes because it grows slowly and is not demanding. It can be trained to a totem pole or trellis or allowed to trail over the edge of a window sill, where its shining green leaves flecked with pink spots and blotches are a pleasant contrast to the all-green foliage of other plants.

Being a jungle plant, it likes tropical temperatures, needs frequent watering, and does not need full sun. One is pictured in Fig. 15.

PITCHER PLANT: *Billbergia, Darlingtonia californica, Neoregelia*

PISTIA Stratiotes   *Araceae*   WATER LETTUCE

This floating aroid from tropical America looks disconcertingly like a head of garden lettuce sitting in your indoor pool. William Bartram, son of John Bartram, describes islands of water lettuce on St. John's River in Florida: "These floating islands present a very entertaining prospect . . . we see not only flowery plants, clumps of shrubs, old, weather-beaten trees, hoary and barbed, with long moss waving from their snags, but we also see them completely inhabited and alive with crocodiles, serpents, frogs, otters, crows, herons, curlews, jackdaws, etc."

Water lettuce can be grown floating or planted in a pot with the rim at water level. They need some sunlight in the winter and must have water temperatures of at least 60°. Indoor water gardeners will have to work hard to keep this plant alive through the winter. Two are discernible in the pool shown in Fig. 18.

PITTOSPORUM Tobira   *Pittosporaceae*   JAPANESE PITTOSPORUM

A handsome, shiny evergreen, and one of the finest house shrubs in cultivation. It can stand heat or cold, and if it can depend on summering outside in partial shade, it will winter well in any light place indoors, not necessarily a window.

Plants grown in full sun all winter flower freely, bearing small cream-colored blooms with a fragrance reminiscent of orange blossom or jasmine. Unpruned plants become ungainly, so be bold with the shears in spring when you put your plant outside.

P. Tobira variegata is pictured in the window garden shown in Fig. 12.

PLATYCERIUM bifurcatum   *Polypodiaceae*   STAGHORN FERN

It is a great temptation to try a staghorn fern indoors, and I know from experience that it can be done. But, since they are jungle epiphytes care must be taken to see that they are not subjected to low humidity and that daily syringing and spraying of the fronds is not neglected. Also, they need bright light and even some winter sun if possible, though this is not an absolute necessity. Night temperatures should not go below 55°, and higher temperatures are preferable, provided the atmosphere is not too dry.

These ferns are grown on slabs of cedar, cork, or other decay-resistant wood, with their roots surrounded by osmunda fiber and the whole ball of roots and fiber firmly wired in place. The forked, fertile fronds grow out and down and give the plants their common name; the sterile ones stay flat against the slab, making a shield to hold tiny particles of decaying vegetation. The new plants that occasionally appear beside the old ones can be potted separately to increase your supply.

The species *bifurcatum* from Australia and Polynesia is the best for indoor growing. Greenhouse owners may want to try some of the other species available. See Fig. 18 for a picture of a four-year-old plant.

PLECTRANTHUS Oertendahelii   *Labiatae*   PROSTRATE COLEUS

This amenable trailer from Natal may someday replace the wandering Jew as the most foolproof trailing plant for indoor growing. Any part of the stem can be rooted in water and will soon make a good-sized plant which will grow in any soil in north or south light. The very dark green leaves are brightened by silvery veins and purple edges. The small lavender flowers, which appear in spring, add nothing whatever, and I always snip them off. (Fig. 14)

Another species, *P. australis*, from Australia and Polynesia, has bright green leaves and the same growing habit. (Fig. 54)

PLUMBAGO capensis   *Plumbaginaceae*

Plumbago without flowers is weedy-looking and has no place in a group of plants crowding each other for a chance at the sunlight in a winter window, but Plumbago covered with pale blue phlox-like blooms is a never-to-be-forgotten sight.

Since summer and fall are the flowering times, some frost-free place other than your indoor garden must be found for Plumbago during the two or three winter months when it is half asleep and needs only occasional watering. In early spring bring it out, repot it if necessary in all-purpose soil, prune it, and put it in as bright a place as possible. In May it can go outside in full sun. I grow mine there until early September, when it comes indoors for several weeks more of bloom in a sunny window. Plumbago will withstand vigorous pruning, so there is no reason to let your plant get any bigger than you want it. If it does, a new one can easily be obtained from a cutting. It is native to South Africa. (Fig. 72)

PLUME FERN: *Polystichum setiferum proliferum*

POCKETBOOK FLOWER: *Calceolaria crenatiflora*

PODOCARPUS   *Taxaceae*

These subtropical conifers are grown for house plants in their immature stage because of their extreme durability. Slow growing, immune to heat or cold, and a pleasant relief from the large-leaved majority of tropical plants,

Podocarpus takes its place as a specimen plant in many a well-lighted hall-way or porch and in its tiniest stage is a standby for dish gardens.

P. Nagi, from China and Japan, has attractive shining leaves, considerably broader than those of the commonly grown *macrophylla Maki*, from Japan. (Fig. 16)

POINSETTIA: *Euphorbia pulcherrima*

POLYPODIUM: See PHLEBODIUM

POLYSCIAS Balfouriana   *Araliaceae*   ARALIA

In its small stages Polyscias is a pretty foliage plant suitable for dish gar-dens, planters, or north windows. Mature plants are said to reach a height of forty feet in their native Polynesia, but the plant grows so slowly indoors that it is hard to see the change from year to year. The small heart-shaped leaves are low and can be used to camouflage the pots of larger plants. The varie-gated form *marginata* is the most generally available. (Fig. 44)

P. Guilfoylei Victoriae has green and white feathery leaves, giving the plant an airy look. Both species are from the Pacific islands and like tropical temperatures.

POLYSTICHUM   *Polypodiaceae*

This genus of ferns is closely allied to both *Aspidium* and *Dryopteris*, and some of its species are apt to turn up with one of those names.

P. adiantiforme is frequently listed as *capense* or *coriaceum;* but its common name, leather fern, seems to be agreed on by all. It has a furry rhizome very like that of *Polypodium aureum*, and its fronds are bright green and stiff. (Fig. 77)

P. setiferum (aculeatum), the English hedge fern, is able to survive cold or warm temperatures as well as low humidity and overwatering. It puts out tiny new ferns along the edges of its fronds in the summertime. (Fig. 77)

P. setiferum proliferum, the plume fern, a graceful native of Australia, is much more fluffy than the species. (Fig. 77)

P. tsus-sinense (simense) is a small, neat, and most satisfactory fern from Japan. It is noteworthy for its triangular fronds with a bright metallic sheen and for its unusual compactness. (Fig. 77)

POMEGRANATE: *Punica Granatum nana*

PONDEROSA LEMON: *Citrus ponderosa*

PONY TAIL: *Beaucarnea recurvata*

FIG. 77.   *Polystichum tsus-sinense, P. adiantiforme, P. setiferum proliferum, P. setiferum.*

PORTULACARIA afra   *Portulacaceae*   ELEPHANT BUSH

A South African succulent called elephant bush because elephants find it good to eat. It looks like a crassula with underdeveloped leaves and is easy to grow, the only caution being to avoid too much water. *P. afra variegata* is called the rainbow bush. Its leaves are pink, white, and green. It does not grow as fast or as large as the species, but I suppose it is just as attractive to elephants.

POTATO VINE: *Solanum jasminoides*

POTHOS: *Scindapsus aureus*

POWDERPUFF: *Calliandra inaequilatera*

PRAYER PLANT: *Maranta leuconeura Kerchoveana*

PRICKLY PEAR: *Opuntia*

PRIMROSE WILLOW: *Jussiaea longifolia*

PRIMULA   *Primulaceae*   PRIMROSE

To raise winter-flowering primroses you will need a cool place, since temperatures suitable for humans are definitely too high for these plants. If you happen to have a cool porch or an unused guest room with a sunny window, you can enjoy the lovely flowers from Christmas through April or May. The primroses the florists sell as gift plants also need a cool location if they are to last more than a few days.

P. malacoides is the fairy primrose from China. It has small flowers in many colors, including white.

Winter blooming *P. obconica* is much larger, both in leaf and flower. It gives some people a bad skin rash.

PROSTRATE COLEUS: *Plectranthus*

PSEUDERANTHEMUM atropurpureum
Acanthaceae

A purple-leaved, croton-like plant from Polynesia, grown for its colorful maroon foliage. It should be planted in all-purpose soil and grown in a warm but not necessarily sunny window. This species and another similar one, *P. bicolor*, are sometimes sold under their former name *Eranthemum*.

PSIDIUM Cattleianum   *Myrtaceae*   STRAWBERRY GUAVA

The strawberry guava has leathery evergreen leaves, and being a small tree, develops a proper trunk and branches while still in a four-inch pot. In spring, usually after it has been moved outside, it bears homely but fragrant white flowers, some of which eventually form a small, spicy, edible fruit.

Native to Brazil, it was taken to China at an early date and is now cultivated extensively in California and Florida to produce fruits for guava jelly.

Several years ago I grew one from a packet of seeds. It has now outgrown its window sill and has moved to the floor where it sits all winter, requiring practically no care beyond a weekly shower to keep its leaves glistening. Yearly pruning will keep this plant compact and bushy. You may prefer to grow it as a tubbed tree.

PTERIS   *Polypodiaceae*   TABLE FERN
                                        BRAKE FERN

These are the ferns that are used in the center of poinsettia pans to hide the fact that many of the lower leaves of the poinsettias have dropped off—which they always do, even for experts. The names are badly mixed up because of the large number of varieties, and to confuse matters further, *Pellaea* and *Doryopteris* are often called *Pteris* and vice versa. All three grow well in the house, in either sunny or sunless windows and in warm or cool places. Use African violet soil and be generous with your humidifying spray, because all are from the tropics and like moist tropical conditions.

The kinds I am listing here are the most generally available.

FIG. 78. A dish garden planted with *Asparagus Sprengeri* and three kinds of *Peperomia*.

P. adiantoides. See *Pellaea viridis.*

P. cretica is a very graceful form with slender fronds. Variety *albo-lineata* has white variegations. *Cristata* and *Wilsonii* are two more varieties, both with club-shaped fans on the ends of the fronds.

P. ensiformis Victoriae is a pretty, small species with variegated fronds.

P. Parkeri is a stiff fern with somewhat broad leathery leaves.

P. quadriaurita argyraea has whitish variegation on its fronds.

P. tremula, the Australian brake, is one of the most common—not at all distinguished looking, but easy to keep alive. (Fig. 72)

PUNICA Granatum nana   *Punicaceae*   DWARF POMEGRANATE

There is something romantic about having a pomegranate tree blooming on the window sill! This it will do, off and on, all year round if given plenty of sun and not kept too hot and dry. When they do appear, the orange flowers and the fruits that sometimes follow seem almost too big for the plant.

Unlike many house plants, a pomegranate is long-lived and does not need periodic replacement. In a sunny window it is evergreen; if grown on an unheated porch or outdoors—where it is hardy as far north as Washington, D. C.—it is deciduous, but being a tree, looks perfectly natural without its small box-like leaves.

Here is the plant for those interested in bonsai. It has been used by the Chinese for this purpose since very early times. The variety 'Chico,' with double flowers, is a dwarf by nature. (Fig. 79)

Pussy Ears: *Cyanotis somaliensis*

Queen-of-the-Night: *Selenicereus Macdonaldiae*

Queens Wreath: *Petrea volubilis*

Rabbits Foot Fern: *Davallia fejeensis plumosus*

Rainbow Bush: *Portulacaria afra variegata*

REBUTIA species   *Cactaceae*   Crown Cactus

The "crown" part of the common name comes from the way the red flowers appear in a circle around this small flat cactus from the mountains of Argentina. It is among the most satisfactory cacti, as it is one of the few that will flower indoors almost every spring. Keep it cool and dry in winter, and in summer put it outside in full sun, where it will respond to daily watering. A number of attractive species and varieties can be had from any cactus and succulent dealer.

FIG. 79.   *Punica Granatum nana,* a ten-year-old dwarf.

Marjorie Wihtol

RECHSTEINERIA   *Gesneriaceae*

If you have grown gloxinias with any success, you will be able to raise these South American tropicals, for their culture is the same and the results are at least as spectacular. As I write this, I am looking at a magnificent *R. cardinalis* blooming on my sunniest window sill with twenty-three brilliant flowers (aptly described by the plant's former name, *Corytholoma*, meaning "helmet-shaped") and as many fat buds waiting their turn. This plant grew from an onion-like tuber planted in late January; the first flower opened June first, and it will continue blooming until the end of summer. After a short and reasonably dry nap its velvety bright green leaves will show again and the cycle will be repeated. New plants can be had from seeds or cuttings. My plant can be seen in flower in Fig. 14.

R. leucotricha is a recently discovered species which is called Brazilian edelweiss in this country because its leaves and stems, like those of the Alpine edelweiss, are covered with thick gray hairs as a protection against the elements in the plant's habitat on the mountain cliffs of Brazil. (In its native land it is called queen of the cliffs.) The small salmon-colored flowers, during their short life, make a lovely picture when grown on a sunny window sill with blue saintpaulias. My plants never rest, but start putting out new growth before the old dies away.

All grow from tubers, most will, but do not need a rest after flowering, and will not tolerate temperatures below 50° or lack of sun. Mine never go outside in summer. The same south window where they grow in winter, shaded by a fly screen, gives just the combination of light and heat they like.

REDBIRD CACTUS: *Pedilanthus tithymaloides*

RED FLAME IVY: *Hemigraphis colorata*

RED-HOT CAT TAIL: *Acalypha hispida*

REINECKIA carnea   *Liliaceae*   HERB OF FELICITY

A grass-like foliage plant from China and Japan, where its presence around the house is believed to bring luck to the family. If it blooms, which it practically never does indoors, it is considered a good omen for all. This plant is hardy down to about 15°, making it a candidate for an unheated porch or north window. The long thin leaves are bigger than those of mondo grass, with which it is often confused. It grows directly out of a creeping rootstock in compact fan-shaped clumps. (Fig. 80)

REINWARDTIA indica   *Linaceae*   YELLOW FLAX

One grower calls this winter-blooming plant from India yellow petunia, a more descriptive name than yellow flax. Sun and high humidity will keep the golden flowers coming thick and fast from Thanksgiving to Easter. While a cool greenhouse is the best place, many gardeners can achieve a creditable effect in a sunny window. Old plants should be renewed each summer by planting them in the garden and making cuttings from the growth that comes

FIG. 80. *Reineckia carnea, Rhaphidophora celatocaulis, Reinwardtia indica, Rhoeo discolor, Rhipsalis cassutha, R. Houlletiana.*

from the base of the plant after the tops are cut back. Tip cuttings tend to bloom too early and wear themselves out. (Fig. 80)

REX BEGONIA VINE: *Cissus discolor*

RHAPHIDOPHORA celatocaulis   *Araceae*   SHINGLE PLANT

The common name, shingle plant, aptly describes the intriguing arrangement of close-set, overlapping leaves that characterizes this large climbing aroid. In its native Brazil it shingles the trunks of the tropical forest trees, but I have never found a place indoors to use it. (Fig. 80)

RHAPIS excelsa   *Palmaceae*   LADY PALM

Vigorous, reedy, and oriental looking—and as tough as any potted palm I know—the graceful lady palm, from China and Japan, should be used as a house plant much more than it is. It produces suckers from the base and in time makes a fine bushy clump. It needs fertilizing only once in each of the four seasons and seldom requires repotting, as it grows slowly and may take years to reach ten-inch pot size. (Fig. 85)

R. humilis is a species that the Chinese have been growing indoors for years and use for dwarfing—another example of how much we can learn from them about house plants.

RHIPSALIS   *Cactaceae*

Although Rhipsalis is a cactus, it is found in the jungle rather than the desert and accordingly needs high humidity and protection from spring and summer sun like any other jungle plant. It makes a good companion for African violets and begonias. When potting, remember that it grows naturally in the trees of the mountain forests of tropical America and should be given epiphyte mixture.

Quite a number of species of Rhipsalis are sold by cactus growers in California and Texas. Mine bloom reluctantly, but they grow slowly and stay small—an important advantage when your plant collection gets into the hundreds.

R. cassutha is sold as mistletoe cactus. (Fig. 80)

R. Houlletiana, the snowdrop cactus, is like a miniature epiphyllum. (Fig. 80)

R. mesembryanthoides has many small succulent leaves growing from drooping stems.

RHODODENDRON obtusum   *Ericaceae*   INDIAN OR INDICA AZALEA

These large-flowered hybrid azaleas are misnamed Indian, since they do not come from India. Also, they are often confused with *R. indicum*, a hardy species suitable only for growing outside. *R. obtusum*, which will grow indoors, is not hardy in the northeastern United States.

If you do get the proper kind, azaleas will flower on a cool sunporch in late winter or early spring. For several years I have had a plant of the Belgian variety 'Albert and Elizabeth' growing on a sunny window sill, where it almost always has one flower, seldom more. This performance, of course, is a far cry from that the florists achieve with the same plants by keeping them cool for a number of weeks and then warming them considerably to bring them into full flower at Easter. (Fig. 23)

RHOEO spathacea   *Commelinaceae*   MOSES-IN-A-BOAT
(*R. discolor*)

Sometimes listed as *Tradescantia discolor*, Rhoeo is related to the wandering Jews and requires about the same culture, though its habit of growth is more tree-like than the usual wandering Jew. The leaves are green on top and purple beneath, and the little white flowers are born between boat-like bracts through most of the year, giving rise to the common name. It is easy to grow and not dependent on full sun. (Fig. 80)

FIG. 81. *Rubus reflexus pictus, Rohdea japonica, Rosmarinus officinalis.*

RIBBON BUSH: *Homalocladium platycladum*

RIVINA humilis   *Phytolaccaceae*   ROUGE PLANT
                                                     BLOOD BERRY

A small plant from tropical America, delicate in appearance and well suited for a sunny window, where it is everblooming and constantly laden with small bright-red berries. The plant is not difficult to grow and new plants are easily raised from cuttings or by planting the berries in pots. I use all-purpose soil and keep the humidity high. A six-month-old plant can be seen in Fig. 14.

ROHDEA japonica   *Liliaceae*

The orientals have been using this very house-hardy foliage plant for centuries. The Chinese call it the "ten-thousand-year-green," the Japanese "Omoto" or "Mannensei." In Japan, where the plant appears to have as many fanciers as we have African violet collectors, there are hundreds of named varieties. In this country it rarely appears in catalogs, and I know of only one supplier who offers a choice of varieties—identified only by number. The distinguishing characteristic of all of them is stiff, dark, and highly decorative leaves.

Rohdea is hardy as far north as Washington, D. C., and can be put in either a warm or a cold window. New plants can be obtained by cutting up the creeping rootstock. (Fig. 81)

ROSARY VINE: *Ceropegia Woodii*

Rose of China: *Hibiscus Rosa-sinensis*

ROSMARINUS officinalis   *Labiatae*   ROSEMARY

Rosemary, "the dew of the sea," grows naturally on the chalk hills of southern France and along the shores of the Mediterranean and is hardy, but not evergreen, in Philadelphia. It is well suited to a sunny winter window or cool sunporch. While not exactly handsome, its white-backed, needle-like leaves are a pleasant change from other large-leaved tropicals, and they give out a perfumed fragrance when bruised. In spring, tiny blue flowers grow in spikes from the tips of the branches. (Fig. 81)

Royal Velvet Plant: *Gynura aurantiaca*

RUBUS reflexus pictus   *Rosaceae*

The large, star-shaped, velvety leaves of *Rubus reflexus pictus*, with their chocolate veins and almost chartreuse background, are as colorful as some of the rex begonias. This vine-like native of Hong Kong can be grown in any warm place which is well lighted—not necessarily sunny. It thrives on my sunporch in African violet soil, and I suspect it would grow very big if I kept it from year to year, but new plants from cuttings each summer are more compact and better suited to my space. (Fig. 81)

RUELLIA Makoyana   *Acanthaceae*

This small South American plant grows grudgingly and is a favorite host for red spiders. Its pink flowers don't match the color of the foliage; and it is apt to have peculiar-looking spots on its leaves unless it is kept quite warm. Doubtless others have more success with it.

Sage: *Salvia*

Sago Palm: *Cycas revoluta*

SAINTPAULIA   *Gesneriaceae*   AFRICAN VIOLET

I doubt if anyone can keep house for long without trying an African violet or two, for this is the one plant that can be kept in flower the year around in the poor light and other adverse growing situations found in many houses. For those who have trouble making violets "do," I have a few suggestions:

1. Give them all the sun and light you can in winter.
2. Use pots with good drainage and set them on pebble trays to increase humidity. (Fig. 3)
3. Try those varieties with blue, purple, or white flowers first; they are the easiest.
4. Check the night temperature; violets like it warm, never less than 65°.

5. Avoid sudden temperature drops of more than 20°.

6. Remove all side shoots as they appear, and grow your plants with a single crown.

All the hybrids grown today have been developed from nine species found in various parts of Africa. Some of these species add a distinguished note to any collection. They have small blue flowers and are generally less flamboyant than their hybrid offspring. The nicest are:

S. Grotei, the trailing violet, which doesn't bloom much in winter, but is covered with light blue flowers the rest of the year.

S. ionantha, the species most resembling the common conception of an African violet.

S. orbicularis, very dainty and able to stand much cooler temperatures than the others. The flowers are a pale blue.

S. tongwensis, a large and fuzzy violet. Its blue flowers are the largest of the species.

SALVIA   *Labiatae*   SAGE

The Latin name means well or healthy, and while I realize this doesn't necessarily apply to either the plants or those who grow them, it does me good to rub the leaves of the scented kinds in passing. All need sunny windows, cool night temperatures, and all-purpose soil. They grow leggy by the end of winter and should be replaced each fall with new plants made from summer cuttings.

Some of my favorites for indoors are *S. dorisianum*, which has large fragrant leaves and rose pink flowers; *S. leucantha*, from Mexico, which has pure white stems on young plants and gray leaves and purple flowers all year round; *S. microphylla*, the cherry sage, with red flowers; and *S. rutilans*, the fragrant pineapple sage. (Fig. 8)

SALVINIA rotundifolia   *Salviniaceae*

A floating plant from tropical America, for an aquarium or indoor pool. Being a fern ally it does not flower. The separate plants, perhaps a quarter of an inch long and half as wide, are fascinatingly intricate; and the overall effect of a mass of them is like figured velvet. If the water temperature falls below 60°, most of it will die. At higher temperatures it multiplies rapidly.

SANSEVIERIA   *Liliaceae*   SNAKE PLANT

A florist's dish garden without a sansevieria has almost never been made—and no wonder, for there is no tougher plant. Flower arrangers use the stiff, long-lasting leaves to accent their creations, and the alternate common name, bow string hemp, suggests that the plant is also useful to archers. Sansevieria is a native of Africa. All the species I have will grow anywhere in anything.

S. cylindrica has cylindrical dark green leaves.

S. Ehrenbergii is small, bluish, and very slow-growing.

S. Nelsonii has dark green, graceful leaves and is a marked improvement over the usual type.

S. nidus-variegata and *S. Hahnii* are low-growing rosette types.

S. parva, the trailing snake plant, is by far the nicest of the group because it can be grown in a hanging basket. Two or three years may be required to produce the desired trailing effect, but it is worth waiting for. (Fig. 82)

S. trifasciata Laurentii and *S. zeylanica* are the dish garden specials. The first has variegated longitudinal stripes, and the second has zebra bands across the leaves.

SARCOCOCCA ruscifolia   *Buxaceae*

A broad-leaved evergreen, native to China and hardy as far north as Washington, D. C., which you will probably acquire sooner or later in a dish garden. Dig it out, pot it separately, and watch it grow into a pretty, shining,

FIG. 82. *Saxifraga sarmentosa tricolor, S. sarmentosa, Sansevieria parva, Bowiea volubilis, Sarcococca ruscifolia, Schefflera actinophylla*

dark-leaved foliage plant, which will do best in a cool window or an unheated porch. (Fig. 82)

SAXIFRAGA sarmentosa   *Saxifragaceae*   STRAWBERRY BEGONIA
STRAWBERRY GERANIUM

Not a strawberry, a begonia, nor a geranium, it gets the strawberry part of its name from the runners that dart out and produce new plantlets, the geranium part from the general shape of the leaves, the begonia from the colorful white veins on the foliage. It is a pretty plant for growing in a basket or trailing over the edge of a window sill. (Fig. 82)

The variety *tricolor* is often called 'Magic Carpet' because of the red and white effect of the variegated leaves. It is much harder to grow and at best stands still all winter. If you see a large plant, you can be sure it is old and has been carefully tended. The genus is native to China and Japan. (Fig. 82)

SCHEFFLERA actinophylla   *Araliaceae*   AUSTRALIAN UMBRELLA TREE

The big commercial growers are offering Schefflera in increasing numbers, often as tree-like specimens several feet high planted in cedar tubs. The umbrella-shaped clusters of leaves are highly decorative, and in a light place the plant will survive for months with a minimum of attention.

If you buy a plant one foot high in a four-inch pot, you can expect it to grow about six inches a year, particularly if you put it outside in partial shade in the summer. All-purpose soil is the kind I use. (Fig. 82)

SCHIZOCENTRON elegans   *Melastomaceae*   SPANISH SHAWL

Growing naturally in the mountains of Mexico, this small-leaved trailer can stand dry conditions but needs sun to produce flowers and to keep from getting stringy. It is a good basket plant for a cool window. The flowers, which appear in late winter and continue through the spring and summer, are vivid purply-pink.

If you have a Schizocentron, it should go into your summer garden, where it will make a colorful carpet until fall. Take cuttings in early August for next winter's plants. (Fig. 48)

SCHLUMBERGERA Bridgesii   *Cactaceae*   EASTER CACTUS
CRAB CACTUS

This cactus is often confused with the very similar Christmas cactus, *Zygocactus truncatus*. A distinguishing characteristic is the sharp teeth on the stems, which are present in Zygocactus but not in Schlumbergera. Of the two, Schlumbergera is much more commonly grown.

Both are epiphytes found in the Brazilian jungle and admirably suited for growing in a hanging basket. They do well in osmunda fiber, or with sphagnum moss packed around the roots, or in any light, well-drained soil. Like most jungle plants, they need high temperature and high humidity, a sunny window in winter and partial shade in summer. Pieces of the stem root easily and will produce blooming plants in about two years.

Appropriately, Zygocactus blooms about Christmas and Schlumbergera a few weeks later. The flowers of Schlumbergera are bright red or purple in color and irregular in shape. Both genera are short-day plants, which means that they need at least ten hours of darkness in the fall to set buds for winter blooming. They will not flower satisfactorily in a room where the lights go on at dusk and stay on till bedtime.

SCINDAPSUS   *Araceae*   POTHOS
DEVILS IVY

The true *Pothos* is a trailing oriental plant, not readily available in this country. Scindapsus, almost universally miscalled pothos, is a somewhat similar plant from the Solomon Islands. It requires about the same treatment as philodendron—warmth and regular watering—and will stand at least as much abuse.

S. aureus (*Rhaphidophora aurea*), the most common, has leaves with yellow variegation. The slower growing variety 'Marble Queen' has white variegation and is brighter. They need very little light and will even grow for considerable time on a mantelpiece in water. (Fig. 92)

S. pictus argyraeus, commonly called ivy arum, is much more difficult to grow well. It seems to need higher humidity and cannot stand temperatures below 60°. It has velvety green leaves spotted and edged with silver. Both species will stick to totem poles or bark. (Fig. 16)

SEDUM   *Crassulaceae*   STONECROP

The name comes from the Latin *sedere*, to sit, which is a fitting description for these low, succulent plants. While most familiar in rock gardens, they are also suited to growing indoors in hanging pots or baskets of one kind or another. All need as much sun as possible and grow best in cool or cold places. There are a great many kinds and I am sure that most of them can be grown under glass. My favorites for indoor growing are:

S. dasyphyllum, which has tiny swollen blue leaves. (Fig. 24)

S. lineare and *lineare variegatum*, with small almost needle-like leaves.

S. Morganianum, called burro tail, an amazing blue-gray trailer with pink flowers in spring and summer. (Fig. 83)

S. pachyphyllum, another blue one which does not seem to require so much sun.

S. rubrotinctum (*guatemalense*), known as Christmas cheer, with fat green leaves that turn quite red in bright sun.

S. Stahlii, a miniature plant with green, slow-growing leaves.

SEERSUCKER PLANT: *Geogenanthus undatus*

SELAGINELLA   *Selaginellaceae*   CLUB MOSS

These fern allies will not live except in continuously moist conditions. They do well in terrariums or in a warm greenhouse where they can be shaded from all but the winter sun.

S. Kraussiana Brownii, native to the Azores, makes bright green mossy cushions. It is the toughest of the group.

S. pallescens (*Emmeliana*), the most commonly seen, has no really striking features. Other species are no more difficult to grow and are much more interesting.

FIG. 83.   *Sedum Morganianum.*

S. uncinata and *S. Willdenovii* are an unbelievable shade of blue. The latter has a distinct stem and is classed as a climber. The former, also called the

FIG. 84.   *Selaginella uncinata.*

rainbow moss, from China, creeps and roots wherever it touches anything moist. I grew it last winter in a terrarium on a side table which was in the shade all day and received only the light from a 75-watt incandescent lamp in the evening. It grew well and was a beautiful color. (Fig. 84)

SELENICEREUS   *Cactaceae*   NIGHT-BLOOMING CEREUS

These night-blooming epiphytes from the jungles of South America have angled trailing or climbing stems and bear their large fragrant flowers on summer nights. During the long months when they are not in bloom, they have little to recommend them, and few window gardeners can spare the room to accommodate them. *S. Macdonaldiae*, listed as queen-of-the-night, is the most commonly seen.

SENECIO   *Compositae*

Senecio is one of the largest genera of plants, with over 12,000 species in all parts of the world. *S. confusus*, the Mexican flame vine, is one of the best for house culture. The shoots are inclined to twine, but plants can be kept bushy by frequent pinching. Flaming orange daisies, with their petals pushed

FIG. 85. *Senecio confusus, Rhapis excelsa.*

backwards, appear from January on if the plants are grown in the full sun of a south window. (Fig. 85)

S. cruentus, from the Canary Islands, is the parent of the cinerarias that florists raise each year by the thousands in 45° to 50° greenhouses and sell at Easter time. Needless to say, the change from that atmosphere to your 70° house is too much for any plant. If you have a cool greenhouse, try them from seed by all means, but forget them as something to raise in your living room.

S. mikanioides, a native of South Africa, called parlor or German ivy, is a traditional house plant that is easy and pretty. It resembles ivy but has much thinner leaves. Don't try to grow it in a north window, but any other exposure will do. (Fig. 16)

S. Petasitis, another Mexican species, is called the California or velvet geranium and is a good plant for a cool greenhouse or sunroom, as it bears its yellow daisies in winter. Renew your plant each spring from rooted cuttings and grow it to six-inch pot size by October, when it will begin flowering.

S. scaposus is an attractive succulent. There is quite a group of succulent Senecios, mostly native to the dry parts of South Africa.

SENSITIVE PLANT: *Mimosa pudica*

SERISSA foetida variegata   *Rubiaceae*

This is a nice small plant from Southeast Asia, resembling a boxwood with yellow-margined leaves. It can be exposed to warm or cool temperatures in winter and does not need sun. Don't be frightened by the species name. The "fetid" odor comes only when the stems are bruised and is then barely discernible. A small one is used in the dish garden shown in Fig. 44.

SETCREASEA   *Commelinaceae*   WANDERING JEW

This is easy to grow, like other wandering Jews. All members of this family will survive in the shade, but good light is necessary for compactness, and even in a sunny place you must pinch them back frequently if you want a really bushy plant.

S. purpurea, variety 'Purple Heart,' is a larger-leaved variety with lavender leaves. (Fig. 89)

S. striata is the striped inch plant.

SHINGLE PLANT: *Rhaphidophora celatocaulis*

SHRIMP PLANT: *Beloperone guttata*

SILK OAK: *Grevillea robusta*

SINNINGIA   *Gesneriaceae*   GLOXINIA

This is an exciting group of tuberous-rooted gesneriads, some of which have been discovered only in the last twenty years. Under natural conditions in the mountains and jungles of South America they do their growing and bear their tubular flowers in the spring and summer, but gloxinia fanciers succeed in inducing them to grow and flower indoors at almost any season.

Gloxinias like well drained African violet soil, temperatures not less than 60°, and a sunny exposure except in summer. Without enough light they are leggy and their leaves curl. When growth stops, gradually withhold water until the soil is practically dry, then store in a warm place, watering occasionally to keep the tuber from drying out. When new growth starts repot in fresh soil—covering the tuber completely and leaving only the new sprout exposed—and bring it back to the light. Sometimes dormancy lasts for a few days, sometimes for several months.

Sinningia can be propagated like African violets from leaf petioles, or from seed.

S. eumorpha (formerly called *Maximiliana*) has a smooth orange tuber, rather shiny corrugated leaves, and large white flowers which, like those of most of the species, are the down-turned kind known as "slippers." Mine blooms four to five months at a time.

S. pusilla is the smallest gesneriad under cultivation. I keep one in the kitchen garden shown in Fig. 13, the only site small enough for its tiny leaves and delicate lavender flowers, no bigger than the end of your little finger.

S. regina has purple slipper flowers and beautiful, velvety, olive leaves with purple backs. It has a long season of bloom, sometimes as much as six months. (Fig. 16)

S. speciosa, usually called blue slipper, is one of the parents of the florist's gloxinia. It is very like *S. regina* but the leaves are not as striking.

While there is one species that is correctly called Gloxinia (namely *G. perennis*), the name is almost universally applied to Sinningia hybrids, new varieties of which appear constantly. The most popular of these hybrids are characterized by upright flowers which may be almost any shade of blue, purple, pink, or white, or a combination. A recent authoritative text gives them the name 'Fyfiana Group.'

I have often been disappointed by the decline of healthy flowering or budded greenhouse gloxinias when they are brought into the house. In contrast, plants that are grown in the house from the start, in a window or under fluorescent lights, seldom fail; and many of them, particularly the slipper types, refuse to go dormant and start sprouting new growth before the old is through.

SKY FLOWER: *Thunbergia grandiflora*

SLIPPER GLOXINIA: *Sinningia speciosa*

SMILAX: *Asparagus asparagoides*

SMITHIANTHA   *Gesneriaceae*   TEMPLE BELLS

The gesneriads have recently undergone a thorough overhauling by the taxonomists. In the process the name of this native of the Mexican mountains was changed from *Naegelia* to *Smithiantha*. Its dark red or purple leaves, with the texture of plush, provide a spot of color during the summer and fall; and its exquisite bell-shaped blooms last from November through February.

I grow Smithiantha on an east or south window sill, using African violet soil and pots from two and a quarter to four inches in diameter, depending on the number of rhizomes. When dormancy begins, I store the small scaly rhizomes in plastic bags in a warm place for the duration of their dormant period, generally two or three months. They are sometimes slow to start again, but placement in a warm, sunny place will usually bring them to life.

S. cinnabarina has red flowers spotted with white, and those of *S. zebrina* are red and yellow. There are also a number of hybrids on the market. Both species and hybrids are noteworthy for their dark textured leaves, beautifully marked with red and green. All need more light than African violets, but like the same soils and temperatures. (Fig. 86)

SNAKE PLANT: *Sansevieria*

SNOWDROP CACTUS: *Rhipsalis Houlletiana*

FIG. 86.   *Smithiantha zebrina.*

SOLANUM   *Solanaceae*

These Brazilian relatives of the potato (whose botanical name is *Solanum tuberosum*) and the eggplant are old favorites. Plants bought from a florist have been grown in a cool greenhouse and are apt to deteriorate when brought into the house, but plants raised in pots from seed sown in the spring can be successfully brought indoors early in September after their fruit is set and before the furnace goes on. If they are kept as cool as possible and given plenty of sun, they should keep their fruit all winter.

S. pseudo-capsicum is the Jerusalem cherry. If possible, get seeds of the dwarf variety *Pattersonii*. There are many other varieties and hybrid forms.

I am going to try *S. jasminoides*, the potato vine, soon. It is said to be a fine climber with fragrant flowers, and to be well-adapted to a cool greenhouse or sunporch.

SPANISH MOSS: *Tillandsia usneoides*

SPATHIPHYLLUM   *Araceae*

Often called white anthuriums, these aroids from South America are easier to handle in the house than their red-flowered cousins. They need a light soil (African violet or begonia mixture), plenty of water and humidity, temperatures of not less than 60°, good light in winter, and shade in summer.

S. Clevelandii has long, thin, shiny leaves and bears its white flowers freely from March to November. This plant gets big in time, but can be divided to make small plants. During its semi-dormancy in late fall and early winter, I water it less frequently. (Fig. 16)

S. floribundum is small, has dull green leaves, and is never without one or more white flowers.

SPIDER PLANT: *Chlorophytum*

SPIRONEMA fragrans   *Commelinaceae*

A large-leaved Mexican cousin of the wandering Jew, admirably suited to growing in baskets or on roomy window sills. Vigorous, bug-resistant, easy to grow, and attractive, it seemingly enjoys any soil and any temperature, will thrive in a bright window, and will also do well without sun. (Fig. 92)

SPLEENWORT: *Asplenium*

STAGHORN FERN: *Platycerium bifurcatum*

STAPELIA   *Asclepiadaceae*   STARFISH

South Africa produces these succulent plants of the milkweed family, which can be hung in a window or used to decorate a shelf. They will grow without direct sun but will not flower except in full sunlight. The five-petalled flowers account for the common name.

S. gigantea is aptly called the carrion flower. Flies will come from miles around to lay their eggs in its enormous evil-smelling blossom. A good plant to avoid bringing into flower indoors.

S. hirsuta, the hairy starfish, is the nicest one I have.

S. variegata is a smaller plant, and the odor of its flowers is not nearly so offensive. A number of species and varieties are available with flowers in different shades of red, purple, and brown. (Fig. 50)

STAR CACTUS: *Astrophytum*

STAR CLUSTERS: *Pentas lanceolata*

STARFISH: *Stapelia*

STAR JASMINE: *Trachelospermum jasminoides*

STAR OF BETHLEHEM: *Campanula isophylla*

ST. AUGUSTINE GRASS: *Stenotaphrum secundatum*

STENANDRIUM Lindenii   *Acanthaceae*

Stenandrium is another member of the acanthus family, producer of so many fine house plants. Small and slow-growing, it is valued primarily for its dark green, corrugated leaves marked with lighter areas around the veins, and for its ground-hugging habit of growth. The small yellow spikes of flowers, which appear off and on throughout the year, are an extra attraction.

Stenandrium is a tropical plant from Peru, needing African violet soil, good light, warmth, and plenty of moisture, both at the roots and in the air. A small plant is growing in the planting box shown in Fig. 15.

STENOCHLEANA palustris   *Polypodiaceae*

This, like so many tropical ferns, is epiphytic. It grows naturally upon a rocky outcrop or high in a tree, rather than with its roots in the ground. In big conservatories it is often encountered climbing up the trunks of the trees, where its brown, hairy rhizomes can be clearly seen. I grow it in a wooden planter six feet long. Each summer I move the box outside into the shade of tall trees, prune the old fronds away and cut back the creeping rhizomes. By September the new growth is well under way. It continues without abatement until the following summer.

STENOTAPHRUM secundatum variegatum
Gramineae   ST. AUGUSTINE GRASS
BUFFALO GRASS

A visitor from the South might not recognize this familiar ground cover in its variegated form. A tougher plant probably does not exist. It makes an attractive hanging basket, lacking pretty flowers, of course, but not at all demanding about heat or humidity. Like all grasses, it must have good light— direct sun if possible—and must be cut now and then. (Fig. 87)

STEPHANOTIS floribunda   *Asclepiadaceae*   MADAGASCAR JASMINE

No sunroom is complete without a Stephanotis vine. It is easy to grow; its leathery, dark green leaves look well all year; and in June, July, and August it bears clusters of exquisitely scented white flowers. A pleasing effect can be achieved by allowing one or two shoots to wind up a piece of string along with a shoot or two of *Asparagus plumosus*. Give the plants a winter rest by watering less often, and grow them at 60° for best results. (Fig. 72)

STRAWBERRY BEGONIA: *Saxifraga sarmentosa*

STRAWBERRY GUAVA: *Psidium Cattleianum*

STRELITZIA Reginae   *Musaceae*   BIRD OF PARADISE

The lovely blue and orange flower of the bird of paradise is familiar to all, but few realize that the plants themselves are tough and good looking. The large, blue-gray, banana-like leaves spring from a thick root stock. Flowers appear in the summer and fall on plants sufficiently mature to have produced ten or more leaves. They can spend the winter in any sunny place, provided the temperature does not fall below 50°, and in summer can go outside in light shade. The plant is native to South Africa. One is shown in Fig. 23.

STREPTOCARPUS   *Gesneriaceae*   CAPE PRIMROSE

Most of the varieties of Streptocarpus grown on window sills are hybrids from a number of species native to South Africa and Madagascar, and this is one gesneriad that can be grown at temperatures as low as 50°. Its other requirements are about the same as for all members of this family—good drainage, a loose, airy growing medium, and plenty of sun in winter. The large gloxinia-like blossoms are held high above the flat, rather coarse foliage.

S. Rexii is the best known species and is commonly called Cape primrose.

FIG. 87. *Stenotaphrum secundatum variegatum, Streptocarpus Rexii.*

It has pale blue flowers. I also have very large hybrid plants with pink, blue, white, and purple flowers. They are easy to propagate from seed (ten months to flower), leaf cuttings, or divisions, and they have no apparent dormant season. (Fig. 87)

S. saxorum is a much smaller plant than the Cape primrose. Its small dark green leaves form clusters around its trailing stem. The flowers are white and pale lavender. Like its robust cousins, it is everblooming and evergrowing.

STREPTOSOLEN Jamesonii   *Solanaceae*   ORANGE BROWALLIA

The endearing trait of this trailing plant is that it blooms in winter rather than in summer. Its main requirement is a place that receives direct sunlight four hours or more each day and gets cool enough at night to remind the Streptosolen of its native mountains in Colombia and Ecuador—55° is ideal. Raise new plants from seed or cuttings each summer, or cut your old plants back severely, prune their roots, repot them, and summer them in a partially shaded place. All-purpose soil is the best growing medium. (Fig. 90)

STRIPED INCH PLANT: *Setcreasea striata*

STROBILANTHES   *Acanthaceae*

Good house plants for a warm sunny place if the humidity is not too low. *S. Dyerianus*, from India, is grown for its foliage, generally purple in color with tinges of silver (Fig. 88). *S. isophyllus*, also from India, looks entirely different; it has long thin leaves and bears small, pale lavender flowers in profusion all winter. Never try to keep these plants more than one season; old ones are woody and not nearly as satisfactory as new plants made from spring and summer cuttings. (Fig. 92)

SURINAM CHERRY: *Eugenia uniflora*

SWEET ALYSSUM: *Lobularia maritima*

SWISS CHEESE PLANT: *Monstera deliciosa*

SYNGONIUM   *Araceae*   NEPHTHYTIS

Resistant to drought and bugs and easy to grow, these trailing or climbing plants are an excellent substitute for philodendron in north windows, on the mantle piece, and in other inhospitable circumstances.

S. podophyllum is the very common arrow-shaped green trailer. The variety 'Imperial White' is small, slow growing, and brightly variegated.

S. Wendlandii is also variegated, small, and slow growing, with satiny dark green leaves decorated with light markings along the veins. Young plants are well suited for a coffee table or dish garden. There are several other species and varieties on the market.

All syngoniums are native to Central and South America, but will tolerate practically any indoor temperature and grow in any soil. They are occasionally confused with philodendrons but can be identified by the presence of milky juice in the stem. Having an aversion to stringy vines, I cut my plants back hard in June so they will put out compact new growth to start the indoor year. (Fig. 88)

TABLE FERN: *Pteris*

FIG. 88. *Tetrapathaea tetrandra, Tillandsia ionantha, Talinum patens variegatum, Tibouchina semidecandra, Strobilanthes Dyerianus, Thunbergia alata, Syngonium Wendlandii, S. podophyllum* 'Imperial White,' *S. podophyllum, Tacca Chantrieri.*

TACCA Chantrieri   *Taccaceae*   BAT PLANT
                                                   DEVIL FLOWER

In the spring and summer this peculiar plant bears black flowers which look like something out of a Charles Addams cartoon and account for its common names. A curious item for a collector, but otherwise not worth the space it takes up. Being a native of the Malayan jungles, it needs high heat and humidity and grows best in African violet or begonia soil. Many dealers selling the bat plant list it wrongly as *T. cristata,* the name of a similar but separate species. (Fig. 88)

TALINUM patens variegatum   *Portulacaceae*   FAME FLOWER

This native of the southern United States is a good house plant as it will grow without much sun, and being succulent, will also withstand a hot, dry atmosphere. The leaves resemble those of the variegated wax plant, with pink and green markings. To my way of thinking, it is better to keep the plant bushy by pruning the flower stalks and the top growth, than to let it get leggy in order to preserve the blooms, which are small and insignificant. It is easy to grow and will do well in almost any bright window. (Fig. 88)

TARO: *Colocasia antiquorum*

TEMPLE BELLS: *Smithiantha*

Tetranema: See *Allophyton*

TETRAPATHAEA tetrandra   *Passifloraceae*

A miniature passion vine from New Zealand whose green and white flowers, while by no means spectacular, are pretty and freely born from spring through fall. Like other passion vines, this one has tendrils which clutch anything at hand. Since new plants flower just as well as old ones, I make cuttings in summer and thus renew my plant every year or so. (Fig. 88)

THUNBERGIA   *Acanthaceae*

Another member of the wonderful acanthus family, but this time with single flowers instead of spikes. I consider Thunbergia indispensable for a sunroom or sunny window. It is not particular as to temperatures between 50° and 70°.

T. alata, the black-eyed Susan, is a small twining vine with black-eyed yellow-orange or white flowers, which it bears at all seasons. It is easy to propagate either from seeds, which can be harvested from your vines in the summer, or from cuttings taken in late winter, spring, or summer. I make new plants each year. This species is native to tropical Africa. (Fig. 88)

T. erecta, also from tropical Africa, is a shrub with small dark green leaves. The flowers are deep blue with yellow throats, and appear at all seasons except the darkest part of the winter.

T. grandiflora, the sky flower, from northern India, is a large twining vine with four-inch pale blue flowers appearing in winter but never in summer. It always causes comment in the greenhouse. I have not yet tried it in the house, but see no reason why it should not bloom in my sunniest window.

TIBOUCHINA semidecandra   *Melastomaceae*   GLORY BUSH
EMPRESS FLOWER

Tibouchina, a native of Brazil, is only fairly satisfactory for indoor growing as it bears its short-lived, purple, clematis-shaped flowers only in summer and fall. However, the velvety pale green leaves always look attractive. Put your Tibouchina in the garden for the summer and make cuttings in August for fall bloom indoors. In winter grow them in the coolest, sunniest place you have. They are leggy plants and need constant pinching and pruning. (Fig. 88)

Tiger Jaws: *Faucaria tigrina*

TILLANDSIA   *Bromeliaceae*

This genus of bromeliads contains one of the most beautiful plants I know, one of the cutest, and one of the most familiar. They are *T. Lindeniana*, a hazy purple pitcher type from Peru with a gorgeous blue inflorescence; *T. ionantha*, a dwarf from Mexico also with a blue flower; and *T. usneoides*, the Spanish moss that festoons trees all over the south. The first two grow well in the house in osmunda fiber, fir bark, or epiphyte soil mixture, if they are sprayed regularly to keep the humidity high. Spanish moss seems happier in the dampness of the greenhouse, where it lives but does not grow much. (Fig. 88)

Ti Plant: *Cordyline terminalis*

TOLMIEA Menziesii   *Saxifragaceae*   Piggy-back Plant

A hardy ground-covering creeper found growing naturally from Alaska to California. New plants ride piggy-back on old leaves to give this plant its common name. It is fine for either a sunny or a sunless window indoors, where it remains evergreen. It is not at all particular; just don't let it get too hot and dry. (Fig. 89)

Tom Thumb Cactus: *Parodia aureispina*

TRACHELOSPERMUM jasminoides
Apocynaceae   Confederate Jasmine
Star Jasmine

This is a Chinese twining vine with small, dark, leathery leaves. When grown in a sunny place it bears fragrant, white or yellow, star-shaped flowers in all but the darkest of the winter months. It can be pinched so as to need no support, or allowed to wind around a trellis. At temperatures below 50° the leaves become chlorotic and the plant stops growing. Pot Trachelospermum in all-purpose soil and propagate from cuttings in the spring and summer. It takes about two years to produce a plant large enough for a four-inch pot. (Fig. 89)

TRADESCANTIA   *Commelinaceae*   Wandering Jew

There are many species and varieties of this easy trailing plant. All are native to Central and South America, where they clamber over the forest floor and in and around stumps and bushes. They do well indoors in any exposure or temperature and in almost any potting soil, but plants grown in the sun are much more highly colored and bushier than those grown in the shade.

T. Blossfeldiana is, true to its name, a riotous spring and summer bloomer.

T. fluminensis is the common all-green variety, with white flowers, and *fluminensis variegata* is the nice green and creamy white variety.

T. laekenensis is a particularly attractive variegated species with leaves of green and white tinged with pink. (Fig. 89)

T. multiflora is a charming miniature with white flowers. It will overrun your window garden if given half a chance.

T. navicularis is a succulent wandering Jew with thick, drought-resistant leaves.

FIG. 89. *Setcreasea purpurea, Tradescantia laekenensis, Tulbaghia fragrans, Trachelospermum jasminoides, Tradescantia fluminensis variegata, Tropaeolum majus, Tolmiea Menziesii.*

TROPAEOLUM majus   *Tropaeolaceae*   NASTURTIUM

The common nasturtium, from Mexico and Chile, will bloom all winter in a cool sunporch or sunny window. The dwarf varieties are better suited for growing in pots, but whichever kind you choose, be sure to propagate new plants from seeds or cuttings in the summertime. Pot them in all-purpose soil and expect to pick off brown leaves every few days. (Fig. 89)

TREVESIA palmata   *Araliaceae*

In Southern China and India this very large-leaved tree grows to 15 feet. It does well as a pot plant, and its deeply cut leaves, up to two feet across, make it a real curiosity.

Sun and cool temperatures are desirable. The stem is spiny, and the new leaves have feltlike protective covering.

TULBAGHIA   *Liliaceae*

Two evergreen bulbs, one worth growing and one not worth the effort.

T. fragrans is commonly called pink agapanthus. Its pale green, narcissus-like leaves always look well, and if grown in the sun, it blooms off and on all year round, bearing pale lavender umbels of exquisite fragrance. (Fig. 89)

The common name of *T. violacea* is society garlic. Perhaps that is comment enough.

UMBRELLA PLANT: *Cyperus alternifolius*

VARIEGATED OAT GRASS: *Arrhenatherum elatius bulbosum*

VELTHEIMIA viridifolia   *Liliaceae*

When grown in a sunny window, these bulbous plants from South Africa produce large shiny green leaves in a graceful rosette. Flower buds appear in early fall and develop with tantalizing slowness until finally, around Christmas time, a pink fountain of flowers emerges and lasts for several weeks. A two- or three-week dry summer rest is essential for flower production. If the plant is not rested, it will stay green but probably will not bloom. (Fig. 90)

VELVET PLANT: *Gynura aurantiaca*

VERBENA peruviana   *Verbenaceae*   PERUVIAN FLAME VERBENA

The common name of this trailing plant aptly describes the flowers. It makes a fine basket plant for a sunny window garden. Cuttings should be made in spring for garden plants and again in August for winter house plants. Pot them in all-purpose soil and keep the plants neat and bushy by occasional pinching.

The common garden verbenas I have tried under glass did not begin to

FIG. 90. *Veltheimia viridifolia, Vinca major, Wedelia trilobata, Vriesia carinata* 'Marie,' *Verbena peruviana, Peristrophe salicifolia aureo-variegata, Streptosolen Jamesonii.*

bloom until February, but the Peruvian flame flowers without regard to season. (Fig. 90)

Veronica: See *Hebe*

VINCA major   *Apocynaceae*

Vinca major, a non-hardy European plant which is not be to confused with its hardy ground-covering cousin, *Vinca minor*, is most often encountered trailing out of summer window boxes. It needs more light and humidity and cooler temperatures than are generally available in the house. A row of small pots, each with three rooted cuttings of *Vinca major* in its variegated form, makes a pretty border for a cool sun room bench. (Fig. 90)

VRIESIA   *Bromeliaceae*

South American epiphytic bromeliads, the aristocrats of the family. Like their cousins, the Billbergias, they have "pitchers" (rosettes of leaves) which must be kept full of water. They grow best for me in osmunda fiber or fir bark and must have some sun if they are to bloom. Each pitcher will flower once in its life, the flower lasting from four to six months. Suckers then appear around the base of the plant, and the old part dies and must eventually be cut away. Each sucker will make a new plant.

V. carinata 'Marie' is a hybrid well worth the substantial price you will have to pay for it. Its leaves are plain green, but its flat yellow and red inflorescence is one you can't forget. (Fig. 90)

V. fenestralis is another fascinating species. It has transversely striped leaves, though not as pronounced as those of *V. splendens*, described below.

V. splendens, the flaming sword, is expensive and beautiful. It does not sucker like the others, but instead produces a new plant in its own center. Its leaves have bizarre, black, transverse stripes.

WANDERING JEW: *Tradescantia, Zebrina pendula*

WATER LETTUCE: *Pistia Stratiotes*

WATER POPPY: *Hydrocleys nymphoides*

WATER SNOWFLAKE: *Nymphoides aquatica*

WAX PLANT: *Hoya carnosa*

WEDELIA trilobata   *Compositae*

A bright ground cover from tropical America with yellow daisies from May to November. It is useful to edge a greenhouse walk or cover a ground bed because it roots anywhere the stems touch ground. It is also suitable for use in a hanging basket or as a trailing window plant. Wedelia should be grown in full sun and pruned back from time to time. It is not particular about temperature. Fast growing plants like these, which are easy to root from cuttings taken in spring and summer, should be renewed frequently. (Fig. 90)

WIRE VINE: *Muehlenbeckia complexa*

WOOD SORREL: *Oxalis*

WOODWARDIA   *Polypodiaceae*   Chain Fern

Woodwardia fimbriata and *W. orientalis* can be grown in a north, east, or west exposure. Their medium-broad fronds are rather stiff and leathery and make a pleasant contrast to the airiness of ferns like the maidenhairs. Mature plants will soon be too big for a window sill. Pot *Woodwardia* in the mixture recommended for African violets and be careful not to overwater them when new fronds are not uncurling. (Fig. 91)

XANTHOSOMA   *Araceae*

X. Lindenii magnificum, the species most commonly available, is a stemless plant from South America requiring high temperature and humidity to produce its beautifully marked green and white foliage. If the thermometer falls below 65°, the plant will drop its leaves entirely and go into protesting dor-

FIG. 91. *Woodwardia orientalis, Xanthosoma violaceum, Schlumbergera Bridgesii, Zebrina pendula, Zingiber officinale, Xanthosoma Lindenii magnificum.*

mancy. New plants can be made by dividing the tuberous underground stem in the summer. Each piece containing an "eye" will grow. (Fig. 91)

X. violaceum can stand lower temperatures. The leaves are a deep smoky green with purple edges. The petioles, which emerge directly from the bulb, are purple. I have grown this plant with the pot immersed in water with good results. (Fig. 91)

Neither species needs sun, but both require good light for the best growth. Both should be planted in African violet mixture in a pot only slightly larger than the tuber or bulb.

YELLOW FLAX: *Reinwardtia indica*

ZEBRINA pendula   *Commelinaceae*   WANDERING JEW

This native of Mexico is but one of several plants called wandering Jew. The flat leaves are striped with silver and purple on the upper side and are solid purple beneath. Reddish-purple flowers appear in spring and summer if the plants get enough sun, and the coloring of the leaves is brighter if they can see the light, but the plant will survive almost anywhere. Soil mixtures are not important, and tip cuttings are frequently seen growing happily in water. (Fig. 91)

FIG. 92. *Strobilanthes isophyllus, Scindapsus aureus, Spironema fragrans, Kohleria amabilis* 'Cecilia,' *Strobilanthes Dyerianus, Scindapsus aureus* 'Marble Queen.'

ZINGIBER officinale   *Zingiberaceae*   CANTON GINGER

Candied ginger is made from the fleshy roots of Zingiber, which is otherwise undistinguished except by its toughness. The plant, which looks a little like bamboo, has a predilection for a midwinter rest, during which it can be virtually forgotten, and even in its growing season it can be left without water for a considerable time. On the other hand, it seems just as impervious to overwatering. It must have warmth at all times. Its equally long-suffering relative, *Amomum Cardamon*, is bushier and somewhat more attractive. Zingiber grows naturally on the Pacific Islands. (Fig. 91)

ZYGOCACTUS truncatus   *Cactaceae*   CRAB CACTUS
CHRISTMAS CACTUS

See discussion under *Schlumbergera Bridgesii*.

Appendices

PLANTS FOR VARIOUS EXPOSURES AND TEMPERATURES

Many people who garden indoors want to know at a glance what plants to try in the particular conditions they have; so I have listed here the plants I have found satisfactory when only certain exposures and temperatures are available. However, there are wide differences between different species—and even between different strains and varieties of the same species—in capacity to withstand adverse conditions. The fact that two plants are included in the same list does not mean that both will react the same way to the same conditions. All the plants in the lists are described in Part III, and you should refer to the description there before deciding on any of them.

No doubt there are those whose experience with certain plants has been different from mine and who would disagree with some of my listings. It may be that they live in a different latitude or a different climate—both of which have a great effect on plant growth. Also, no two windows are alike as far as all the factors affecting growth are concerned, and no two gardeners apply their horticultural skill in the same way. These lists are intended only as guides. If a plant does not do well for you in one location, by all means try it in another.

If you live in the northern part of the country, you will find that all the plants, even those listed for sunless north windows, will grow best if they have sun in the winter months, from October to March. Later in the year the jungle plants will need protection from the strong rays of the noonday sun.

NIGHT TEMPERATURE OF 50° TO 60°

These plants do best where the night temperature is between 50° and 60°. However, many will survive temperatures as low as 45° for considerable periods, and most will grow satisfactorily at temperatures above 60° if the relative humidity is 25 percent or higher.

239

At least five hours of winter sun needed for flowers and best growth

Abutilon
Acacia
Acalypha
Adromischus
Aeonium
Allophyton
Arrhenatherum
Bougainvillea
Cactus
Campanula
Capsicum
Centradenia
Cephalocereus
Cestrum
Citrus
Coleus
Cotyledon
Cuphea
Cymbalaria
Diplacus
Drosanthemum
Echeveria
Exacum
Felicia

Fuchsia
Gazania
Graptopetalum
Heliotropium
Iboza
Impatiens
Iresine
Jasmine
Lampranthus
Lippia
Lobularia
Lotus
Mahernia
Mammillaria
Manettia
Nepeta
Nicotiana
Ochna
Oplismenus
Osmanthus
Oxalis
Oxypetalum
Pachyphytum
Pachyveria

Pandorea
Passiflora
Pelargonium
Pentas
Pereskia
Plumbago
Primula
Reinwardtia
Rivina
Salvia
Schizocentron
Sedum
Senecio
Solanum
Streptocarpus
Streptosolen
Tetrapathaea
Thunbergia
Tibouchina
Tropaeolum
Tulbaghia
Verbena
Vinca
Wedelia

At least two hours of winter sun needed for flowers and best growth

Acanthostachys
Aechmea
Agave
Aloe
Asparagus
Astrophytum
Billbergia
Bowiea
Camellia
Carissa
Ceropegia
Clivia
Crassula
Cyanotis
Cyclamen

Eugenia
Eurya
Gasteria
Greigia
Hebe
Helxine
Kalanchoe
Kleinia
Michelia
Muehlenbeckia
Musa
Myrtus
Narcissus
Neomarica

Nerium
Opuntia
Othonna
Pedilanthus
Psidium
Punica
Rhododendron
Rosmarinus
Stenotaphrum
Strelitzia
Talinum
Tillandsia
Veltheimia
Vriesia
Zingiber

North light sufficient during winter months

Acorus	Euonymus	Reineckia
Adiantum	Hedera	Rhapis
Araucaria	Hoya	Rohdea
Ardisia	Ligularia	Sarcococca
Aucuba	Ophiopogon	Serissa
Chlorophytum	Pittosporum	Syngonium
Cycas	Plectranthus	Tolmiea
Cyperus	Podocarpus	Trevesia
Davallia	Polystichum	Zebrina

MINIMUM NIGHT TEMPERATURE OF 60°

These plants do best where the temperature does not go below 60° at night. While most of them will survive an occasional drop below this point, they will either stop growing or die if routinely subjected to colder temperatures. Higher night temperatures do not bother any of them and are preferred by some.

At least five hours of winter sun needed for flowers and best growth

Chirita	Eucharis	Lantana
Columnea	Gardenia	Petrea
Crossandra	Gloxinera	Sinningia
Episcia	Hypocyrta	Strobilanthes

At least two hours of winter sun needed for flowers and best growth

Achimenes	Kohleria	Rubus
Aeschynanthus	Maranta	Saintpaulia
Anthurium	Medinilla	Schlumbergera
Aphelandra	Nautilocalyx	Smithiantha
Calathea	Peristrophe	Stenandrium
Coffea	Persea	Stephanotis
Dizygotheca	Rechsteineria	Tacca
Gynura	Rhipsalis	Zygocactus
Kaempfera		

North light sufficient during winter months

Aglaonema	Codiaeum	Ficus
Alocasia	Collinia	Hemigraphis
Aspidistra	Crassula	Hoffmania
Caladium	Ctenanthe	Homalomena
Chamaedorea	Cyperus	Howea
Chrysalidocarpus	Dieffenbachia	Monstera
Cissus	Dracaena	Nephrolepis
		Pandanus

Peperomia	Rhaphidophora	Selaginella
Philodendron	Sansevieria	Spathiphyllum
Polyscias	Schefflera	Syngonium
Pseuderanthemum	Scindapsus	Xanthosoma

UNHEATED SUNPORCHES AND OTHER PLACES PROTECTED FROM FREEZING

A number of the plants listed here will withstand several degrees of frost; others will not. All prefer night temperatures below 60°. Experimentation is the key to success with an unheated place, as no two are exactly alike.

At least five hours of winter sun needed for flowers and best growth

Acacia	Felicia	Nicotiana
Arrhenatherum	Gazania	Osmanthus
Cactus	Jasmine	Plumbago
Campanula	Lippia	Primula
Citrus	Lobularia	Sedum

At least two hours of winter sun needed for flowers and best growth

Agave	Eurya	Nerium
Aloe	Gasteria	Punica
Camellia	Greigia	Rhododendron
Cleyera	Hebe	Rohdea
Clivia	Michelia	Rosmarinus
Cyclamen	Myrtus	Stenotaphrum

North light sufficient during winter months

Acorus	Hoya	Podocarpus
Ardisia	Ligularia	Reineckia
Aucuba	Ophiopogon	Sarcococca
Hedera	Pittosporum	Tolmiea

MANTELPIECES AND DARK CORNERS

Here are the very tough plants that can survive on a coffee table or mantelpiece with poor light and no pebble tray to relieve the dryness. Remember that even they cannot be expected to grow in such conditions. Move them into a lighter place as often as you can and be sure to put them outside in a shady place in the summertime.

Night temperature—60° to 70°

Aglaonema	Chamaedorea	Collinia
Aspidistra	Cissus	Crassula

Cyperus
Dieffenbachia
Howea
Monstera

Nephrolepis
Pandanus
Peperomia
Philodendron

Sansevieria
Schefflera
Scindapsus
Syngonium

Night temperature—below 60°

Hedera

Ophiopogon

Pittosporum
Podocarpus

INDOOR POOLS AND WATER GARDENS

Water temperatures above 58° and as much sun as possible are the requisites for success in indoor water gardens, although some (Acorus and Myriophyllum) will grow in cooler water and others (Aglaonema and Cyperus) will survive and look attractive with no direct sunlight in winter.

Acorus
Aglaonema
Azolla
Ceratopteris

Colocasia
Cyperus
Hydrocleys
Jussiaea
Myriophyllum

Nymphaea
Nymphoides
Pistia
Salvinia

WOODY PLANTS TO GROW AS INDOOR TREES

Acacia
Araucaria
Calliandra
Camellia
Chamaedorea
Chrysalidocarpus
Citrus
Coffea

Cordyline
Cyphomandra
Dizygotheca
Dracaena
Ficus
Grevillea
Hibiscus
Howea

Jacaranda
Nerium
Pandanus
Podocarpus
Rhapis
Schefflera
Trevesia

POTTING MIXTURES AND GROWING MEDIUMS

Despite the impression of preciseness conveyed by the formulas set out below, the preparation of potting soils is not an exact matter, because the soil components vary in character and composition. The essential thing is the soil structure. Chemical analysis—so important out-of-doors—is of relatively little significance inside because of the regular fertilizing which is part of pot culture. Acidity, another constant concern of the outdoor gardener, can almost be ignored by the indoor gardener because virtually all his plants grow best in mildly acid soil (pH 5.8 to 6.5), and the large proportions of peat and humus in these mixtures hold the acidity at about this level.

I have described below the ingredients most commonly used in potting soils, both those mixed at home and the pre-mixed, packaged soils which I have found so satisfactory. I have also indicated the characteristics that the various ingredients contribute to the final product. If you mix your own soils, make it a habit to examine the components closely and to adjust the formulas to compensate for variations and deficiencies. If you prefer ready-mixed preparations, a reading of the labels in the light of the following descriptions should help you to predict their characteristics and the results they will yield.

Compost is partially decomposed vegetable matter—grass clippings, weeds, leaves, and other garden refuse—generally with a substantial proportion of soil mixed in. In outdoor gardens, compost is added to the soil to increase the content of organic matter and improve the structure. Indoors, compost is itself the basic soil, to which is added even more organic matter, such as leafmold or peat moss. Obviously, batches of compost will differ depending on the proportion and kind of soil used in the compost pile, the extent of decomposition, and the nature of the vegetable matter included.

Leafmold is, of course, well decayed leaves. It varies considerably in acidity, oak leaves and pine needles forming a more acid mold than the leaves of

244

most other trees. In view of the preference for acid soil on the part of the majority of house plants, oak leaf mold is best for indoor use.

Peat moss (also known as German or imported peat) is the partially carbonized residue of sphagnum mosses which have decomposed under water or in a bog. So-called "domestic peat" is the residue of other types of bog plants. It is darker in color, finer in texture, and less desirable for use indoors. While peat moss is an excellent source of organic matter, its principal function in potting mixtures is to improve the structure of the soil and increase its capacity to retain moisture. Like oak leaf mold, it is markedly acid. The secret of handling peat moss is to open the bale, loosen the tightly packed fibers, and wet them thoroughly with a sprinkler head on the hose or watering can. The damp moss can then be left in the open outside or stored inside in a moisture resistant container.

Builder's sand is the kind sold for making mortar. It is perferable to sand from natural deposits because it has been washed clean of soil and weed seeds. The particles are coarse and sharp—quite different from beach sand, which is too smooth and fine for use in potting soil and is also apt to be salty no matter how carefully you wash it.

Bone meal is an organic source of phosphorus, the element that promotes the formation of roots and flowers. Unlike nitrogen, phosphorus does not leach, so top dressings will not wash down to the roots. This means that the phosphatic material should be incorporated in the soil when the potting mixture is made. If a long-term supply of soil is to be mixed in advance, bone meal is appropriate because, like other organics, it becomes available slowly. If the soil is to be used immediately, quick acting superphosphate may be substituted.

Perlite is a pelletized white volcanic rock, which is extremely porous and readily absorbs many times its own weight in water. It is often used as a rooting medium for vegetative propagation and is added to potting mixtures primarily to retain moisture and promote aeration. Do not confuse it with styrofoam, to which it bears a superficial resemblance. Styrofoam is a plastic used by florists for Christmas decorations and flower arrangements and also by nurserymen for mixing with peat moss in the propagation of woody cuttings. It repels water and is of doubtful value in potting mixtures.

Sphagnum moss, *shredded bark*, *and osmunda fiber* are sometimes used without soil for growing bromeliads and other epiphytes. Since they are relatively inert and supply little or no nutrient matter for the roots, plants grown in these mediums should be fertilized regularly. Osmunda fiber, the fibrous aerial roots of osmunda ferns, is more difficult to handle than the others, but is the best of the three for use on cork bark, driftwood, stumps, or crevices in masonry. It is more amenable if it is fresh and thoroughly damp.

All-purpose mixture—for plants with a vigorous fibrous root system

Compost or topsoil	3 parts
Leafmold or peat moss	3 parts
Builder's sand	2 parts
Superphosphate or bone meal	1 pint per bushel

African violet mixture—for African violets and other jungle plants

Compost	2 parts
Leafmold or peat moss	3 parts
Builder's sand	½ part
Broken crock or cinders	1 part
Chopped charcoal	½ part

Begonia mixture—for begonias and tropical plants

Compost	4 parts
Leafmold or peat moss	4 parts
Builder's sand	2 parts
Chopped charcoal	½ part

Epiphyte mixture

a)
Peat moss	3 parts
Perlite	3 parts
Chopped charcoal	1 part

b) Sphagnum moss

Bromeliad mixture

a)
Peat moss	3 parts
Builder's sand or perlite	3 parts
Shredded fir or cedar bark	1 part

b) Shredded fir bark

c) Osmunda fiber (particularly for use on cork bark, driftwood, etc.)

d) Sphagnum moss

Desert mixture—for cacti and succulents

a)
Compost	2 parts
Leafmold or peat moss	2 parts
Builder's sand	2 parts
Broken crocks or pebbles	2 parts
Bone meal	1 pint per bushel
Ground limestone	1 pint per bushel

b) All-purpose mixture

SOURCES OF SUPPLY FOR HOUSE PLANTS

Few indoor gardeners are lucky enough to live near a greenhouse with any variety of unusual and desirable house plants for sale. Those who are not must shop by mail to obtain the plants they read about in their garden books and magazines. The following is a list of the suppliers I have used to build my collection; all of them accept mail orders.

Most of these suppliers offer primarily small plants, usually in 2¼-inch plastic pots or paper bands. There are two reasons for this. In the first place, few buyers want to pay more than the price of a small plant. Secondly, larger plants are difficult and expensive to ship.

Don't expect dealers to send you plants during the freezing winter months. Some refuse to deliver at this time of year, and those who accept orders make it clear that their responsibility ends when the package leaves their greenhouse. Thereafter, all that stands between your plants and the weather is the vigilance of the Post Office Department, the Railway Express, or the airlines; and while these carriers are remarkably conscientious, they cannot always keep the shipment from freezing. The same cautions apply to ordering in July and August, when shipments are apt to dry out or even cook.

I have had most success with plants ordered and received in early spring. They have the spring and summer months (the best growing season) to get over the shock of the journey, and with good fortune, they attain a respectable size by the time fall comes and indoor gardening begins in earnest.

Plants ordered and received in the fall are slower to adjust to house life and are apt to look even less vigorous by January than they did when they arrived. Often they do not start growing until the following spring, and so a whole season is lost.

Many of these greenhouses are located near vacation spots, and if you find yourself in their vicinity, you will enjoy a visit to any of them. While I have not seen them all, I have spent many happy hours browsing in those within my reach and talking to the men and women who run them. House plant growers are always ready to give you helpful information about their plants.

Also, of course, you may find something that looks much more attractive in the ground than it did in the catalog; or, indeed, something the grower did not list because of short supply or lack of demand.

SOURCES OF SUPPLY FOR HOUSE PLANTS AND HOUSE PLANT SUPPLIES

Alberts & Merkle Bros., Inc.
2210 S. Federal Hwy.
Boynton Beach, Florida 33435 — Tropical foliage plants, Bromeliads, Orchids

Arthur Eames Allgrove
N. Wilmington, Mass. 01887 — Terrarium plants

Buell's Greenhouses
Eastford, Connecticut 06242 — Gloxinias, African violets

Burgess Seed & Plant Co.
Galesburg, Michigan 49053 — Seeds, various plants

California Jungle Gardens
11977 San Vicente Boulevard
Los Angeles, California 90049 — Tropical foliage plants, Bromeliads

L. Easterbrook Greenhouses
10 Craig Street
Butler, Ohio 44822 — House plants

Edelweiss Gardens
54 Robbinsville-Allentown Road
Robbinsville, New Jersey 08691 — House plants

Fantastic Gardens
9550 S.W. 67th Avenue
South Miami, Florida 33156 — Bromeliads

Fennel Orchid Co. Inc.
26715 S.W. 157th Avenue
Homestead, Florida 33030 — Orchids

Fischer Greenhouses
Linwood, New Jersey 08221 — Gesneriads, house plants

Flora Greenhouses
Box 1191
Burlingame, California 94010 — Geraniums, begonias, African violets

Fruitland Nurseries
Augusta, Georgia 30901   Flowering trees and shrubs

Henrietta's Nursery
1345 North Brawley Avenue
Fresno, California 93705   Gesneriads

The House Plant Corner
P.O. Box 810
Oxford, Maryland 21654   Supplies, plants

Margaret Ilgenfritz
Box 665
Monroe, Michigan 48161   Orchids

Johnson Cactus Gardens
Box 458
Paramount, California 90723   Cacti, succulents

Kartuz Greenhouses
92 Chestnut Street
Wilmington, Mass. 01887   Gesneriads

Lager & Hurrell
426 Morris Avenue
Summit, New Jersey 07901   Orchids

Leatherman's Gardens
2637 N. Lee Avenue
South El Monte, California 91733   Ferns, Begonias

Logee's Greenhouses
55 North Street
Danielson, Connecticut 06239   House plants, Begonias

Lyndon Lyon
14 Mutchler Street
Dolgeville, New York 13329   African violets, Gesneriads

Merry Gardens
Camden, Maine 04843   House plants, Begonias

Oakhurst Gardens
P.O. Box 444
Arcadia, California 91006   Bulbs, Bromeliads

Orinda Nursery
Bridgeville, Delaware 19933   Camellias

George W. Park Seed Co.
Greenwood, South Carolina 29646　　Seeds, bulbs, plants, heating cables

Julius Roehrs Co.
E. Rutherford, New Jersey 07073　　Exotic plants

Tinari Greenhouses
2325 Valley Road
Huntingdon Valley, Pa. 19006　　African violets, Episcias

William Tricker, Inc.
Allendale Avenue
Saddle River, New Jersey 07458　　Water plants

Whistling Hill
M. C. Cogswell
Box 27
Hamburg, New York 14075　　Gesneriads

Wilson Brothers
Roachdale, Indiana 46172　　Geraniums

Wyrtzen Exotic Plants
165 Bryant Avenue
Floral Park, New York 11001　　Gesneriads, Begonias

INFORMATION ON PLANT SOCIETIES
FOR THE INDOOR GARDENER

African Violet Society of America, Inc.
Mrs. Edward A. Nelson, Secretary
603 E. Essex Avenue
St. Louis, Mo. 63122
Membership $6.00,
 includes 5 magazines yearly

American Begonia Society, Inc.
Mrs. E. W. Benell, Membership Secretary
10331 S. Colima Road
Whittier, Calif. 90604
Membership $4.00 per year,
 includes monthly publication

The American Bonsai Society
Box 78
Bedford, New York 10506
Membership $5.00 per year,
 includes quarterly journal

American Fern Society
LeRoy K. Henry, Treasurer
Division of Plants, Carnegie Museum
Pittsburgh, Pa. 15213
Membership $5.00 per year,
 includes quarterly journal

The American Gesneria Society
Worldway Postal Center
Box 91192
Los Angeles, Calif. 90009
Membership $4.00 per year,
 includes bi-monthly bulletin

The American Gloxinia and Gesneriad Society, Inc.
Mrs. Diantha B. Buell, Secretary
Dept. P.F.S.O.
Eastford, Conn. 06242
Membership $4.00 per year,
 includes bi-monthly magazine

The American Orchid Society, Inc.
Botanical Museum of Harvard University
Cambridge, Mass. 02138
Membership $10.00 per year,
    includes monthly bulletin

Bromeliad Society
Joanne Woodbury
1811 Edgecliffe Drive
Los Angeles, Calif. 90026
Membership $5.00 per year,
    includes six bulletins

Cactus and Succulent Society of America, Inc.
Box 167
Reseda, Calif. 91335
Membership $6.00 per year,
    includes bi-monthly journal

The Indoor Light Gardening Society of America, Inc.
Mrs. Fred D. Peden, Secretary
4 Wildwood Road
Greenville, South Carolina 29607
Membership $4.00 per year,
    includes quarterly magazine

Los Angeles International Fern Society
Wilbur Olson
13715 Corary Avenue
Hawthorne, Calif. 90250
Membership $2.50 per year
    includes monthly fern lessons

Saintpaulia International
P.O. Box 10604
Knoxville, Tennessee 37919
Membership $4.00 per year,
    includes bi-monthly magazine

The Palm Society
Mrs. Lucita H. Wait
7229 S.W. 54th Avenue
Miami, Florida 33143
Membership $10.00 per year,
    includes quarterly journal

INDEX

Plants are omitted from this index because they are listed alphabetically by botanical and common names in Part III, which also contains cultural practices and cross references to illustrations.

255

74 75 10 9 8 7 6 5 4 3